Devil's Den
A History and Guide

MAY 10, 1998

To Tony,

by
Garry E. Adelman
and
Timothy H. Smith

Best wishes

Timothy H. Smith

Thomas Publications
Gettysburg, PA

Copyright © 1997 Garry E. Adelman and Timothy H. Smith

Printed and bound in the United States of America

Published by THOMAS PUBLICATIONS
          P.O. Box 3031
          Gettysburg, Pa. 17325

ISBN-1-57747-017-6

Cover design by Thomas A. Desjardin

To our parents—

Eleanor Sarah Bomberg Smith
Howard James Smith
Eve S. Adelman
Robert Adelman

Contents

Introduction

Devil's Den. Over the years this name has evoked a variety of images in the minds of visitors to the Gettysburg Battlefield. To many people, it represents a place of wild, scenic beauty. Others are attracted by the folklore which presents images of evil spirits and vicious reptiles residing nearby. And, of course, it reminds some of the sinister fighting that took place in and around this jumble of boulders. It is because of Devil's Den's particularly wide appeal that this book has been written.

Obviously, the area of Devil's Den would not attract the number of visitors it currently does without the prominent role it played in the battle. But oddly enough, the fighting there has received very little notice. The attack and defense of Little Round Top has attracted longtime national attention while the fight for Devil's Den has been relegated to a position of lesser prominence. Recognized for little more than the notion of Southern sharpshooters, picking off hapless Yankees from the safety of the rocks, the eerie appearance of the Den coupled with the rapid evolution of its myth, lore and legend, has overshadowed the actual fighting that took place there.

Yet there are many aspects of Devil's Den which have contributed to its popularity. In addition to the battle, the history of the site and the fascinating story of its evolution into a tourist attraction are detailed on the following pages. Finally, a tour is provided for those who wish to visit Devil's Den. It is by simply visiting the Den, that we first became enamored with its wondrous beauty and rich history.

Photography is an integral part of the story of Devil's Den, and thus, numerous views are included to illustrate the site through time. The maps herein also reflect the changing Devil's Den through the years. This is not the first narrative on this subject, nor will it be the last. We have tried, however, to view Devil's Den in a unique and broad fashion.

We were first captivated by the unnatural appearance of the area. As students of the battle, we learned of the chaotic nature of the fighting and folklore surrounding it. As Licensed Battlefield Guides we came to understand the popularity of Devil's Den and the need to place it into its proper historical context. This volume is a result of our love of history, the Battle of Gettysburg and of our favorite place in the world—Devil's Den.

Gettysburg, PA
May, 1997

Acknowledgements

Over the last four years, many individuals and institutions generously assisted us during the research, writing and publication of this book. Given the span of time which has elapsed since this project began and the large number of people who have contributed to the final product, we apologize to anyone we have missed.

First and foremost we would like to acknowledge William A. Frassanito. He not only has our greatest respect, but his *Gettysburg: A Journey in Time* was the spark which ignited our interest in the Civil War. A good friend and a scholar with no equal in his field, his writings laid much of the foundation for our present understanding of Devil's Den. At every turn he provided important photographs and much valuable insight.

Thomas Publications was, indeed, extremely helpful in editing and preparing the manuscript. The staff includes Dean Thomas, Jim Thomas, Sarah Rodgers, Tom Desjardin, Scott Wolf and Barbara Grant.

David L. Richards of Gettysburg read over the battle section of this book and made numerous suggestions and corrections. His knowledge of that part of the field was most useful.

Many thanks go out to Ken and Sue Boardman of Sunbury, Pennsylvania, for allowing us access to their vast photographic collection of the Gettysburg battlefield.

One of the most valuable and least used repositories for material concerning the battlefield is the Adams County Historical Society (ACHS). Its director, Dr. Charles H. Glatfelter, and assistant director, Elwood W. Christ, as well as the entire staff greatly assisted in our research.

We spent numerous hours at the Gettysburg Naitonal Military Park (GNMP) library and archives and were greatly assisted by Kathy Georg, D. Scott Hartwig, Eric Campbell, Hal Greenlee, Troy Harman, Winona Peterson and Randy Krichton.

Another institution which made contributions to this work was the United States Army Military History Institute (USAMHI). The particularly helpful staff members include Michael J. Winey, Randy Hackenberg, Richard J. Sommers and Louise Arnold-Friend.

Michael Musick, Deanne Blanton, Michael E. Pilgrim and the rest of the staff of the National Archives and Records Administration (NARA) helped us sort through the treasure troves of information in their collections.

Contributions were also made by the following: Warren Motts, Motts Photographic Center; Paul W. Romaine and Sandra Trenholm, The Gilder Lehrman Collection; Lori Gilbert and Marilyn Palmeri, The Pierpont Morgan Library; David T. Hedrick, Gettysburg College; Andrea Mark, Chicago Public Library; Laura O'Keefe and Melanie Yolles, New York Public Library; Dwight Van Nitz and Herbert O. Brown, Fields of Glory; the Small family, The Horse Soldier; Beverly Allen, Emory University; Library of Congress; Maine State Archives; and the Food For Thought Cafe and Coffeehouse.

We are indebted to our colleagues and friends in the Association of Licensed Battlefield Guides, all of whom have helped us in one way or another. Most helpful were: Robert Cammaroto, James Clouse, Dr. Charles Fennell, Roy Frampton, Edward Guy, Frederick Hawthorne, Mike Kanazawich, Timothy Krapf, Wayne Motts, George Shealer, James Tate and David Weaver.

Thanks also to: Frank Antonucci, Dr. Finely Bryan, Craig Caba, Gregory A. Coco, Chris Daw, Steve Doyle, Sam Floca, Larry Fryer, Dale Gallon, the Heberling family, George Joiner, Walter Powell, Justin A. Shaw, Bryan Smith, Dean Thieret, David E. Welsh, Robert Williamson, Steve L. Zerbe and the man, whose name is unknown, who helped Garry find the original Dead Sharpshooter position upon his first trip to Gettysburg.

Garry cannot close without mentioning the kind understanding he received from Erin K. Barr. She assisted him in correcting portions of the manuscript, listened patiently to his seemingly endless stream of Civil War monologues and was most supportive during this exhaustive work.

Tim would also like to extend his appreciation to his wife Diane J. Smith. She managed to spend untold hours reading and correcting draft copies of the manuscript despite her busy schedule. Her patience and understanding were vital in dealing with his obsession with Devil's Den.

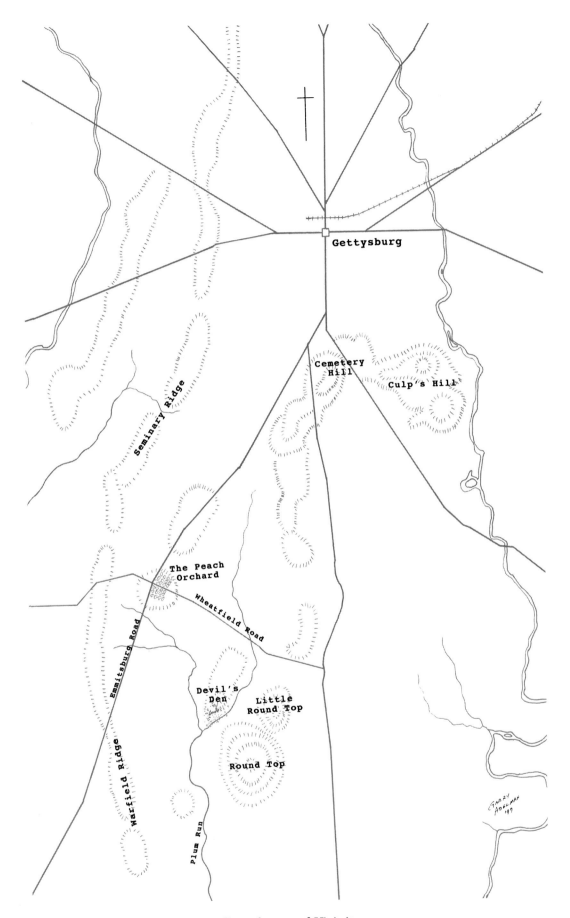

Gettysburg and Vicinity.

Pre-Battle History

Geology

As long as man has inhabited the area surrounding Devil's Den, there have been questions concerning its origin. One story still commonly heard on the battlefield is that the Den was formed by glacial activity during the Ice Age.[1] Over the years however, much has been written by geologists concerning this formation. Michael Jacobs, professor of mathematics and science at Pennsylvania (now Gettysburg) College, explained it concisely in 1864:

> When the forces which folded and raised up the strata which form the South Mountain was in action, it produced fissures in the strata of red shale which covers the surface of this region of country, permitting the fused material from beneath to rise and fill them, on cooling, with trap dykes, or greenstone and syenetic greenstone. This rock, being for the most part very hard, remained as the axes and crests of hills and ridges when the softer shale in the intervening spaces was excavated by great water-currents into valleys and plains.[2]

Over 180 million years old, the diabase boulders of Devil's Den continue to erode.

Devil's Den, the most famous of these rock formations, is actually an "outcropping of a diabase sill, appropriately enough called the Gettysburg Sill." This sheet of igneous rock, forced upward between existing strata, is about a mile wide, 1,800 feet thick, and runs southwest to northeast for almost 40 miles passing directly through the middle of what is now the Gettysburg National Military Park.[3] As one geologist has correctly pointed out, the second day of "the battle of Gettysburg was essentially an effort by the Confederates to drive the Union army" from the diabase outcroppings of this sill.[4] Diabase is a coarse-grained and granular rock, very similar to granite in appearance and composition.[5] The diabase was formed over 180 million years ago under and within the beds of sandstone and shale that covered this area. Over time, the erosion of these softer sediments and the removal of pressure from above has allowed the underlying rock mass to expand; the cracks and joints becoming prime conduits for the infiltration of water.

Since their exposure to the surface millions of years ago, the diabase has slowly weathered. The "swelling of decomposing and oxidizing minerals" causes the surface of the boulders to flake off in thin sheets. The "daily and seasonal temperature changes" and the freezing of water in the crevices and cracks, breaks the rocks into smaller fragments. Sheets at their corners develop into "curved plates and concentric layers," and as the rocks weather they take on a spheroidal shape, or as some have suggested, become "Round Tops."[6] Other types of visible erosion include the "breaking apart and splitting of rocks by plants (tree and root wedging) and the encrustation of a pale gray-green scale-like primitive plant, lichens, which draws various chemical elements for the rock."[7] Erosion in these rocks also "occurs at different or irregular rates with varying amounts of intensity within the same rock mass. This is called "differential weathering" and is caused by variations existing in the chemical composition of the rocks and their susceptibility to wind, moisture, and frost.[8] Devil's Den has been eroding for millions of years and it will continue to erode. By comparing photographs taken just a hundred years ago with the same scenes today, one is able to detect this process of erosion, going on unabated, before our very eyes.

The First Battle of Gettysburg

The fact that Native Americans did at one time hunt over the ground on which the battle was fought is not in dispute. Local museums exhibit many arrowheads and other early stone objects found on the fields around Gettysburg (many by persons in search of Civil War relics). As an example, the Gettysburg *Star & Sentinel* ran an item in 1906 entitled "Found Tomahawk."

> While showing some friends through Devil's Den the other day, John Thorn found a tomahawk in a crevice of the rocks, which has probably been there for a hundred years. The relic gives the den a little more historic interest concerning the earlier haunts of the Red Man.[9]

Articles describing Indian artifacts found in the area of the Round Tops can be easily found in local newspapers. Some claim that relics have been found near Gettysburg ever since the first pioneers settled here. In 1869, an article (originally printed in the York *Press*) appeared in the Gettysburg *Compiler* stating that:

> An archeological investigation of the country around Gettysburg, conducted by a learned antiquarian, has proved the truth of a belief long entertained by residents that the battlefield of Gettysburg had in the distant past been the scene of a bloody struggle between the Indians or some unknown or long extinct race. This fact is attested by the exhumation of the military implements of the combatants, and the remains of the dead in what is known as Indian field, about a mile southwest of Roundtop.... The relics are found thickly imbedded in the soil over the whole area of territory which was the scene of the battles in 1863.[10]

An 1869 publication by *Star & Sentinel* also mentioned the "relics of the first battle of Gettysburg," and further speculated that they could not have been produced by the North American Indians as we know them, but from some long extinct civilization, such as "a northern Aztec empire."[11] Emanuel Bushman, a resident of Gettysburg who knew the area of the Round Tops well, told a number of stories concerning these early Americans. In several articles for the Gettysburg *Compiler*, he also wrote of the "Indian Field" on his grandfather's farm.

A half a century ago [about 1830] it was a clearing of about six acres, in the midst of a dense forest.... There is an old Indian tradition that there was a great battle fought there, which seems very reasonable from the fact that the early settlers found two different kinds of arrows on each side of a stony ridge, which would indicate that there were two tribes or two great nations at war; that the loss was so great that it took this spot to bury the chiefs alone.... It is a remarkable coincidence that in the dim twilight of the past, the greatest battle fought on this continent by the savages, and one of the greatest battles of modern times, were fought on nearly the same, if not quite, the same ground.[12]

Bushman wrote that the long-forgotten conflict was referred to as "the Battle of the Crows," and it was estimated there were one hundred Indians engaged. During his youth he "picked up scores of arrows of both kinds in Indian Field." And while hunting with his father on the western slope of Round Top he had once found an "Indian tomahawk." He speculated that the relics found in the area were "many centuries" old and "belonged to the stone age of tools."[13] "Still another tradition" suggested that the site was "sacred ground for religious festivals, where they [the Indians] observed their moons; the new moons, full moons, and old moons...." Bushman's knowledge of the area came from his parents, grandparents, and neighbors, whose families had lived in the area since the 1700s.[14]

> There is an old tradition that an Indian hunter was passing the "Big Rocks" [Bushman's name for Devil's Den] and a huge black bear came out from the cave and sprang upon him with his capacious mouth open to take in his head. The Indian thrust his arm down his throat and partially choked and tore the bear's entrails. The Indian's arm was terribly lacerated. They both struggled until they were glad to quit. In a day or two the Indian brought a member of his tribe, and they tracked a bear to a pine tree, for it had snowed. Was it reason or instinct which led the bear to the pine tree to get pitch to heal his wounds, for he had swallowed two considerable pitch balls?[15]

Emanuel also wrote of the many "unnatural and supernatural sights and sounds heard and seen on Round Top and the Indian Field."[16] The early settlers would tell "wonderful stories of ghosts and hobgoblins seen there in the still hours of the night," and occasionally "the Indian warwhoop could be heard, and the hunters chasing the prowling wolf."[17] Undoubtedly influenced by early lore, and his belief in the existence of an ancient tribe of Indians, such as the 1869 *Star & Sentinel* had suggested, Emanuel had his own theory as to the origins of Devil's Den. In 1884 he wrote:

> I have always had a curiosity in those rocks. They should be examined by a competent geologist. My own opinion is that they were a solid pyramid many hundred feet high. That they were broken is very evident from the crevices. If they were pressed together every one would have its place to fit. There was some force more powerful than dynamite that broke them up. My impression is it was a deep canon [sic], filled with broken rocks. Any one going to the trouble will find that it is entirely filled with broken rocks. Did the explosion take place when the veil of the temple was rent, or was it long ages before that?[18]

Of course, with the emphasis on the battle in July of 1863, no serious study has ever been undertaken by the National Park Service to investigate the prehistoric sites that may exist on the battlefield. Over the past few years however, the park archeologists are continually confronted with Native American artifacts while on routine digs on the southern portions of the battlefield.

The Early Settlers of Round Top

The first European settlers in the area surrounding the Den were primarily Scots-Irish and German immigrants, during the 1720s and 30s.[19] In 1741 this area was part of a 43,500 acre tract set aside by the sons of William Penn as "The Manor of Maske," and by the 1760s the first warrants were issued for the land which now comprises the area around Gettysburg.[20] Because of the nature of the ground and its inadequacy for agricultural use, the area of the Round Tops was one of the last parts of the Manor to be settled. Consisting of smaller-than-average size tracts, no fewer than ten properties intersected on or near the Round Tops.[21]

The early families that settled this area included those of Jacob Sherfy (or Sherfig), Jacob and Andrew Bushman, Quinten Armstrong, Hugh Woods, Adam Linn, Adam Black, Daniel McPike, Robert Work, and Michael Miller.[22] Like many place names used today to describe features on the battlefield, Little Round Top is a postwar name, and accounts written before and just after the battle rarely distinguish between the two hills.[23] With a height of 785 feet above sea level, it is not surprising that Big Round Top was frequently used as a landmark in the early deeds and warrants of the area.[24] In January 1766, surveyors referred to it as "Adam Lynn's Hill." One of the earliest settlers of the Manor, Adam

Linn (or Lynn), who died in 1767, was the first recorded owner of the Round Tops.[25] Other early records, including the will of Quinten Armstrong, Sr. (1793), indicate its name as "Round Hill," and several other documents, such as a 1799 survey, indicate it as the "Rocky Hill."[26]

Emanuel Bushman's reminiscences also recall the early history of Round Top. He was told that its original name was "Sally McPike's Hill," and indeed, according to early land records, a spinster named Sarah McPike did own Big Round Top as early as 1805.[27] The old settlers also told Bushman of "a spring at the southwest side of Round top near the summit: the water flowed down over the rocks. And in winter while frozen, it was a beautiful sight when the sun shown upon it."[28] In 1886 Bushman wrote of an incident told to him by his father concerning a fire on Round Top:

> It was in November 1806. Father [Henry Bushman], with two of the Armstrongs went coon hunting; after rambling around the hills awhile without much success, they got cold, it being a cold night. They made a fire against a big log to warm themselves near the big rocks now called Devil's Den. When they were thawed out or warmed up, there was a gust of wind, or whirlwind, came down the hollow or valley. The leaves of the trees were nearly all down and dry, and the wind scattered the fire among the leaves in every direction, and soon all of Round Top was in a blaze. The effects of

Emanuel Paul Bushman (1821-1899).
(Star and Sentinel, *ACHS*)

that fire could be seen forty years afterwards in the bare pine trees, some standing blackened and charred felled.... A heavy rain set in and put the fire out before it spread through the settlement.[29]

By the time of the Civil War the owners of Little Round Top included Ephraim Hanaway, who in 1858 purchased about 30 acres on the western face of the hill, and Jacob Weikert who owned its eastern face. The base of Big Round Top was intersected by several properties, the summit hill itself (about 35 acres), was owned jointly by Hugh G. Scott and the heirs of John Guinn.[30] Over the years much has been written concerning the barren appearance of Little Round Top during the battle. In *High Tide At Gettysburg* (1958), Glenn Tucker repeated an "old guide story" relating that "the Weikert brothers, Charles and John, had taken off the timber in the fall of 1862 to help meet the war's ravenous demands for lumber."[31] More recently however, accounts have been uncovered to suggest that the hill might have been barren for years prior to that date.[32] In 1886, a Confederate veteran named William H. Swallow made some interesting comments on the Round Tops.

The Writer, just here, would like to speak of the prominent land-mark directly in front of Longstreet's corps. On looking to the southward, about half a mile from the Emmittsburg road, there looms up into view a rugged mountain, nearly bare, along whose sides are seen deep ledges of rocks and many stones of great size. It has for over a hundred years been known by the name of Round Top. Due east of it, and connected with it, there rises a smaller projecting spur called Little Round Top. The latter seems to sleep on the bosom of the former. History has made their names immortal, and will transmit them to the remotest ages of time. Around the northern front of these mountains a small creek runs to the eastward. At their base a valley filled with rocks and cliffs, skirted with underbrush, separates the main landscape from the mountain. Seen in the stillness of the night it presents a most desolate appearance, an impression which long clings to the memory. The writer well remembers, while a boy of eleven years of age, attending school at Mount St. Mary's, near Emmittsburg, Maryland, passing over the road from the latter place to Gettysburg in the fall of the year 1839. It was growing late when the stage reached the front of Round Top, and he still remembers the fear that seized him while the stage was passing their front, and the relief experienced when these objects of his terror had been passed and left behind. He often wondered, when a boy, why the Creator had placed those rugged mountains upon the open landscape, little dreaming, at the time, of the many thousand heroic spirits in the distant future, and in his presence, who would dispute with their lives and seal with their blood the right to possess their stony slopes....[33]

"Granite Ridge & Round Top," c. 1865. This engraving was printed on early memberships certificates to the Gettysburg Battlefield Memorial Association. (ACHS)

While the first owners of the Round Tops can be established through existing records, the Devil's Den is a different matter altogether. The Den is part of another, more elusive tract of land, and its first recorded owner is difficult to establish. It is known, however, that in 1805 it was part of the 350-acre tract of land located in Cumberland Township, Adams County, Pennsylvania, that was granted to Jacob Sherfy.[34] Sherfy, who had been a squatter on the land since 1795, owned the property until his death. During his fifty years of ownership many improvements were made, including a huge two-story stone dwelling built for his wife and eleven children.[35] With the death of Jacob Sherfy in 1842, and his wife Catherine in 1844, the property was transferred in 1845 to Jacob Benner.[36] During Benner's subsequent ownership several large tracts of land were separated and sold off. Among these were 47 acres located at the property's southeastern edge which Benner transferred on March 29, 1848, to John Houck and Samuel McCreary.[37] Houck and McCreary were Gettysburg business partners who owned a brickyard on the edge of town.[38] As the years passed, Houck bought out his partner's interest, and on April 5, 1861, a few days prior to the firing on Fort Sumter, he established sole ownership of the property that was to become a landmark in American history. Although not yet named as such, Devil's Den, the Slaughter Pen, Plum Run, and the Valley of Death were all part of Houck's 47 acre tract.[39]

Houck's Ridge and its Surroundings

In 1863 John Houck was a 76-year old resident of Gettysburg. He owned several properties in and around the town, including the one-and-a-half-story brick dwelling in which young Mary Virginia "Jennie" Wade would be killed on July 3, 1863.[40] The Houck family itself lived in a house located on Baltimore Street, two doors south of the Presbyterian Church. John was born in Maryland, and in census records is described as a farmer. His family in 1863 consisted of his wife Elizabeth (age 68) who was apparently "sick in bed" during the battle, his son David (age 37), and his daughter Jane (age 45).[41] Houck was an influential member of Gettysburg society, an "excellent citizen and a consistent member of the Presbyterian church." During his life he held several elected posts including county coroner in 1827, town councilman in 1827 and 1833, and director of the poor in 1846.[42]

Houck's 47 acre tract was roughly in the shape of a rectangle, bordered on the north by a county road, referred to since the battle as the Wheatfield Road. The eastern edge of his property ran along the base of the Round Tops (bordering properties

View from Little Round Top, M. B. Brady, July 1863. This view looks southwest across the property owned by John Houck. The Table Rock at Devil's Den can be discerned between the limbs of the pine tree at the extreme left of the photograph. (USAMHI)

owned by Ephraim Hanaway and John Musser), with its southern edge located near the confluence of Plum Run and Rose Run (bordering the lands of Philip Snyder and Joseph Sherfy). On the west, his property bordered a triangular-shaped field (owned at that time by George W. Weikert), the Rose Woods, and the soon-to-be-famous Wheatfield (owned by George Rose).[43] The western edge of his property formed the ridge on which the Union left flank would be positioned on July 2, 1863. Today this ridge is appropriately known as Houck's Ridge.[44]

A small stream trickled southward through John Houck's land. Today the stream is popularly known as Plum Run, but as is the case with many other place names now related to the field, there seems to be no pre-battle reference for that designation. On an 1813 deed the stream is called "John Linn's Run," after a man who owned property through which it ran.[45] On the 1821 *Map of York and Adams Counties* and an 1846 history of South-Central Pennsylvania it is referred to as Rock Run, which makes perfect sense, considering its rock-strewn nature and the fact that it flows into Rock Creek.[46] On the 1832, 1848, and 1850 *Map of Pennsylvania* it is shown as "Bear" Run, which goes along with Bushman's story of the bear.[47] The name Plum Run is not associated with this stream on either the *1858 Adams County Map*, the *1872 Atlas of Adams County*, the Warren Map (ca. 1869), or in the *1886 History of Adams County*.[48] It first appears as Plum Run on early battlefield maps. Maps published by E. B. Cope and Theodore Ditterline in the fall of 1863, and John Bachelder's Isometrical Map, published the following year, all show the stream as Plum Run. In his 1873 guide to the Gettysburg Battlefield, Bachelder referred to "Plumb Run" as "a small un-

Plum Run and the Valley of Death, Tipton, c. 1890. The rock in the right foreground can be located today near the footbridge over Plum Run at Devil's Den. (GNMP)

important stream" that "drains a marshy swale in front of Little Round Top."[49] Years after the war, battlefield guides began referring to the area between Houck's Ridge and the Round Tops by the more colorful name, "Valley of Death." And it was probably guides who popularized the story that Plum Run ran so red with blood for days after the battle, that it was renamed Bloody Run.[50]

As Plum Run flows southward, it passes through an area just east of Devil's Den filled with hundreds of huge, broken rocks. This area is commonly referred to, in the accounts of participants of the battle, as the "Gorge."[51] The sight of bloated human remains along the rock-choked banks of Plum Run following the battle caused this area to be nicknamed "The Slaughter Pen."[52]

The entire length of Houck's property consisted of undulating, rocky and swampy ground. No part of his land could be considered a field and the rocky terrain made it unsuitable for crops. Union accounts of the battle, and a photograph taken by M. B. Brady shortly afterward, do however, indicate that cattle were grazing on the property at that time. Since neither John Houck nor his son David appear to have owned livestock in the tax records or the 1860 agricultural census, it is likely that the ground was being leased to someone else.[53] Perhaps Houck & McCreary originally purchased the land in connection with their brickyard. According to the *1886 History of Adams County*:

> Wolf's Hill, Culp's Hill, Big Round Top, Little Round Top, and Houck's Ridge, of which Devil's Den forms a projecting spur, furnish a

supply of this rock [diabase] that is practically inexhaustible. This rock, however massive and unbroken it may appear, has a tendency to divide more easily in certain directions than in others, and is traversed by parallel seams, separating readily into blocks more or less symmetrical. It is a rock of great durability—hard and compact, and the finer varieties of it are susceptible of a good polish. It is easily split into blocks of any size by a very simple process. These blocks, thus quarried or split out, are conveyed to the granite yards.[54]

The "disintegration and decomposition" of the diabase in the vicinity also "produced immense deposits of an excellent quality of yellow sand much used for building purposes." All of these factors would have made Devil's Den more valuable for a dealer in building supplies than a farmer.[55]

But what importance did Devil's Den have to Gettysburg citizens before the battle? There is some suggestion that the area of the Round Tops was, in fact, a popular local picnic area years before the Civil War. In an 1843 Gettysburg diary, reference is made to a 4th of July picnic on "round top." A pleasant day was spent among "the large rocks that were half as large as a common house."[56] In 1844 the Gettysburg Methodist Church had its "camp meeting" on the "lands of Peter Trostle, near Round Top." And in the summer of 1855 the Methodist Sunday Schools of the Gettysburg Circuit had a large "picnic in Trostle's woods near Round Top."[57] Carvings on rocks in the Devil's Den area predate the Civil War, also suggesting it was popular before the battle. An 1898 tourbook states that "since 1837, the earliest date inscribed, it had become common practice to place inscriptions" on the rocks of the Den.[58] One carving dated 1849 can still be seen atop a large rock at the southern edge of the Plum Run Gorge (See Rock Carving section). Although the Den may have attracted attention before the battle, no one at that time could have envisioned the heavy visitation that would occur in the decades to follow.

The Lore of the Den

According to popular tradition, the name Devil's Den was given to that outcropping of large rocks long before the battle was fought there. However, at present there is no direct evidence to support this claim. No documentation dated prior to the battle has yet surfaced which makes reference to the nickname. All records of the word "Devil" being used to describe the area in question are post-battle. The term evolves soon afterward, the earliest such reference appearing in the official report of Captain James E. Smith of the 4th New York Independent Battery. From a "Camp near Sandy Hook," Maryland on July 20, 1863, he wrote that at Gettysburg on July 2nd, a part of his battery was placed "on a hill (near the Devil's Cave)."[59] The first documented usage of the name "Devil's Den" to describe the rocks in front of Round Top comes from a Pennsylvania soldier named Francis M. Stoke who was stationed at Camp Letterman General Hospital after the battle. On October 26, 1863 he wrote a letter to his brother in which he describes an area in front of Little Round Top which seemed "as though nature in some wild freak had forgotten herself and piled great rocks in mad confusion together. This place is known as the Devil's Den."[60]

Within weeks of the battle, historian John Bachelder arrived on the field and began research for his well-known Isometrical Map. The "drawing was the result of eighty-four days spent on the field immediately after the battle, during which time" he "sketched carefully the twenty-five square miles which it represents." Although many have searched, only a few of these sketches have ever been found. Among those that have survived include a watercolor of Devil's Den, signed and dated July 23, 1863.[61] Afterward, he spent months interviewing the soldiers involved, noting their positions and the movement of their commands during the battle. When the Isometrical Map was published in 1864 the words "Devil's Den" were printed just above the position occupied by the left of General J. H. Hobart Ward's Brigade on July 2, 1863.[62] In his 1873 *Gettysburg: What to See And How To See It*, Bachelder described the area in more detail.

John B. Bachelder and his wife Elizabeth at Devil's Den. (GNMP)

West of...[Little Round Top] is a stony, precipitous undulation called Houck's Ridge, along which the Third corps line of battle ran on July 3 [*sic*]. The evidences are, that by some mighty convulsion of nature, this ridge was rent asunder at its intersection with the base of Round Top, thereby draining an extensive body of water in front of the Little Round Top. The gorge thus produced is called the Devil's Den, and presents a scene of the wildest character. Huge syenitic boulders are crowded into this narrow ravine, through which struggle the waters of Plumb Run; while yawning chasms suggest to the visitor the haunts of the lurking sharp-shooters, who occupied them during the battle.[63]

When questioned in 1894, Bachelder stated that "the Devil's Den is not a new name; it was a name given to the locality before the battle."[64] There is little doubt that the use of this designation on his maps, during his lectures, and in his writings, popularized the term. It is also possible that early visitors to the area, Francis Stoke for instance, could have picked up the term from Bachelder. But whether it was commonly referred to as Devil's Den before Bachelder used it is difficult to determine.

Watercolor of Devil's Den, Rock Ridge and Round Top, Bachelder, July 23, 1863. It is uncertain if the words "Devil's Den" were originally in the title or if that designation was added later. (GLC2670.01, The Gilder Lehrman Collection on deposit at the Pierpont Morgan Library, New York)

At least one early writer who toured the field shortly after the battle with a local guide, was misinformed as to its location. In Benson Lossing's 1866 pictorial history of the Civil War, an engraving of a curious rock formation (actually on Little Round Top), is captioned "The Devil's Den." From the text provided in a footnote to the caption, it is obvious that he believed the Den was a part of Little Round Top, and not a group of rocks 500 yards across the valley.

This little sketch shows a mass of rocks forming a sort of dark inclosure, which is called the Devil's Den. It gives a good idea of the masses of huge rocks among which the Confederates struggled up the steep slopes of Little Round Top. This heap was in front of Hazlett's battery, a little way down the hill.[65]

This confusion regarding the location of the Den was not widespread, and most early writers and guides support Bachelder's site and suggestion that it was given its name prior to the battle. In 1874, the Comte de Paris, who compiled one of the first complete histories of the American Civil War, wrote that "the colonists, jealous, no doubt, of the legends of the mother-country, in the middle of the eighteenth

Engraving of rocks on Little Round Top entitled "The Devil's Den," Benson Lossing, 1866. (Timothy H. Smith Collection)

century gave the name of Devil's Den to one of the numerous caverns that are to be found there."[66] In the 1883 history of Company F, 1st United States Sharpshooters, the author makes reference to the Den as a point known by an "altogether suggestive and appropriate name."

> Devil's Den—a name well applied, for a more desolate, ghostly place, or one more suggestive of the home of evil spirits can hardly be imagined. Barren of tree or shrub, and almost destitute of any green thing, it seems cursed of God and abandoned of man.[67]

All early references to the origin of the name "Devil's Den" refer to the sinister appearance of the area. For instance, an 1885 battlefield tour book stated that "Devil's Den" was "named, possibly, from the ominous character of its rocks, with their hard and ragged faces, and the gloom of their deep recesses."[68] In *Maine at Gettysburg*, printed in 1898, a passage describing the position of the 4th Maine Infantry also testifies to this fact.

> The official report of the regiment, made directly after the battle and before history had made famous every hill and valley on the field, speaks of taking position on a "rocky hill." This was the hill to the right of Devil's Den, that wonderful ravine where nature has disposed precipices and huge bowlders in a wild combination meriting the name which is given it.[69]

Among the Confederate soldiers who faced the 4th Maine during the battle were the men of the 44th Alabama commanded by Colonel William F. Perry. In 1901 he wrote of the "wild, rocky labyrinth, which from its weird uncanny features, has long been called by the people of the vicinity the "Devil's Den.""[70] Another source recorded it as "a chasm named by the country folk."[71] And *New York at Gettysburg*, published in 1902, states that:

> Devil's Den is a wild, rocky, partly wooded eminence which, owing to its weird and impressive appearance, had been known by this name for many generations before the battle. Around its base huge boulders, some of them as large as a small house, rest in an irregular, confused mass, forming nooks and cavernous recesses suggestive of its uncanny name.[72]

Not everyone, however, was so convinced that the Devil's Den was a pre-battle designation. On July 1, 1884 a poem entitled "Col. Egan's Charge" was published in the Gettysburg *Compiler* recounting the exploits of the 40th New York Infantry in the Valley of Death. The article was reprinted in the same paper a month later, this time entitled "Round-

Top." In one of its final passages the poet, W. W. Jacobs, mentioned that "That day of strife named the 'Devil's Den,'" suggesting that the name was derived from the heavy fighting on July 2, 1863. At the end of this sentence the editor of the *Compiler*, Henry J. Stahle, added an asterisk to which he attached a footnote at the bottom of the poem with the following correction: "The place has been spoken of as the "Devil's Den" for at least forty years [ca. 1844]."[73] It was at this point that one Gettysburg citizen finally had enough. Emanuel Bushman, a 42 year-old cabinet maker in 1863, was in a very good position to know about the Den. His grandfather (Jacob Bushman) was one of the early settlers of the area and his father (Henry Bushman) was born on the family farm a short distance southwest of the Den. At the time of the battle, this farm was owned by Emanuel's brother, Michael Bushman (1812-1893).[74] As a youth Emanuel spent much time on "Round Top" and in the rocks on its western base. On August 19, 1884 his response was printed in the *Compiler*.

> MR. STAHLE: The so-called "Devil's Den" was not known by that name in my early recollection. I heard my father [Henry Bushman], the elder Sherfy, and Armstrongs always call it "The Big Rocks." I do not know how or when it got that name. I sometimes heard it called "Raccoon Den." Was told there was a man named DeGroft went in to see who lived there. He saw three big raccoons inside, and they charged on him for trespassing. After a time he came out with a torn shirt and minus some flesh and a good deal of blood. The story was that he was nearly killed.[75]

Bushman concluded that regardless of what the rocks were called before the battle, the use of the term since the battle, and in "Mr. Jacobs's great poem, will perpetuate the name of 'Devil's Den' until the 'Big Rocks' shall crumble."[76] One would suppose that it was at least possible that a few in Gettysburg were calling it Devil's Den before the battle, but the term was not widespread and was not commonly used. In the midst of this controversy, confusion grew over what exactly the Devil's Den consisted of. Most assumed the name applied to the massive group of boulders itself. One writer in 1886 had another idea:

> ...the Devil's Den, a gloomy cavern, into whose grim shadows many poor fellows crawled, wounded and dying, blue and gray, while the fight was raging, and side by side lain down to escape the iron and leaden storm that whistled and thundered overhead. It is said that long after, when the war had stayed

its havoc, and the sword and bayonet were quietly asleep in their sheath and scabbard, in this lonely and dismal cave a score of skeletons were found. How one's heart sickens at the thought that a cup of water or a morsel of bread might have saved these lives, and paint if you can the agony of these suffering and abandoned wretches, when the fight was over, listening to the rumble of the departing trains, too faint to utter the feeble cry that would have brought them relief. This cave is within the shadow of Little Round Top, and about two hundred yards to the east, in a rocky ravine, where the boulders are piled one upon the other in absolute grandeur....[77]

In response to these comments made by one who had apparently "never visited the Gettysburg Battlefield," an article from the Lancaster *Intelligencer* fired back.

"Devil's Den" is no such cave or cavern. It is a lot of boulders piled into battlements and tumbled around promiscuously with clefts and hollows, and even a rude sort of shelves, and chambers, all tossed topsy-torvy upon a pile, across the meadow from the Round-Tops. Behind these rocks lay sharpshooters picking off the soldiery on Little Round-Top, and the faces of the boulders are pitted and streaked to this day with bullet marks. Among them were found a number of dead bodies after the battle,

two or three fallen down one of the fissures; but the story of twenty skeletons in a cave is bosh.[78]

With this apparent confusion over the nickname, it is fortunate that in 1894, but a few months before his death, John Bachelder was questioned about the Devil's Den, and gave an explanation to clear up the confusion concerning the name that he had popularized 30 years earlier. It appears that he had never intended the name to be applied to the outcropping of rocks itself. His use of the name was designed to mark something far more specific.

The Devil's Den is seldom visited, and very few people know what it is.... The Devil's Den is a hole under ledges in which there is a spring. The front of it is masked by a big bowlder, and you cannot see it until you get within ten feet of it. You see the rocks about there, and people go home and say they have seen the Devil's Den, but they have not been within a hundred yards of it. The Devil's Den is seldom visited by anyone.... The Den is not a new name; it was a name given to the locality before the battle. It is a gorge, or rather it is a hole in the ground, and it is very difficult to get into it. There is a spring at its mouth, but those big rocks that stand up there are not the Devil's Den. ...The whole gorge is the region of the Devil's Den, and the ridge in front of it, west of it, or rather the ridge which

"The Spring at Devil's Den," Tipton, c. 1888. (ACHS)

commencing at the Devil's Den extends northward, I have called in history the Rocky Ridge, because it is so characterized in quite a number of official reports of Confederate officers. Being strangers here, they named things from what they saw, and they called that the Rocky Ridge, and as there is no rocky ridge on the battle-field except that, I shall accept their name and call it so in history.[79]

Heap Big Snake

By the turn of the century the term Devil's Den was used in virtually every book published on the battle. For the first fifty years after the battle all articles and publications on the topic suggested that the name was derived because of the formation's eerie or irregular appearance. Today, however, one cannot visit the Den without hearing of the reptiles that infested it. Emanuel Bushman, who in 1884 refuted the idea that the "Big Rocks" were known as Devil's Den before the battle, was also one of the first to tell stories of snakes that lived in the area. In an 1875 letter to a Baltimore newspaper, he described the now famous "Round Top" as a "rendezvous" for a "monster snake."

One sunny day in April in 1833 my brother with six others, were exploring Round Top for the first time. The hill and surroundings were covered with a dense forest. As they were ascending the west side they suddenly came upon a monster snake, sunning itself upon the rocks. Part of them took to flight, but brother and two others stood to see how it would end. They described it as a black snake, apparently turning gray with age. Brother hissed the dog on it, and he thought from the capacious mouth that he would swallow the dog. They estimated its length to be from fifteen to twenty feet, and the thickness of an ordinary man's waist. They threw at it from above and it rolled down into its den. Frank Armstrong saw it and was badly frightened. Father saw it before that about a mile from there at the big rocks, called the Devil's Den. Grandfather saw it in his time, and Mother says the Indians used to speak of it as "heap big snake." Mr. Michael Fry [Frey], living near Round Top, saw it about thirty years ago [1845], which is the last time I heard of it. How old do they get? Father says tradition traced it back one hundred years. Brother and Mr. Fry are the only two living who claim to have seen it.[80]

There is no doubt that the rocky terrain near Round Top makes an ideal habitat for snakes. Eight species of snakes (two of which are poisonous) are documented to inhabit the Gettysburg National Military Park.[81] The largest of these is the Northern Black Racer (Coluber constrictor) and is commonly seen on the battlefield, preferring dry areas full of bushes and rocky crevices into which it may seek quick shelter. The blacksnake is an alert, active and locally abundant reptile. A very good climber, it feeds on small mice, birds, and any eggs it can steal from the nests of its prey. Over the years many romantic stories have exaggerated the prowess of this creature; some have even suggested it has the power of hypnotism. If cornered, it will strike out at humans, but more likely it will dash with great speed at the first sign of danger. Today, the Northern Black Racer is known to grow about six feet in length. Unless it was a mutation, or was some other species that no longer exists, Bushman's fifteen to twenty foot snake seems a bit exaggerated.[82]

The most popular story for the naming of Devil's Den, and that tourists to Gettysburg are most likely to hear today, is an account given by Salome Myers Stewart for an article in the *Chattanooga News* on October 30, 1913. Sallie was a twenty-year-old resident of Gettysburg in 1863, who became a heroine for her work as a volunteer nurse in the hospitals around town after the battle.[83] In her version, the story of the snake is incorporated with the fact that the Den had been given its name before the battle.

There is another wrong impression which I wish to correct, and that refers to the name "Devil's Den." Many persons have been told that the name was given to those immense rocks because of the fierce fighting there during the battle of Gettysburg. My uncle, John Plank, was one of the early settlers of the County, and his farm included a part of the "Round Tops." As a child, I have heard him tell of the snakes which infested the country, and had their "den" among those huge rocks. Parties of men were organized to rid the neighborhood of these dangerous reptiles. One big old snake persistently eluded them. They could never kill or capture him, and they called him "The Devil." He finally disappeared, and it was supposed that he died in his "Den." So, to Gettysburgers, that has always been "Devil's Den."[84]

Regardless of how it got its name, Devil's Den has its share of interesting lore. On tours of the field, questions concerning the origins of the Den and its surroundings are common. In many ways its popularity has transcended the battle. With its rich history and wild appearance, one is left to ponder a thought-provoking question. What would Devil's Den be like today if there had never been a battle at Gettysburg?

The Battle for Devil's Den

The event which gave the Devil's Den its national significance was, of course, the fighting on July 2, 1863. Producing far more casualties than the attack and defense of Little Round Top, the struggle for the Den has, by comparison, been largely overshadowed. Over the years, this aspect of the battle has been misinterpreted, glossed over or ignored altogether. The comparatively few narratives which contain detailed accounts of the fighting at Devil's Den are often vague, out of sequence or focused only on a single unit. This section places the flow of the battle into its proper chronological order and explains many complicated and fascinating details of the fight, some of which are compiled here for the first time. The scope is deliberately narrow and focuses solely upon those units that participated in the fighting in and around the Den—largely Ward's Brigade and Hood's Division. When discussing general events such as the march to Gettysburg, every attempt has been made to limit the quotations within the text to the words of these soldiers.

Where applicable, maps and photographs are included in order to give the reader a more complete understanding of the engagement. The objective is to answer who it was that fought, what they did, and when and how specific events occurred. Without standardized time, the great disparity in the recollections of participants on both sides regarding the timing of events is not surprising when one considers the confusion that reigned during the fighting. However, with a sequential relationship between events in Devil's Den and the surrounding areas, the issue of time falls into its context. The focus, therefore, is on the chronolgical placement of events rather than on the unreliable timepieces of the soldiers.

The following short biographies of the units and the men within who fought at Devil's Den, are presented to assist the reader in understanding the battle as well as to provide some information about the commanders who would lead these units at Gettysburg. For more detail, the order of battle for both armies is located in Appendix I, while the strengths and losses of each unit that fought at Devil's Den can be found in Appendix II.

The Army of the Potomac

Ward and his Brigade—First Division, Third Corps. John Henry Hobart Ward came from a family with a long military tradition. His grandfather was mortally wounded in the Revolutionary War and his father was wounded in the War with Mexico. Entering the army at the age of eighteen, young Ward attained the rank of sergeant major, which he held until he, like his father, was wounded during the Mexican War. Remaining in military service until the outbreak of the Civil War, he was soon commissioned colonel of the 38th New York; a regiment he led throughout 1861 and most of 1862. In October of that year he was promoted to brigadier general and was given command of David Bell Birney's Brigade, part of the gallant Major General Phil Kearny's famed "red diamond division."

Ward marched to Gettysburg with more men and more regiments than any brigade in the Union army. Almost 2600 strong, the eight regiments could be considered a small division.[1]

The 124th New York, Ward's Brigade. The 124th New York was recruited in Orange County, New York in the summer of 1862, but saw no severe action until desperately engaged at Chancellorsville. At that battle, Colonel Augustus Van Horne Ellis first referred to the regiment by its nickname—the "Orange Blossoms." At Chancellorsville, the 124th lost over 37% of its men and would march to Gettysburg with scarcely 300 soldiers. Scores of men were lost along the way and the regiment could muster but 238 officers and men on July 2nd, 1863.

Augustus Van Horne Ellis was a sea captain before the war and was, at one point, offered the command of the Hawaiian Navy. To his chagrin, however, that navy had not even a single ship or the means to purchase one, so he soon made his way back to his home state of New York. In 1861 Ellis became a captain in the 71st New York State Militia. When the 124th N. Y. was formed the following year, he became its colonel, a post which he held until his last breath.[2]

The 4th Maine, Ward's Brigade. The 4th Maine Volunteers was raised in Knox, Waldo and Lincoln Counties in the summer of 1861. Also known as the "Limerock Regiment" it arrived in Washington on June 21st under the command of Colonel Hiram J. Berry, the former mayor of Rockland, Maine. Berry was destined to rise to the rank of major general but was killed shortly thereafter, leading a bayonet charge at Chancellorsville.

In March 1862, as a result of Berry's promotion to brigadier, Elijah Walker became the 4th Maine's colonel. The former lumber merchant from Rockland "accepted the honor reluctantly, conscious of [his] inability to adequately fill [Berry's] place." Walker, however, filled the position more than "adequately," leading his men through the Seven Days Battles, Chantilly, Fredericksburg and Chancellorsville. As the 2nd days fight at Gettysburg opened, his force of less than 300 men would be the left flank of the entire Army of the Potomac.[3]

The 86th New York, Ward's Brigade. The 86th was organized at Elmira, New York in November of 1861 and mustered into the United States service for three years. Eight of its ten companies were recruited in Steuben County, hence its nickname— the "Steuben Rangers." The regiment departed its home state with 960 men. After almost a year of provost duty it was fiercely engaged at the Second Battle of Bull Run. Fighting through Fredericksburg and Chancellorsville it would march to Gettysburg as merely a skeleton of its former strength, with but 287 officers and men—the same number as the 4th Maine. At the head of the 86th was Lieutenant Colonel Benjamin L. Higgins. The former Syracuse fire chief would be in the center of Ward's Brigade at Gettysburg.[4]

The 99th Pennsylvania, Ward's Brigade. The 99th Pennsylvania was recruited from Philadelphia and Lancaster County. Fighting with the Army of the Potomac throughout 1862 and early 1863, the men were seasoned veterans by the time they reached Gettysburg. Like most experienced regiments, however, it was reduced in numbers. Upon reaching the field the 99th could boast but 277 officers and men. At Gettysburg, the 99th was ably led by Major John William Moore of Philadelphia. He was the sole field officer in his regiment as the fight for Devil's Den opened.[5]

The 20th Indiana, Ward's Brigade. The 20th Indiana Volunteer Infantry was organized in July of 1861 at Camp Tippecanoe in Lafayette, Indiana. The 20th was composed of ten companies from ten different counties. These 401 men marched to Gettysburg under the command of Colonel John Wheeler. Born in New Milford, Connecticut on February 6, 1825, Wheeler moved to Indiana, and in 1857 founded a newspaper in Crown Point. He soon gave up the newspaper business to raise a unit of infantry which became Company B, 20th Indiana. Ascending to the colonelcy, Wheeler was admired by both his men and his superiors. He commanded Ward's largest regiment at Gettysburg.[6]

The 2nd United States Sharpshooters, Ward's Brigade. In the fall and winter of 1861, a diverse group of men were brought together under the leadership of Hiram Berdan. All were expert marksmen. Coming from as far east as Maine and as far west as Minnesota, they were issued green uniforms and were eventually armed with Sharps breechloading rifles. Organized as the 1st and 2nd United States Sharpshooters, they saw serious action in 1862.

The 2nd regiment marched to Pennsylvania under Major Homer Richard Stoughton. The regiment contained only eight companies and mustered just 169 men for action at Gettysburg. Primarily employed as skirmishers, the sharpshooters had much experience in this area, as well as the ability and arms to make good of it.[7]

The 4th New York Independent Battery, Third Corps Artillery Brigade. Leaving New York City in the fall of 1861, Smith's Battery, styled after its Captain, James Edward Smith, rendered valuable service with the Union Third Corps throughout 1862 and 1863. Captain Smith served as division chief of artillery for a time but only had charge of his battery at Gettysburg. His battery contained over 120 veterans with which to serve its six Parrott rifles. His lieutenants, however, were both on detached service with other units at the time of the battle and he had two officers attached to replace them. 1st Lieutenant Thomas Goodman from the 6th New Jersey Volunteers and 2nd Lieutenant Jeremiah S. Clark of Turnbull's Battery filled the ranks. With this uncertain leadership structure, The 4th New York Battery marched to the battlefield and toward an opportunity for intense and notable service.[8]

The 40th New York, DeTrobriand's Brigade, First Division, Third Corps. Although the 40th New York Infantry was the largest regiment in the Third Corps, it was by no means an inexperienced unit. Organized with support from the Democratic political faction known as the Mozart Hall Committee, it was mustered in for three years on June 27, 1861. Distinctive in that it contained companies from three different states, New York, Massachusetts and Pennsylvania, it marched off to war with just over 1000 men. The "Mozart Regiment" was brigaded under General John Sedgwick along with the 3rd and 4th Maine and the 38th New York. Thomas Wilberforce Egan commanded the unit at Gettysburg.

Egan had been commissioned colonel of the 40th when, as lieutenant colonel, he put his commander under arrest for misconduct at the Battle of Seven Pines. Throughout 1862 the regiment performed gallantly under Egan and as a result, became seriously depleted in numbers. It was consolidated with the 87th New York in the fall, and after Chancellorsville, with the 37th, 38th, 55th and 101st from the same state. Like the 40th, these regiments had become greatly depleted through hard fighting. Hence, at Gettysburg, Egan marched with 431 veterans of six different regiments and from three different states, all under the flag of the 40th New York.[9]

The 6th New Jersey, Burling's Brigade, Second Division, Third Corps. A small body of 207 men at Gettysburg, the regiment was over four times larger when it left Trenton, New Jersey in the fall of 1861. Fighting with the Army of the Potomac in all of the battles, save one, from Williamsburg to Petersburg they did their duty nobly. Commanded by Colonel Stephen R. Gilkyson, a former lumber merchant, at Gettysburg the brigade would be distributed to various parts of the Third Corps line until it ceased to be a brigade.[10]

The Army of Northern Virginia

The 1st Texas, Robertson's Brigade, Hood's Division, Longstreet's Corps. Recruited in June 1861 and strengthened in the following months, the 1st Texas became the only regiment in the Army of Northern Virginia with a dozen companies. It was initially brigaded with Texas and Georgia regiments under its original commander Lewis T. Wigfall. Wigfall soon returned to political life and the brigade received a new commander—John Bell Hood. Although Hood commanded the brigade for less than six months, the 1st, 4th and 5th Texas and the 3rd Arkansas regiments would be forever known as "Hood's Texas Brigade." This famed unit was renowned for its ferocious and reckless demeanor and had distinguished itself on many battlefields.

The 1st Texas was "sacrificed" at Sharpsburg, losing over 80% of its men. Strengthened thereafter, it fought at Gettysburg under Lieutenant Colonel Phillip A. Work. Its 426 men were under a new brigade commander (Hood was promoted to command the division). Brigadier General Jerome Bonaparte

Robertson, a former medical doctor and politician, took command of the Texas Brigade. A well-mannered, courageous man, his abilities were largely untested when his men marched to Gettysburg.[11]

The 3rd Arkansas, Robertson's Brigade. This regiment was mustered into Confederate service on July 5, 1861 for the duration of the war. Some of the men of Company H were actually recruited from Kentucky but the remainder were Arkansans. The 3rd saw little fighting for over fourteen months until they were intensely "baptized" at the Battle of Antietam. During the organizational changes which followed that battle, the Arkansans were brigaded with Hood's famed Texans and were eventually made to feel a true part of the Texas Brigade by earning their nickname, the "3rd Texas."

At just 23 years of age Vannoy Hartrog Manning (the youngest colonel to fight around the Devil's Den) had been in charge of the Arkansans since March of the previous year. With 479 men the 3rd was the largest regiment, Northern or Southern, to fight around the Devil's Den. It would take an able man to command this regiment at Gettysburg; the 3rd Arkansas would represent the exposed left flank of the first Confederate attack column—one which the Yankees tried energetically to overrun.[12]

The 44th Alabama, Law's Brigade, Hood's Division. Recruited in March 1862, the 44th saw serious action in the late summer and early fall of that year. After Fredericksburg, and until the end of the war, the 44th fought side by side along with the 4th, 15th, 47th and 48th regiments as Evander M. Law's Alabama Brigade. Its colonel, William F. Perry, a former educator who before the war laid the foundation for Alabama's public school system, enlisted as a private upon the forming of the regiment. By September of 1862, Perry had risen to the colonelcy and was destined to retain that title with valor for some time. On July 2nd, the 363 men of the 44th would be separated from much of their brigade.[13]

The 48th Alabama, Law's Brigade. Like the 44th, the 48th Alabama was recruited in the spring of 1862 and saw its share of fighting that year. The 48th boasted 374 men at Gettysburg under James Lawrence Sheffield, a former sheriff and state legislator who was the original colonel of the regiment. He equipped the men himself, spending sixty thousand dollars in gold from his own fortune. His bravery had earned the senior colonel of Law's Brigade the admiration of his soldiers on many occasions.[14]

The 2nd Georgia, Benning's Brigade, Hood's Division. The 2nd Georgia was recruited from nine different counties spread throughout the state. When the regiment was organized in May of 1861, its colonel was Paul J. Semmes who was subsequently promoted to the rank of brigadier general. At the Battle of Sharpsburg, the 2nd regiment, along with the 20th Georgia, distinguished itself in the defense of Burnside's Bridge. With the loss of its fourth commander, William R. Holmes, during the battle, William Terrell Harris took command. Harris had been a planter, lawyer and state legislator before the war. He was 33 years old and a lieutenant colonel when he marched his veterans into Pennsylvania. Although not a full colonel, and thus the lowest ranking of Benning's regimental commanders, he was the only one who had been in charge of his regiment as early as 1862.[15]

The 15th Georgia, Benning's Brigade. Organized in July 1861, the 15th regiment came from the northeastern counties of Georgia. 1862 saw the disability of one and the death of two of its colonels. On the first day of 1863 the regiment got a young, new colonel named Dudley McIver DuBose. The 28 year-old had been admitted to the bar and was married to the daughter of brigade commander Robert Toombs. DuBose commanded the largest regiment of Benning's Brigade at Gettysburg (with the most seniority at the rank of colonel) with about 368 officers and men.[16]

The 17th Georgia, Benning's Brigade. Recruited in the southern and western regions of Georgia in the summer of 1861, its original colonel was none other than Henry Lewis Benning himself. A successful lawyer and politician before the war, Benning was of impressive physique and had a commanding presence. "Old Rock," as he was known, led the regiment with distinction throughout the first half of the war. In January of 1863, at the age of 48, he was promoted to the command of the brigade.

When Benning was advanced, Wesley C. Hodges took his place. Colonel Hodges, having been a Mexican war veteran and cotton merchant, was the only one of Benning's colonels who had not been a lawyer or politician before the war.[17]

The 20th Georgia, Benning's Brigade. The 20th regiment was organized in the summer of 1861 with William Duncan Smith as its colonel. Like all of the other regiments in this brigade, the 20th produced a general officer. Smith was soon promoted to brigadier and fought in the western theater. The regiment fought hard throughout 1862 and immortalized itself in the defense of Burnside's Bridge. In May of 1863, the 20th received a new colonel—John Augustus Jones. He had been the 20th's major as early as 1861 and had earned the respect of the regiment. Gettysburg would be his first battle at his new rank.[18]

The March to Gettysburg

"The first day of July broke clear and bright, and the sun as it moved toward its zenith, had an angry look and sent down upon us blistering rays."[19] Captain Charles H. Weygant of the 124th New York Infantry, put forth the feelings of thousands of men on that fateful day in 1863. Nearly two months after the demoralizing Union defeat at Chancellorsville, Confederate General Robert E. Lee was in the process of invading Northern soil with his Army of Northern Virginia. The Union Army of the Potomac, forced to follow Lee, had done little more than march through the sweltering heat and pouring rain for three straight weeks. The hardships of the march to Gettysburg did not go unrecorded by the men of the Union Army. The 124th New York Regiment lost nearly 30% of its men to fatigue and exposure during the movement north.[20] Henry Leach, a Sergeant in the 4th Maine, was afflicted with severe sunstroke during this prolonged marching. After violent actions for five days, Leach regained his composure to fight in the battle, but the affliction would follow him beyond Gettysburg, into Rebel prisons and eventually lead him to suicide.[21] Often, the true glory of war is a disheartening and lifelong struggle that has little to do with valor on the battlefield.

By the afternoon of July 1, 1863, Union General Daniel Sickles' Third Corps arrived at Emmitsburg, Maryland. His roughly 10,000 men prepared to bivouac after what had been, at last, a relatively short jaunt of but a few miles. But soon, Sickles received a plea from Major General Oliver O. Howard, who was in desperate need of help at a town not ten miles distant. With his response to Howard, "I shall move to Gettysburg immediately," Sickles approached the most important day of his life.[22]

The position at Emmitsburg, however, was yet an extremely important point and Sickles had no plans to abandon it against orders. DeTrobriand's Brigade of Birney's Division and Burling's Brigade of Humphreys' Division along with two New York Batteries, were left near Emmitsburg to cover the rear of the Army. The remainder of the Third Corps (four brigades and three batteries strong) marched through the humid July heat on the muddy and worn roads to Gettysburg.[23]

As the men marched, the sound of cannon fire became more pronounced and the ranks of the column became thin. Some remembered this "forced march," although not particularly long, as "one of the hardest of the war."[24] Men fell by the roadside, unable to stand the sweltering heat and the intense humidity.[25] "Louder and fiercer boomed the yet distant guns, and forward men, forward, shouted the officers."[26] Knapsacks, blankets, guns, and most no-

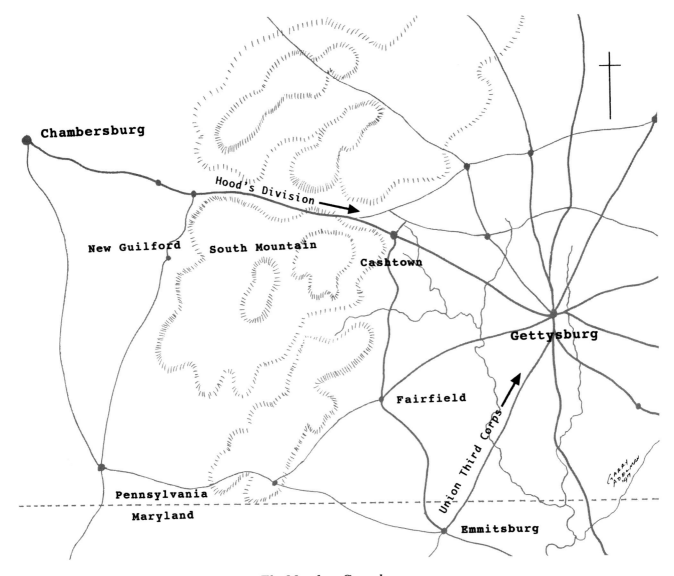

The March to Gettysburg.

tably, stragglers could be found amid the shade at every patch of woods and every field of timothy. Canteens could provide no succor, as the water therein was "steaming hot."[27] By the time the exhausted men reached the southern end of the battlefield, it was too late to participate in the fighting that day. The 4th Maine was one of two Third Corps regiments that spent the night of July 1st on picket duty, guarding the Emmitsburg Road.[28] The remainder of the Third Corps took position near the George Weikert farm, and were only somewhat luckier. Sergeant J. Harvey Hanford, of the 124th New York recalled:

> We lay down in an open field, with orders to sleep on our arms, and not take off an article of clothing or any of our accouterments. This was hard sauce after such a march as we had had; but, soldier like, we had to take it out in grumbling.[29]

Just as the Yankees had to march hard to reach the field, the advance of their counterparts was equally grueling. The Army of Northern Virginia moved farther (throughout the month of June) although not as fast as the Union army. The previous weeks had held many difficulties for the invaders. Private Theodore Fogle of Benning's Georgia brigade recalled the invasion of Pennsylvania:

> ... this last campaign exceeds in hardships anything I have ever experienced. I have been cold, hot, wet, dry, ragged, dirty, hungry & thirsty, marched through clouds of dust, waded mud knee deep & suffered from fatigue & loss of sleep & through it all I have *kept my health*, there is only one thing I can't stand, that is hunger—it makes me crazy almost...[30]

The unscathed land, however, and the plentiful crops eased the trials of marching. Most Southerners chose to remember the pleasures of Pennsylvania farmland and its harvests more than the hard marching. One man recalled his satisfaction over such a luxury.

> One canteen of skimmed milk was turned up to the mouth of this private soldier, who never stopped to breathe until the entire contents—three pints—had passed into his stomach; and then, with a sigh of satisfaction, he was ready to go to sleep.[31]

Of Robert E. Lee's nine divisions of infantry, only one would be involved in the fighting at Devil's Den. Unfortunately for the Union soldiers, this was Major General John Bell Hood's Division of 7800 battle-hardened soldiers. Hood's Division contained two brigades of Georgians, one of Alabamians and one composed of Texans and Arkansans. Attached to the division was an artillery battalion commanded by Major Mathis Henry. With the exception of Law's Brigade of Alabamians and Bachman's Battery, who were positioned at New Guilford, July 1 found Hood's Division around Greenwood, Pennsylvania about fourteen miles from Gettysburg.

The marching orders that day provided for a division of Ewell's Corps to pass first, but a wagon train of that corps was also allowed to proceed on the overcrowded Chambersburg Pike ahead of Hood's and McLaws' Divisions. Longstreet's men were "greatly delayed" waiting for the long train to pass.[32] Meanwhile, advance elements of Lee's Army were smashing the Union First and Eleventh Corps north and west of Gettysburg. Unable to be of any help on July 1, Hood's men relaxed, held a dress parade and poked fun at the teamsters passing by.[33]

Finally, at around 5:00 p.m., Hood's veterans took to the road behind McLaws' Division and started for the battlefield. Several of the soldiers recalled that the "stop and go" nature of this miserable ordeal made it much worse than steady marching. Private William T. Fluker of the 15th Georgia recalled this endeavor:

> We began to suspect by this time that we were going somewhere for something, as we failed to get our usual ten minutes rest every hour, which had been the regular order of General Lee's march since we commenced our march from Culpepper Courthouse, Va., which was to march fifty minutes and rest ten. The tired men would cry out "rest, rest," but no order came to rest. Men fell asleep marching only to wake as they stumbled or bumped against their file leaders and get cussed for tramping on his heels.[34]

The exhausted men tramped through the darkness until around midnight when they reached the vicinity of Marsh Creek.[35] Upon completion of their march, the men of Hood's Division shared many of the same conditions as their Yankee counterparts in the Union Third Corps. One Georgian recalled:

> ...we filed to the right of the turnpike and went some 300 yards and halted in a clover field. As soon as we stopped every man dropped to the ground where he stood and was soon asleep. As he fell no man unrolled a blanket to lie on or cover with, but slept with every buckle and strap in place, ready to rise and move at the command.[36]

Most of Hood's Division slept less than five miles away from the men of Ward's Brigade that night. It was a night spent in full uniform, equipment and all, on the damp Pennsylvania ground into which so many of them, Northern and Southern, would be interred within the next few days.

Morning, July 2nd

While most of Hood's Division spent the early morning hours of July 2 resting near Marsh Creek, Brigadier General Evander M. Law's Alabamians were still "on picket at New Guilford, on the road leading toward Emmitsburg."[37] On the previous evening, few, if any of Law's men were allowed more than a couple hours of sleep before the early morning march on July 2. These men, who marched farther than any Confederate unit who fought that day, did most of their tramping before the heat became most oppressive. Private William C. Ward, of the 4th Alabama recalled the 2:00 a.m. reveille and the march.

> Promptly we were aroused, and began the most fatiguing march of the war. At daylight we were ascending the mountains; and, without halting, we went over the crest and down into the valley at Cashtown. Then we began to realize what this march meant. Passing rapidly to the rear were hundreds of Federal prisoners taken in the battle of July 1....The roads were the roughest and the long, sloping hills the steepest. The day was hot, and we were thirsty and had not stopped to rest or drink.[38]

Law's men did some respectable marching that morning, and covered the seventeen miles from New Guilford, through the South Mountain range, to Marsh Creek in about ten hours.[39] Unfortunately, they needed to march still farther to get into position for the upcoming attack, with little rest beforehand.

As if the entire battle were orchestrated from

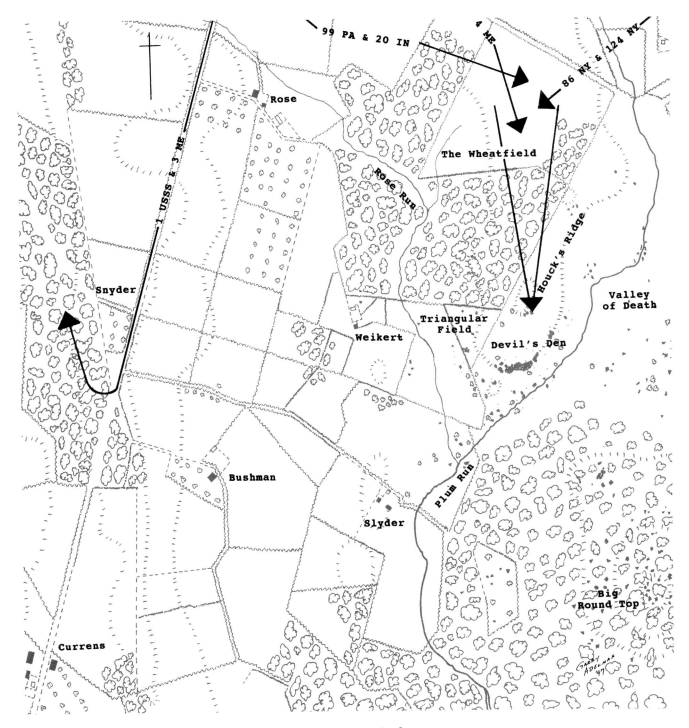

Morning, July 2nd.

above, Union soldiers who had been left behind at Emmitsburg were also marching to the scene. The Third Corps brigades of DeTrobriand and Burling as well as Smith's and Winslow's New York Batteries received orders to make the ten-mile jaunt to Gettysburg at the same time that Law's men were making their lengthy march to the battlefield. The Union forces at Emmitsburg were scattered and it took several hours before they were on the move. If this march was particularly event-

ful, all commanding officers failed to report it. What was significant, however, was their arrival. Smith and Burling arrived at around 9:00 a.m. to find preparations for battle underway. Captain Smith remembered:

> As we approached the ground between the two armies in the vicinity of the "Peach Orchard," I noticed that the fences had been cleared away, and all preparations made that

usually precede a battle; even then the pickets and skirmishers were uneasy and kept up a desultory fire, little puffs of thin blue smoke dotting the plain before us, indicating quite distinctly the respective lines of the two greatest armies on earth, at this hour.[40]

Smith and Burling, heading for what was soon to be a no man's land, left the Emmitsburg Road and parked near the Wheatfield. DeTrobriand's Brigade and Winslow's Battery reached the field sometime later and took a similar path eastward.

Earlier that morning, General Ward had formed his brigade in line of battle, along a stone wall south of the George Weikert farm. Not knowing when or where the battle would take place, he issued orders to several of his regimental commanders. Lieutenant Colonel Benjamin L. Higgins of the 86th New York recalled:

> After remaining inactive until 10 a.m., I was ordered by General Ward to send forward a sufficient body of men, under charge of a commissioned officer, to demolish all stone walls and fences in our front to the Emmitsburg Road. I immediately sent Captain Baker, of Company G, with 35 men on that duty.[41]

Before noon, Ward's commanding officer, Major General David B. Birney, asked for General Sickles' permission to do some reconnaissance in his front. Receiving the affirmative, he chose Ward's men for the task. Ward detached 100 men of the 1st United States Sharpshooters, along with the 3rd Maine Regiment, and this force, under Colonel Hiram Berdan, advanced southwesterly and entered Biesecker's Woods. Additionally, the 99th Pennsylvania and the 20th Indiana were sent forward toward the Emmitsburg Road as support.[42] The sharpshooters in front, with the Maine men following, moved north through the woods when they encountered Confederate skirmishers and drove them in. Soon, they came upon three columns of Alabamians moving toward them and brisk fighting ensued for a short time, with both sides inflicting casualties.[43] Having accomplished his objective and being heavily outnumbered, Berdan ordered his force to retire. Neither of these regiments would rejoin Ward's Brigade in the struggle for Devil's Den.

It was now clear to the Yankees that the Confederates were, in fact, extending their lines southward. General Ward concentrated the remainder of his brigade: the 4th Maine (who had been on picket duty all night), the 99th Pennsylvania, and the 20th Indiana were pulled back from their advanced positions, while the 86th and 124th New York regiments were moved forward from the protection of their stone wall. One New Yorker remembered the advance:

> ...after crossing one or two fields we came to the famous Wheatfield,—and, by the way, it was one of the finest I ever saw—the wheat breast high and ready to cut,—but we marched through and over it in line of battle, and on looking back not a stalk could be found, for it was all trodden out of sight.[44]

The two regiments of New Yorkers rested in the trampled wheat for about thirty minutes when they were joined by Ward's three regiments that had been near the Emmitsburg Road. These five regiments: the 4th Maine, the 124th New York, the 86th New York, the 20th Indiana and the 99th Pennsylvania, in the order named from left to right, now moved to the south, and into position along the rocky ridge owned by John Houck.

In the meantime, Robert E. Lee decided that the main thrust of his attack would be made upon the Union left flank by the divisions of Hood and McLaws. He issued orders to Longstreet to march his two divisions southward without being detected, and envelop the Union left flank. Having no competent guide, much time was wasted on the march and even more frustration and exhaustion ensued. The outcome of this "flank march," is important due to the countermarching and the delays that resulted.[45] It was between three and four o'clock before Hood and McLaws were in position. Lee, Longstreet and many other officers were concerned that the hour was becoming too late to mount an attack before darkness covered the battlefield.

When Longstreet's men finally arrived in position along Warfield and Seminary Ridges, it was supposed that they would be entirely on the flank of the enemy. This was not the case at all and it became painfully obvious that Lee's plans would have to change. Northern soldiers were posted in force in the Peach Orchard and the Union line appeared to extend all the way to Big Round Top. It had not been as such for long. The commander of the 3rd Army Corps did not find the ground that his men were to occupy to his liking. According to General Sickles himself:

> The early morning of July 2 was spent reconnoitering my front on the left, choosing positions, gathering information about the roads, and learning something of the force and dispositions of the enemy. The prolongation of the line of Cemetery Ridge, perhaps the more desirable tactical position for me to occupy, unless overruled by superior considerations, proved upon examination to be an unsatisfactory line because of its marked depression and the swampy character of the ground between Cemetery Ridge and Little Round Top. The most commanding position on the field was

Little Round Top and the ridge running from it towards the Emmittsburg road. Moreover, to abandon the Emmittsburg road to the enemy would be unpardonable.[46]

As the afternoon wore on, Sickles, still having not received the orders he desired, decided to make the move forward. "Impossible to wait longer without giving the enemy serious advantages in his attack," Sickles recalled, "I advanced my line towards the highest ground in my front, occupying the Emmittsburg road."[47] This relocation placed his men in front of the rest of the army, with his flanks less than secure. The Peach Orchard became the center of Sickles' line with his second division, commanded by Brigadier General Andrew A. Humphreys, on the right and Birney's first division bending back and filling the space between the Peach Orchard and the strange, rocky bulwark, nearly destitute of trees, now known as Devil's Den. In occupying this line, Sickles created a hazardous salient with his corps and all but abandoned Little Round Top. For better or for worse, the responsibility for holding this line now rested with the officers and men of the Third Corps. The position of Devil's Den, now on the left of the Army of the Potomac, was entrusted to the care of Brigadier General John Henry Hobart Ward. Ironically, the Den was a place of little value to Adams County farmers before the battle, but on July 2, 1863, it was the end of the Union line and men from as far away as Texas and Maine would fight, maim and kill each other for the privilege of standing atop its rock-strewn crest.

The Eve of Battle

As Hood's Division and Ward's Brigade prepared to do battle, the Federals had at least one distinct advantage. The men of Ward's Brigade arrived in their positions about two hours earlier than their Southern adversaries. Instead of greatly strengthening their line, however, most of the men spent the hours relaxing and eating. A member of the 124th New York explained:

> We had not yet learned by bitter experience the inestimable value of building breastworks, and instead of spending our leisure time in rolling together the loose stones and throwing over them such a quantity of earth as would have made a bullet proof line, we lounged about on the grass and rocks, quietly awaiting the coming shock, which many declared themselves ready and anxious to receive. But there were undoubtedly those among us who ardently wished and perhaps secretly prayed that when the battle opened, it might rage the most furiously along some other portion of the line.[48]

Gettysburg, perhaps, proved to be just the "bitter experience" necessary to teach these men to build breastworks. Having not yet learned to appreciate them, though, Ward's men made the best of the time. Ammunition was distributed and the battle lines were perfected. One soldier of the 124th New York recalled that each man of his regiment was "ordered to take at least 80 rounds of ammunition, of which there was numerous supply." He went on to speculate that most men took over 100 and some as many as 200 rounds "putting the extra cartridges in their empty haversacks in lieu of rations."[49] Others wasted no time, however, in filling their stomachs instead of their haversacks. Colonel Elijah Walker of the 4th Maine recalled:

> It was now 3 o'clock and my men were hungry, having drank water for supper, breakfast and dinner. Fires were kindled, a heifer was found near by and slaughtered, coffee was steeped and beef impaled on sticks was warmed over the blaze. We drank our coffee and ate the very rare and thoroughly smoked meat, sprinkling it with salt, of which condiment every soldier carried a little in his pocket.[50]

John Henry Hobart Ward. (USAMHI)

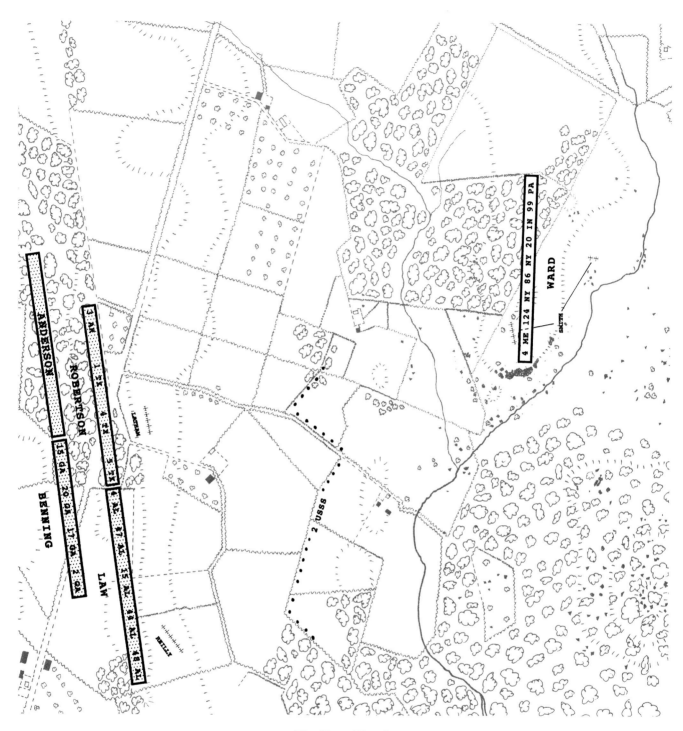

The Eve of Battle.

Cattle must have been plentiful in that area, for the 124th New York and 99th Pennsylvania also mentioned slaughtering steer. The 99th, however, did not have time to enjoy their feast: "...the meat was cut up and distributed to the men, who did not have the time to cook the same, but put the raw and bloody meat in their haversacks just as the order was given to move forward."[51] Many of these men would soon be as bloodied as the fare in their pouches.

While the infantrymen passed the time, the men of Captain James E. Smith's 4th New York Light Artillery labored to get their guns into position atop Devil's Den. Third Corps Artillery Commander, Captain George E. Randolph had ordered Smith to the position at around 2 p.m.[52] It was a difficult location and the placement of the guns took over an hour. Union Chief of Artillery Brigadier General Henry Hunt proceeded to Devil's Den to observe the movement and

"On climbing to the summit...found that Smith had just got his guns, one by one, over the rocks and chasms, into an excellent position."[53] It was a good site but the nature of the ground allowed the placement of only four of Smith's six, ten-pounder Parrott rifles atop its crest. The left of Smith's four guns was probably placed just west of where the 99th Pennsylvania monument currently stands atop Devil's Den. In Smith's words, "The remaining two guns were stationed in rear about seventy-five yards, where they could be used to advantage, covering the Plum Run Gorge passage, which lies to the south of and below the crest."[54] The caissons and horses of the battery were placed north and east of the two guns in the rear.[55] (For more on the location of Smith's Guns, see Appendix III.)

The position atop Devil's Den was a good one with a sweeping field of fire and numerous rocks and boulders which afforded some protection to the artillerymen. The spot, however, had its weaknesses. The gunners would become vulnerable to enemy snipers if they reached the base of the hill, and the close proximity to woodlots on the north, south and east gave Smith some worry (even Brigadier General Hunt told Smith that, if attacked, he would most likely lose his guns).[56] The four guns themselves were important in the fight for Devil's Den, but the spot upon which they rested held the key to the position. Whoever held the crest controlled the ground around it, and thus, the left flank of the Union army.

As the fight approached, the 4th Maine was stationed directly behind Smith's guns. Its left was positioned near the large rocks at the Den, its center was just on the eastern side of Houck's Ridge and its right extended northward toward the 124th New York which was atop the crest in the mostly open ground. Company A, on the right of the 124th, entered Rose Woods several yards east of the modern avenue.[57] Whether the left of the 86th New York connected with the right of the 124th New York is questionable. Captain Charles H. Weygant, of Company A of the latter regiment recalled, "The 86th New York was posted in a piece of woods, to the right of the 124th, but between that regiment and ours there was an unoccupied space of about a hundred yards."[58] Lieutenant Colonel Higgins of the 86th New York described his line as, "in the woods" excepting his left company.[59] It seems unlikely that a gap as large as 100 yards would have been left in a line of less than 500 yards in length, especially considering that Ward had five regiments in line to fill the space. Perhaps the 86th was somewhat behind the 124th and was sticking out of the woods east of the crest.

In any event, the right of the 86th touched the left of the 20th Indiana, who prolonged the line northward, connecting with the 99th Pennsylvania, who extended along the ridge to the southern boundary of the Wheatfield. Posted in the Wheatfield to the right of the 99th were the six Napoleons of Winslow's Battery.

General Ward's line was well-manned, boasting about one infantryman per foot of ground covered and they had plenty of ammunition with which to load and fire their Springfield, Enfield and Austrian muskets.[60] To his advantage, Ward held high ground upon which were posted four rifled guns under a capable artilleryman. The weakness of his line was in being the left flank of the army. His left and rear were guarded somewhat by Smith's rear section but his men were still exceedingly vulnerable to flank attack.

Unlike their Union adversaries, the Southerners arrived in position just before the battle opened. After their frustrating march, Hood's men aligned themselves upon the right of McLaws' Division, and formed the right of the Army of Northern Virginia along Warfield Ridge. Hood and McLaws positioned their divisions similarly with two brigades in front and two in rear. The Southerners were not very explicit as to exactly where units went into position immediately before the attack on July 2nd. They were there but a short time and took relatively few casualties on the ridge. Therefore, the following positions, especially on the regimental level, are somewhat general.

Brigadier General Jerome Bonaparte Robertson's Texas Brigade connected with the right of McLaws' Division. The brigade's only non-Texas regiment, the 3rd Arkansas, formed the left of Hood's Division. Covering a space of about 200 yards, the Arkansans stretched from McLaws' right and approached the Emmitsburg Road.

The 1st Texas continued the line southward. The Texans formed in columns on the west slope of Warfield Ridge but were soon put into battle line atop the ridge. They extended their line southward on the east side of the road to connect with the 4th Texas. The 4th continued southward to touch Robertson's right regiment, the 5th Texas.[61]

Law's Alabama Brigade prolonged the line to the south in the following order from left to right: the 4th, 47th, 15th, 44th and 48th Alabama regiments.[62] Centered about 200 yards behind both Law and Robertson were the four Georgia regiments of Brigadier General Henry L. "Rock" Benning, and on his right flank was the 2nd Georgia Infantry. The line extended northward with the 17th, 20th and 15th Georgia regiments. Benning later indicated that his brigade straddled the Emmitsburg road. If so, his left center was west of the modern south-end comfort station on the Emmitsburg Road.[63] Hood's final brigade, that of George "Tige" Anderson, was behind and to the left of Robertson's Brigade.

Bolstering Hood's line in front of Robertson and Law were two batteries of Major Mathis W. Henry's Battalion. In front of the Texans were three Napoleons, a 12-pounder Howitzer and a lighter 6-pounder bronze gun of Captain Alexander C. Latham's Branch (North Carolina) Artillery. In front of the Alabamians was Captain James Reilly's Rowan (North Carolina) Artillery which boasted two each of Napoleons, 10-pounder Parrott rifles and 3-inch rifles.[64]

After the formation of his line, John Bell Hood remained near his former Texas Brigade for most of the time before the fight. Although he had a strong line of veteran regiments along with eleven pieces of artillery posted, Hood was reluctant to carry out a frontal assault on what appeared to be a very strong position. Hood sent some of his "picked Texas scouts" to reconnoiter the Union line; they brought back information that the land east of the Round Tops was devoid of Yankees and that their vast supply trains sat helplessly for the taking.[65] Hood, excited by this report, requested three times to be allowed to go around Big Round Top and assault the Union Army in "flank and rear." He later remembered:

> In fact, it seemed to me that the enemy occupied a position by nature so strong—I may

say impregnable—that, independently of their flank fire, they could easily repel our attack by merely throwing and rolling stones down the mountain side as we approached.[66]

It is important to note that Hood's commander, James Longstreet, also voiced concerns about making this charge, and preferred a wider sweeping movement around the Union army.[67] Finally, Hood's plan was rejected by Lee, and he was ordered forward.[68] Upon being ordered to the attack, Hood was heard to say, "Very well; when we get under fire I will have a digression."[69] John Bell Hood had no opportunity to "digress" at Gettysburg and his men assaulted the "impregnable" heights of which he spoke. Ironically, although Hood and Longstreet opposed this plan, the attack was made with vigor. Longstreet later called the assault on July 2, "the best three hours' fighting ever done by any troops on any battle-field."[70]

Earlier in the afternoon, General Ward ordered his 2nd United States Sharpshooters to screen his left and front. They took position as a thin skirmish line with their center near the John Slyder House. Their position changed somewhat throughout the afternoon, but one man wrote that they used the protection of the stone and rail fences along Slyder's lane.[71] The right of their line probably stretched to near the George W. Weikert farm with their left bending back along the Slyder lane to one of the many foothills of Big Round Top. These select marksmen, armed with Sharps rifles, were extremely effective skirmishers.

As Hood's men formed, the 2nd United States Sharpshooters saw skirmishers appear at "the top of the hill in front."[72] A Confederate battery, probably Reilly's, unlimbered as well. The guns, however, were out of the range of the sharpshooters, so Major Homer Stoughton, "sent forward a few men under cover of woods on the left, and silenced one piece nearest [him]."[73] As for the skirmishers that Stoughton's men saw, they belonged to Robertson's and Law's brigades. Robertson's skirmish line was probably made up of one company from each of his regiments, while Law's consisted of a total of five companies from the 47th and 48th Alabama.[74]

Ward's was the largest brigade in the Union Army but the 3rd Maine and the 1st United States Sharpshooters were detached near the Peach Orchard, which left him with six regiments totaling about 1650 men. In the initial assault the Confederates brought four regiments (two of Law's and two of Robertson's), about 1650 men as well, to the fight at Devil's Den. The numbers, however, do not tell the entire story. Ward held commanding ground, remained mostly on the defensive and had a battery of six guns to bolster his line. The Confederates inadvertently overcame this disadvantage by sending more reinforcements to the area. The arrival of

John Bell Hood. (GNMP)

Benning's Brigade at a critical moment added another 1400 men to the Confederate assault. During the fight, the Yankees received but 640 men to strengthen their line. Thus, the aggregate strengths gave the Rebels a distinct numerical advantage, pitting more than 3000 men against the 2300 Union soldiers around Devil's Den.[75]

The plans made, the troops in line and the orders given, the fight for Devil's Den began as one between brigades. As the battle progressed, the difficult terrain and subsequent confusion broke formations and rendered it a fight of regiment against regiment. Eventually the fray became one of man against man. In this chaotic situation involving thousands of men, acts of individual courage and valor altered the outcome of the struggle for the Den and the Battle of Gettysburg.

Rare wartime photograph of Captain James Edward Smith. (Rodney B. Taylor Collection, USAMHI)

The Bombardment

Sergeant J. Harvey Hanford of the 124th New York sat among the Yankees on Houck's Ridge anticipating the coming fight. "Presently" he recalled, "a shell came shrieking, and bursting near us, we needed no order or invitation to get behind the rocks...."[76] The relaxation, foraging and lounging for the regiments in the Devil's Den area abruptly halted. Reilly's Rowan Artillery on Warfield Ridge began lobbing iron and lead to their counterparts on Houck's Ridge with the aim of ascertaining the location of the enemy's left.[77] One of General Ward's aides brought orders for Captain Smith to return the favor to the Confederates and the artillerymen began the laborious task of bringing each round of ammunition from the base of Houck's Ridge — at least 50 yards up the steep and rocky slope.[78] As his guns returned fire, Captain Smith stood atop Devil's Den, on a large rock with General Henry Hunt, observing the effect of the fire.[79] Not many shots were fired, however, before another Confederate battery joined in. Smith recalled:

...a battery of six light 12-pounders marched from the woods near the Emmitsburg Road, and went into battery in the field in front, about 1400 yards distant. A spirited duel immediately began between this battery and my own, lasting nearly twenty minutes....[80]

What followed was a "trial of skill between artillerists." One member of the 124th New York recalled, "The heroic Captain gave every order in a clear, distinct tone, that could be heard above the tumult." Captain Smith reported, "the accuracy of the enemy's aim was astonishing...."[81] Indeed its aim was impressive as the 124th New York received "several casualties" as a result of being so close to Smith's Battery. This prompted Colonel Augustus

Van Horne Ellis of the 124th to move his men "by the right-flank into the woods on which [their] right rested." Apparently, however, he found this to be equally or more dangerous and moved the regiment back to its original position.[82] There his regiment presented a show of force to the Confederates on the opposite ridge.[83]

General Hunt, satisfied with Smith's position, descended Houck's Ridge.

I left to seek infantry supports, very doubtful if I would find my horse, for the storm of shell bursting over the place was enough to drive any animal wild. On reaching the foot of the cliff, I found myself in a plight at once ludicrous, painful and dangerous. A herd of horned cattle had been driven into the valley between Devil's Den and Round Top, from which they could not escape. A shell had exploded in the body of one of them, tearing it to pieces; others were torn and wounded. All were stampeded, and were bellowing and rushing in their terror, first to one side and then to the other, to escape the shells that were bursting over them and among them. Cross I must, and in doing so I had my most trying experience of that battle-field.[84]

Hunt escaped harm but was rendered "badly demoralized" as a result of the episode.

Meanwhile, things along the Confederate line were lively. Although a strip of woods hid his troops completely from the eye of the enemy, General Benning remembered that it, "did not prevent their shells from reaching us and producing some casualties."[85] One of Robertson's Texans, laying a short distance behind Latham's Battery remembered that the replies, "knock[ed]...out a man here and there."[86]

Another recalled, "one shell killed and wounded fifteen men."[87] Another "shot," recalled John C. West of Company E, 4th Texas, "hit our line about eight feet in front of me, knocking off one soldier's head and cutting another in two, bespattering us with blood."[88]

Just as memorable to the common soldier, though, were amusing incidents that did not involve death. During the cannonade, Dick Childers of the 1st Texas, who was particularly efficient at acquiring food from locals, was turned with his side toward the enemy. Over his right shoulder hung his haversack full of fresh biscuits which he had recently been given by a kind Dutch lady. Soon a shell came in from Smith's Battery and:

> ...as Dick happened to be just in the line of fire, it struck him, or rather his haversack, fairly, and scattered biscuits all over that end of Pennsylvania. But the strange part of it is, that it did not knock the man down, but so paralyzed him that he fell, after it had passed, and lay there unable to move a muscle. The litter bearers picked him up and laid him on a stretcher, as if he had been a log. The boys all contended, however, that it was the destruction of Dick's rations, and not any shock the shell gave, that paralyzed him.[89]

Dick Childers regained the strength to fight at Gettysburg, only to be captured by the enemy.[90]

The duel between these batteries was only a portion of a much larger and lengthier artillery fight involving batteries along the entire Union and Confederate lines. Casualties for Reilly, Latham and Smith (who also came under intense infantry fire) were not particularly high. Smith later defended the low casualty rate:

> ...the close proximity of the boulders to the guns made it possible for the cannoneers to step behind them during the discharge of their respective pieces. I believe in this manner the enemy's artillery was cheated, for not withstanding their excellent and accurate aim, not one man in the battery was touched by their numerous shot and shells which landed on the crest...[91]

The outcome of the cannonade, however, showed the severity of the contest. One of Smith's guns on the crest near Devil's Den was struck and disabled. Two of Latham's guns, a 6 pounder bronze gun, the only such gun used at Gettysburg, and one 12 pounder Howitzer were rendered useless. Also, one of Reilly's rifled guns was disabled. Unfortunately for Smith, Reilly and Latham received replacement guns before the close of the battle. The greater effect of the duel was some demoralization to the Confederate infantry

who were lying helplessly in the heat, unable to return fire, knowing that soon they would be face to face with the projectiles, which at that time, were only accidentally landing among them.

Then came a lull in the action, and, "the cannonading seemed to stop as by mutual consent, as though for a breathing spell; but it was of short duration"[92]

Hood's Charge

With skirmishers in front, officers screaming orders above the din and the sun blazing down on their backs, John Bell Hood's soldiers stood in readiness to make the initial infantry assault of the day—one which would severely impact the success or failure of Lee's entire Pennsylvania Campaign. General Hood, standing in his stirrups, hat in hand, at the edge of the woods, shouted the order to advance.[93] For the the tired, hot, yet spirited Southerners, the waiting was over. In awe of the formidable task ahead of them, they moved from the crest of Warfield Ridge. The Union Infantry could do little more than await the coming shock. One soldier atop Houck's Ridge recalled:

> We could see emerge from the woods, along the Emmitsburg Road a deployed Rebel skirmish line. Within supporting distance was a long line of battle extending in either direction as far as the eye could reach. It was followed by a second and third line, each in supporting distance.[94]

The Confederate batteries ceased firing when Law and Robertson passed through their guns. As the Southerners moved onward, however, Smith, Winslow and the other Union batteries along the Wheatfield Road, had no obstructions and wasted no time in firing at the long, gray lines. The 4th New York Independent Battery opened up with case shot and "tore gap after gap throughout the ranks of the Confederate foe."[95] Captain Smith "never saw the men do better work: every shot told."[96] The Confederates, anxious to escape the shot and shell raining upon them, had to cross some 700 yards of ground toward the enemy before reaching the comparative safety of woods and rocks below the Union line.

A soldier of the 4th Maine remebered that the Texans let loose a piercing, Rebel yell at the outset of their advance while the Alabamians advanced "more silently."[97] They did not advance together for long. A major breakdown in the plan of attack occurred only minutes after it began. Robertson had orders, "to keep ...[his]... right closed on Brigadier-General Law's left, and to let [his] left rest on the Emmitsburg Pike."[98] As the advance continued, this became increasingly difficult as Robertson's Brigade

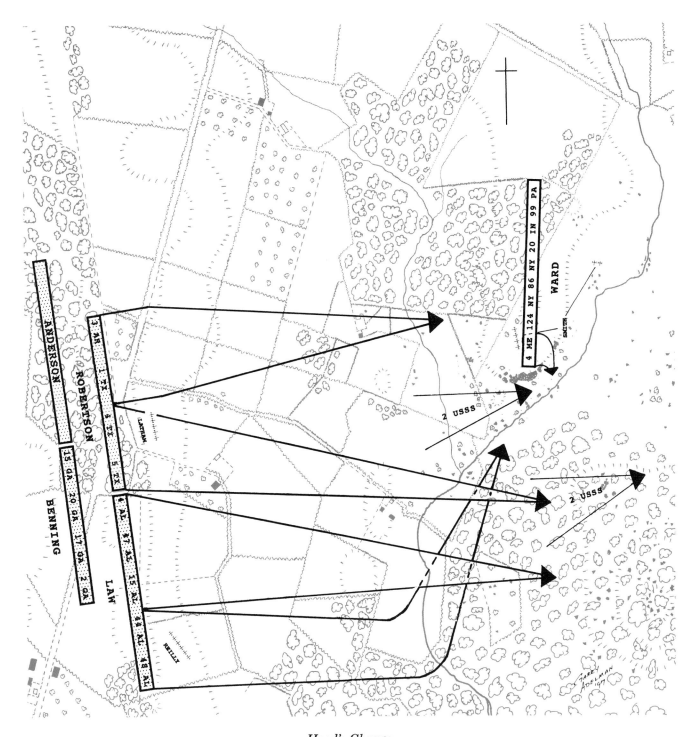

Hood's Charge.

found itself unable to cover the distance from the road to the left of Law's Brigade, which was moving farther to the right. His unit was splitting down the center, the 4th and 5th Texas on the right and the 1st Texas and 3rd Arkansas on the left. Robertson made the decision to abandon the road and stay with Law's Brigade. This choice was partially influenced by Robertson's impression that McLaws' Division would advance on his left. This change in plans, coupled with the "numerous stone and rail fences

that intersected the field" rendered Hood's line jagged and disorganized, even before it reached the truly difficult terrain.[99]

Needed at this point was a general who had the authority, bearing and ability to command a Confederate division; an experienced, clear-headed, military man able to react to the changing circumstances and remedy situations as they occurred—someone like Major General John Bell Hood. Hood remained mounted at the onset of the assault and was in the

View of the Round Tops from the Confederate position, J. I. Mumper, c. 1900.   At the base of Little Round Top (center), can be seen the Slyder Farm, and Houck's Ridge (far left). Note the expanse of open ground. (New York at Gettysburg)

View looking southwest from summit of Little Round Top across the ground over which Hood's Division advanced, Tipton, c. 1888. (ACHS)

vicinity of the Michael Bushman Farm when a spherical case shot burst above his head and tore a painful wound into his left arm.[100] Hood reeled in the saddle, was caught by some of his staff and carried from the field. An extremely effective shot by the Union Army, it forced one of the most important men in the Confederate assault to the rear. Command shifted to Hood's senior brigade commander Evander M. Law.[101] Evidence is scant as to exactly when and how Law exercised command of the division but no Confederate brigade commander wrote of receiving an order from Law until the fighting was essentially over for the day.[102]

Adding to the disorder in the Confederate advance was the annoyance of the Union skirmishers. The 2nd United States Sharpshooters were posted along a rise in front of and several hundred yards both north and south of the Slyder House.[103] Many had the additional protection of a stone wall, making the position all the more formidable. So impressive was their fire that many Southerners considered it to be the enemy's first line of infantry rather than a skirmish line. Confederate reports frequently mention this advanced force. The 4th Alabama succeeded in "carrying ...[the position]... with the bayonet," while other Confederates simply advanced, and overwhelmed the Yankees.[104] The sharpshooters began to fall back, but continued their "splendid execution killing and wounding a great many."[105] One Confederate regiment "broke three times before they would come on, under the well-aimed fire of the sharpshooters."[106] After a short but stubborn resistance, the Union sharpshooters retired up the slope of Big Round Top and toward Devil's Den. William C. Ward, one of the Alabamians, remembered racing with another private who, upon reaching Plum Run, stopped, "supporting himself on his left hand, without kneeling, holding his musket in his right hand, and drank as an animal might have done."[107]

Meanwhile, General Law did his best to maintain order in the rocky and undulating Plum Run Valley. James Sheffield, Colonel of the 48th Alabama, remembered the advance as "very rough and rugged ... the worst cliffs of rocks there could have been traveled over."[108] Law himself remembered that, "the rugged nature of the ground ... increased fourfold the difficulties of the attack."[109] At about the time that his brigade reached the Slyder Farm, Law decided to rearrange it. He ordered Colonel William F. Perry of the 44th and Colonel Sheffield, of the 48th, to march from their positions on the right, "by the left flank" across the rear of the brigade.[110] This shift represents the extent of Law's known contributions to the fighting for Devil's Den. The separation of the 44th and 48th from the rest of the brigade propelled the 15th, 47th and 4th Alabama into their own notoriety—on the slopes of Little Round Top.

Law's Brigade continued eastward, and Robertson, in dealing with Stoughton's force, had trouble closing up his brigade upon Law. The 4th and 5th Texas continued to move with Law, while the 1st Texas and 3rd Arkansas veered northeastward widening a gap between them and the remainder of their brigade. At this point, Company I of the 4th Texas, along the skirmish line, fell in with the 1st Texas and remained with them throughout the fight.[111]

As the Union infantry waited for the advancing Confederates to close within range, they were by no means idle. From the moment the Confederate advance was apparent, Captain Smith realized that the enemy outflanked his position and was extremely concerned about the safety of his guns. He reported: "I requested the officer in command of the Fourth Maine Regiment to place his regiment in the woods on my left, telling him I could take care of my front."[112] Colonel Walker refused, reasoning that he could better protect the guns from the more elevated position. Walker's reluctance to abandon a commanding position such as Houck's Ridge for the area to which Smith referred is understandable. If Walker moved the 4th Maine as Smith suggested, the Confederate column would still outflank his left by several hundred yards. But Smith did not give up easily. He found General Ward, and implored him to order the Maine men into the woods along the base of Big Round Top. While Smith did not get exactly what he wanted, Ward saw some utility in the idea and sent his adjutant (Captain J. M. Cooney) to order the 4th Maine, "to the left into the Devil's Den."[113] Walker objected, "with all the power of speech [he] could command" but with the enemy near, and time running out, he reluctantly obeyed and moved his regiment into the "Gorge" between the Devil's Den and the woods on the western slopes of Big Round Top. The 4th Maine's movement, however, created a dangerous gap in the line near Smith's guns. Captain Cooney promised to close the gap, but for a short time it remained open, long enough for some daring Alabamians to exploit it.[114]

To protect his line, Walker threw out skirmishers under Captain Arthur Libby of Company B to the left. In a short time, Company H under Lieutenant Nathaniel Robbins was sent to cover his front. Not the entire 4th Maine went into the Gorge. The 3 officers and 33 men of Company F remained atop the Den, perched advantageously in the nooks and crannies of the rock formation.[115]

Shortly after Walker went into position, Vincent's Brigade of the Union 5th Corps arrived on Little Round Top and sent skirmishers into the woods on Walker's left. Walker felt certain that the force on Little Round Top would extend itself down the slope and join on the 4th Maine's left. Considering his flank secure, he withdrew his skirmishers from that area and eagerly awaited the connection of Vincent's brigade, which never occurred. Walker's Adjutant, Charles F. Sawyer, unrealistically recalled, "Had the brigade seen advancing connected on our left, we could have held the position without any doubt."[116]

As Hood's advanced force reached the Union position, Benning's Georgia brigade stepped onto the crest of Warfield Ridge having dispensed "with everything but canteen, cartridge boxes and haversacks."[117] "As soon as [they] came in sight a furious blast of cannon broke from the tops of the hills and mountains around and the terrific cry and screams of shells began."[118] Smith found it increasingly difficult to fire at the advanced Confederate line in the wooded, low ground, and re-directed his efforts toward this new and appealing target. He ordered his gunners to use five and six second fuses but the contest had taken its toll. Informed that all of the case shot and shrapnel were gone, Smith exclaimed with frustration, "Give them shell; give them solid shot; d—n them, give them anything!"[119] The men of Ward's Brigade were even more impressed and concerned than before. General Ward saw that "the supports of the first two lines of the enemy were now coming up in columns en masse, while we had but a single line to receive the shock."[120] Benning's "Rock Brigade" marched on, "undismayed by the terrors that seemed to awake from the infernal regions."[121] On the left of the brigade, the 15th Georgia advanced more quickly than the other regiments. Benning twice ordered its colonel to halt, under fire, and await the remainder of the brigade.[122] With their front clear of infantry, the batteries of Reilly and Latham reopened on Union position. Smith, however, saw the Southern infantry as the true threat and kept his guns trained upon them, ignoring the opportunity for counter-battery fire.[123]

Mounted officers presented an especially vulnerable target for artillerymen. Lieutenant Colonel William T. Harris of the 2nd Georgia had only moments earlier announced his premonition of death. Private John Maliachi Bowden, of Company D, recalled that his commander's horse was shot from under him.

> It was an inspiring spectacle. He straightened himself in the saddle and leaped like an antelope, striking the ground some ten feet in front of his dead horse. Drawing his sword, apparently before he reached the ground, and lifting it high in the air, as he struck the ground he called out — "Forward Men."[124]

Fortunately, Harris' premonition remained unfulfilled, at least for the moment.

The Advance of the 1st Texas and 3rd Arkansas

Although the 3rd Arkansas and 1st Texas encountered difficulty in their advance, they were a spirited, strong and ferocious force—one which caused great concern to the Union troops in their front. General Ward ordered "the regiments on the right, who were sheltered in a wood...not to fire until they could plainly see the enemy" and "to those who were on the left, not to fire at a longer distance than 200 yards."[125] Ward recalled that the patience and obedience of his men paid off in the form of one horrendous volley which was poured into the Southerners once they reached the prescribed distance. "This checked the enemy's advance suddenly which gave our men an opportunity to reload, when another volley was fired into them."[126] Private H. Watters Berryman and his brother, Newt, of Company I, 1st Texas, were charging side by side when the latter took a minnie ball to the forehead. His brother recalled: "It knocked him down, I thought he was killed, but he jumped up and kept to fighting harder than ever. I tried to persuade him to leave the field, but he would not leave. He told me if every man left for a slight wound we would never gain a battle."[127]

Lieutenant Colonel Phillip Alexander Work, 1st Texas Infantry. (Hill College Collection, USAMHI)

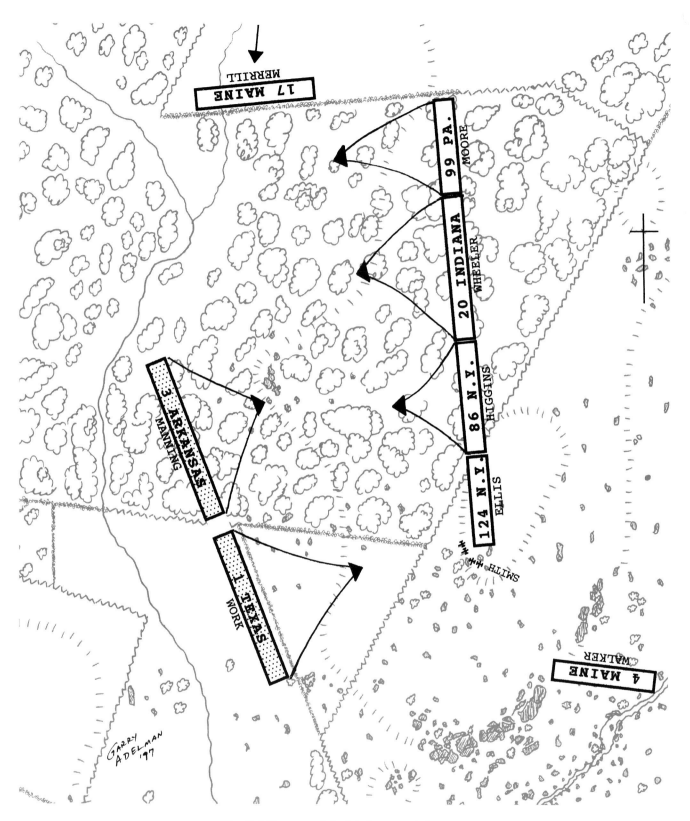

The 1st Texas and 3rd Arkansas Advance.

After the initial volleys, Ward advanced his right regiments (the 99th Pennsylvania, 20th Indiana and 86th New York) to a slight rise overlooking a wooded ravine about 75 yards in their front. This put them in a position to enfilade and overwhelm Robertson's left flank. The effects of this movement became painfully apparent to Colonel Manning of the 3rd Arkansas, who reported:

> ...I ascertained that I was suffering from a fire to my left and rear. Thereupon I ordered a change of front to the rear on first company, but the noise consequent upon the heavy firing then going on swallowed up my command, and I contented myself with the irregular drawing back of the left wing, giving it an excellent fire...[128]

One Arkansan was untroubled by the surrounding chaos. Hidden behind a stump, he fired his gun "steadily and methodically" as he merrily sang:

> Now let the wide world wag as it will,
> I'll be gay and happy still![129]

With its new alignment, the 3rd Arkansas advanced and dueled with Ward's right regiments. During this struggle, a shell fragment tore through the left shoulder of Lieutenant Colonel Benjamin Higgins of the 86th New York, forcing him to turn command over to Major Jacob Lansing.[130] Higgins was but one of several of Ward's field officers to fall that day.

To Manning's right, the 1st Texas advanced through a storm of Smith's canister. Many soldiers recalled the deafening sound of the iron smashing against the rocks. As the Texans reached the stone wall at the base of the Triangular Field, however, Smith's men were unable to depress their guns sufficiently. The Southerners, now positioned in the low ground, under cover of boulders, opened a menacing fire upon the artillerymen, and silenced the guns of the 4th New York Independent Battery atop the crest of Houck's Ridge for the rest of the day.

Not intimidated by this fire was Private Michael Broderick of the 11th Massachusetts, who was detailed to Smith's Battery as a driver. As many of the cannoneers fell back, Broderick left his wagon team and found a rifle which had been dropped by an infantryman. He proceeded to the crest where he began a spirited duel with a Texan in his front. When Smith ordered him back to his team he begged, "Let me stay here, Captain, sure there are plenty back there to look after the horses." Smith allowed him to stay, and Broderick taunted his enemy until he was eventually captured. Later that evening he escaped, walking though the lines dressed as a Southerner.[131]

With the threat of the artillery diminished, the Texans began a more determined advance up the deadly slope in their front. Captain George T. Todd and Private E. P. Derrick, both of Company A, were sheltered together behind a large boulder. A Yankee bullet smashed into Derrick's head and splattered his brains in the face of his company commander.[132]

Slowly, foot by foot, the Rebels moved up the slope exchanging shots with the 124th New York. One Texan recalled that near the top of the ridge was, "a hot situation, almost like the bad place."[133] The men of the 1st Texas received the order to "halt." One soldier recalled, "No one seemed to know whence it came, nor from whom—It cost us dearly... without awaiting orders, every man became his own commander and sprang forward...."[134] Desperate, and now short on artillerymen, Smith begged the infantrymen for help. A sergeant of the 124th remembered Smith, with tears in his eyes, pleading, "For God's sake, men, don't let them take my guns away from me!"[135]

As the fighting intensified, Union Colonel Regis DeTrobriand, commanding the 2nd Brigade, Birney's Division, was ordered to send a regiment forward to strengthen Ward's position. He selected the 17th Maine Infantry, a choice that neither he nor Ward would regret. The 17th moved quickly, and took position on the south boundary of the Wheatfield behind a stone wall. Its left approached the 99th Pennsylvania while its right extended along the wall to the western side of the Wheatfield. Upon taking position, the men of the 3rd Arkansas were visible, advancing through the woods, with their exposed left at a distance of about 100 yards. The men of the 17th joined the action and opened an enfilading fire through the trees.[136] The unfortunate Arkansans now faced at least three veteran regiments, one of which was on their flank and rear. Colonel Manning, having advanced to a ledge of rocks in front, wisely ordered his men to fall back some 75 yards.[137] This movement rendered the left of the 1st Texas "uncovered and exposed."

Both Colonels Manning and Work as well as General Robertson appreciated the perilous situation on their left and all took steps to rectify it. Robertson reported:

> On discovering this heavy force on my left flank, and seeing that no attack was being made by any of our forces on my left, I at once sent a courier to Major-General Hood, stating that I was hard pressed on my left: that General McLaws' forces were not engaging the enemy to my left (which enabled him to move fresh troops from that part of his line down on me), and that I must have re-enforcements.[138]

To protect his flank and to aid Colonel Manning, Lieutenant Colonel Work, "threw out upon [his] left and rear Company G, commanded by Lieutenant B[enjamin] A. Campbell (some 40 men), which soon engaged the enemy."[139] Company G protected the flank of the Texans and drove the 86th New York back a short distance, but not before a minie ball pierced the heart of the brave Lieutenant Campbell.

Colonel Manning, with his front now partially cleared, reported, "...I stretched out my front twice its legitimate length, guarding well my left, and advanced to the ledge of rocks from which we had been previously dislodged by the enemy's movement upon my flank."[140] While this new arrangement helped the Arkansans, they could advance no further without help. Remaining in their position, however, they occupied the attention of two or three times their number until help could arrive. This was a bloody task, as their casualty figures at the end of the fight attest.

With plenty of men on his right, General Ward endeavored to fill the gap in the line created when the 4th Maine moved from the top of the Den into the valley below. For this, he chose the 99th Pennsylvania on the extreme right of the brigade line. They were ordered to move, "by the left flank, left in front, in rear of the brigade, double quick."[141] By the time the Pennsylvanians moved to the contested area, one Union and two Confederate regiments had already arrived.

The 20th Indiana was now on the right of Ward's brigade and was forced to fill the space vacated by the 99th. Colonel John Wheeler deployed Companies B and H on his right for this purpose.[142] These were probably the last orders uttered by the colonel. While Wheeler rode behind the regiment, the enemy advanced "with a rush" to within fifty yards. Suddenly, a bullet passed through his "right temple," and he fell dead from his horse.[143] Lieutenant Colonel William Calvin Linton Taylor took command, but a short while later was wounded himself. Riding over to the ranking captain, Erasmus C. Gilbreath of Company I, he said, "Gil you will have to take charge of the line, as I am wounded."[144] With ammunition running low, the new regimental commander sent to General Ward for more lead. Soon, "Lt. Raphael [*sic*] of General Ward's staff rode bravely up to the line to inform Captain Gilbreath that no more could be supplied. As he did so a shot struck him in the right arm and he fell off his horse into Gilbreath's arms."[145]

The chaos in Rose Woods was equaled by the confusion in the neighboring Triangular Field. Few participants agreed on what happened in this area. With the smoke-filled, undulating terrain, and the breakdown of the Southern command structure, this is not surprising. These peculiarities momentarily favored the Northerners, who atop the hill, had a much better view of the deadly work happening before them.

Ledge of rocks in Rose Woods over which the 3rd Arkansas advanced.

The Charge of the 124th New York Infantry

The men of the 124th New York remained atop the Devil's Den Hill relatively unscathed. Smith's four guns stood silent, the Texans having picked off and intimidated the artillerymen. The battle to their right raged and additional Southern troops advanced beyond the Texans. Colonel Augustus Van Horne Ellis stood behind the center of his line and surveyed the wild scene. His major, twenty-two year old James Cromwell, commanded of the left of the regiment while Lieutenant Colonel Francis Cummins led the right. Cromwell felt that the 124th should attack the somewhat disorganized Texans who were struggling up the field below them. He hurried to the center and requested Colonel Ellis to order a charge, but was sent back to his post. Captain Charles H. Weygant of Company A, who later became the regiment's colonel and historian, recalled that Cromwell went to Ellis a second time and was, again, sent back to his place. But soon afterward, horses were brought up for Ellis and Cromwell. This sparked protest from several soldiers including Captain Silliman of Company C. To these remonstrations, Major Cromwell simply responded, "The men must see us to-day."[146]

Weygant recalled that Ellis simply nodded to Cromwell, and gave the major permission to charge. Cromwell then rode to the left of the regiment, waved his sword twice above his head, screamed the order to charge and dashed out in front of the New York-

Major James Cromwell, 124th New York. (Roger Hunt Collection, USAMHI)

ers, who responded with a "defiant cheer" as they followed him down the slope.[147] Albert Wellington Tucker of Company B remembered that the Texans "ran like sheep" before them.[148]

Lieutenant Colonel Cummins remained on foot with the right of the regiment. Meanwhile, "Ellis sits in his saddle and looks on as if in proud admiration of both his loved Major and gallant sons of Orange, until the regiment is fairly under way, and then rushes with them into the thickest of the fray."[149] The open, undulating slope of the Triangular Field, already littered with dead and wounded, soon became a virtual carpet of blue, gray and red. Sergeant Thomas W. Bradley of Company H remembered the charge as "...a gallant rush into the jaws of hell."[150]

The conflict at this point defies description. Roaring cannon, crashing riflery, screeching shots, bursting shells, hissing bullets, cheers, shouts, shrieks and groans were the notes of the song of death which greeted the grim reaper, as with mighty sweeps he leveled down the richest field of scarlet human grain ever garnered on this continent.[151]

As the 124th was on the mostly barren slope, Lieutenant Colonel Cummins, "with the experience and eye of an old soldier" recognized the likelihood

Colonel Augustus Van Horne Ellis, 124th New York. (USAMHI)

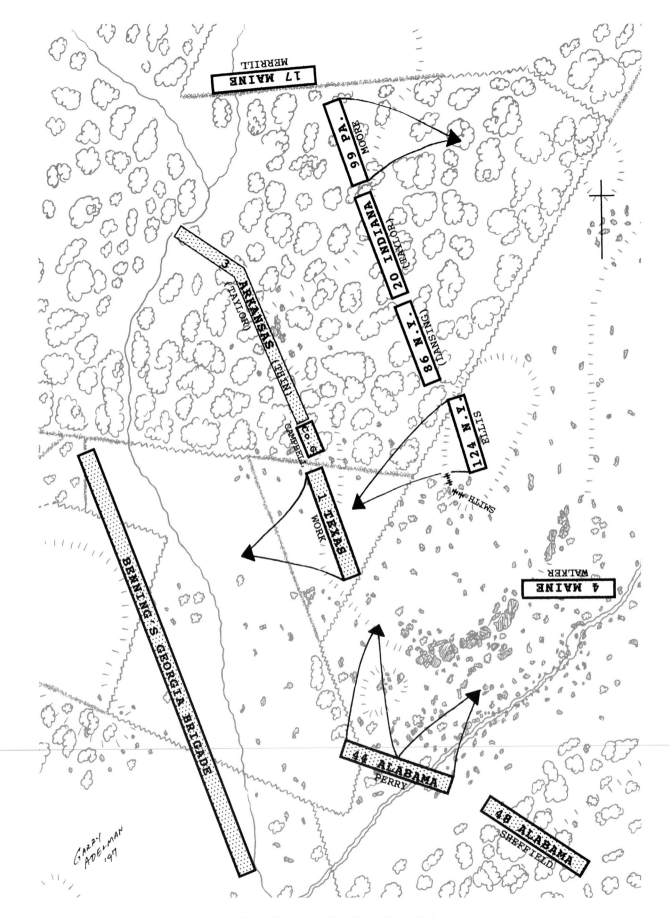

The Charge of the 124th New York.

of being overwhelmed. Concerned about Smith's guns, he hurried up the slope with the aim of getting the pieces pulled off the hill. While near one of the four Parrott rifles atop the hill, a shell came in from the Southern line, struck the gun and hurled its carriage against him. As Cummins was borne from the field, the successful attack of the Orange Blossoms drove the Texans to the valley floor. This respite allowed Smith's men time to remove the disabled gun from the crest.[152]

In the center of the fray, Major Cromwell, "...his noble face flushed with victory, and his extended right arm waving his flashing sabre—uttered a shout of triumph." Just as the young major spoke, some of the Texans reformed and poured into the New Yorkers a withering fire, "which seemed in an instant to bring down a full quarter" of the regiment. The charge of the 124th was stalled, but still Cromwell encouraged his patriotic men. One soldier remembered the young major screaming amid the smoke. Suddenly "his brave heart is pierced by a rebel bullet, his right arm drops powerless, his lifeless body falls backward from his saddle."[153]

The reaction to the death of such a beloved soldier was horror. Ellis screamed above the din of battle, "My God! My God men! Your Major's down; save him! save him!"[154] With that, the New Yorkers charged again and poured lead into anything that moved. Corporal James Scott, at the head of Company B, had already received a wound in the arm. He was so horrified by the death of Cromwell that he turned into a "wild beast." His face and hands were covered with blood but "he did not seem to know anything about it."[155] He fought on until a ball passed clear though his chest, paralyzing him. As he lay helpless on the slope, a piece of shell entered his left arm, a minnie ball struck his side and another piece of shell crashed into his back.[156] Captain Isaac Nicoll fell at the head of Company G with three wounds. His body, wedged in between two rocks, somberly denoted the farthest point to which the Orange Blossoms advanced. Two men of his company tried to rescue his body but were shot in the process.[157]

Although in a desperate position, Ellis still commanded his regiment with zeal. He directed his men to fire into the enemy once more, rose up in his stirrups, pointed his sword upward and began to give an order when a bullet crashed into his head. Captain Charles Weygant remembered:

> ...suddenly his trusty blade falls point downward, his chin drops on his breast, and his body with a weave pitches forward, head foremost among the rocks; at which his wounded beast rears and with a mad plunge dashes away, staggering blindly through the ranks of the foe, who is now giving ground again, firing wildly as he goes.[158]

After the death of Ellis, men fell even more rapidly than before and the situation looked hopeless. Corporal Noah B. Kimbark of Company H was shot in the chest just after Ellis fell. He lost consciousness and was then shot in both of his ankles.[159] Sergeant John Drake was killed, but as a man on the burial detail recalled, "...his death was amply avenged; for within three rods of where he lay were thirteen dead rebs."[160] The New Yorkers fought on, collected as many of their wounded as possible, and saved the lifeless remains of Cromwell and Ellis. Cromwell was particularly difficult to reach as his horse had carried him at least twenty yards toward the enemy line before he fell off. Four or five men of Company E, "dashed out and brought in his body."[161] At this juncture, Sergeant Hanford described the scene:

> As I was kneeling behind a rock and loading my gun, a Lt. [James O.] Denniston of the next company, had picked up a gun, and, there being a rock to my left hand, he jumped over my arms and caught his toe in my ramrod, bending it so I could not use it. I scolded him for it, but on looking around I picked up another one. The Lieutenant squatted behind the rock and was in the act of firing his gun when he was struck by a bullet in the leg. With a cry, "I've got it," "I've got it," he started for the rear, but before getting far another one struck him, so he had to be carried off the field.[162]

It seemed as if things could not get much worse for the 124th, but they, and particularly the men of Company B on the left, were in for a surprise. Part of the 44th Alabama were, at that very moment, charging onto the field in accordance with General Law's orders that redirected them into the fight for Smith's guns. The nature of the terrain prevented any earlier detection of this flanking force. It is doubtful whether the Alabamians had any knowledge of the New Yorkers' presence on the slope. A. W. Tucker of the 124th remembered, "...the enemy poured out in vast numbers from the Devil's Den, not more than 150 yards from us, on our left flank, and opened an enfilading fire. No troops could long stand such a storm." Sergeant Bradley wrote: "flanked at the Devil's Den by the turning of our line at that point, we were swept from the position and the crest and guns were for a brief time in possession of the enemy."[163] Sergeant Hanford, who claimed that when the fight began he was the last man on the extreme left of the army, recalled, "I know that at one time the enemy had passed our left flank and were enfilading us; but it was only for a minute or two."[164] With the arrival of the Alabamians,

Houck's Ridge from the base of the Triangular Field. The 124th New York charged across this ground.

"...it would have been the work of but a few minutes to have annihilated the 124th N.Y."[165] When they retired, there were not many of the Orange Blossoms left to rally atop the ridge. Tucker wrote:

> ...we did not occupy the same ground as when the fight opened. By the loss occasioned during the battle we had kept closing to the right, so that when relieved, my company, which was on the left of the regiment, was where the right of the regiment was when the fight opened.[166]

This new position, entirely in the woods, rendered Smith's guns, as well as the crest, open to the Alabamians.

The charge of the 124th was, "a merciless order." Advancing down an open slope with no protection on either flank into hundreds of Confederates was no less than suicide for many. Men who years later wrote of the assault felt that the charge should not have been made. Still, it took some punch out of the Confederate attack, and bought much-needed time for the Union cause. Sergeant Bradley summed up the sentiment years later.

> I have often thought of the seeming recklessness, and as I at one time thought, uselessness of our charges that day. In the last years of our service we would not have been called on to make them... At any rate, we felt that day as we never felt before or after, that on us, the veterans of the Army of the Potomac, rested in the coming fight the future of the American Republic, and every man was ready to die that day to save it. If ever he shirked before or after, he was the soul of sacrifice in that battle.[167]

The 44th and 48th Alabama Advance

While the New Yorkers had their hands full with Texans, the men from Maine faced nearly twice as many Alabamians. After the shifting of the 44th and 48th Alabama, these two regiments headed northeast toward Little Round Top. Colonel Perry of the 44th reported:

> When at a short distance from the stone fence at the base of the mountain, General Law informed me that he expected my regiment to take a battery which had been playing on our line from the moment the advance began. This battery was situated not on the mountain itself, but on a rugged cliff which formed the abrupt termination of a ridge that proceeded from the mountain...[168]

The 44th was "wheeled to the left, so as to confront that position, its left opposite the battery, and its right extending toward the base of the mountain," the 48th forming on its right.[169] This movement, executed under fire, left the Alabamians facing northward.[170] Perry ordered his men forward and they "responded...with an alacrity and courage seldom, if ever, excelled on the battle-field."[171] The shifting of these two regiments plugged much of the gap which was widening in that area and placed two strong regiments of Alabamians where Ward's line was the weakest—his left flank.

As the 44th Alabama burst from the sparsely wooded area south of Devil's Den, Union skirmishers opened fire, but not in unison.[172] These were men of the 2nd United States Sharpshooters and the 4th Maine who were positioned in the rocks of the Den. According to Colonel Perry, this initial "volley... killed or disabled one-fourth" of his men.[173] He noted, however, that, "A few scattering shots in the

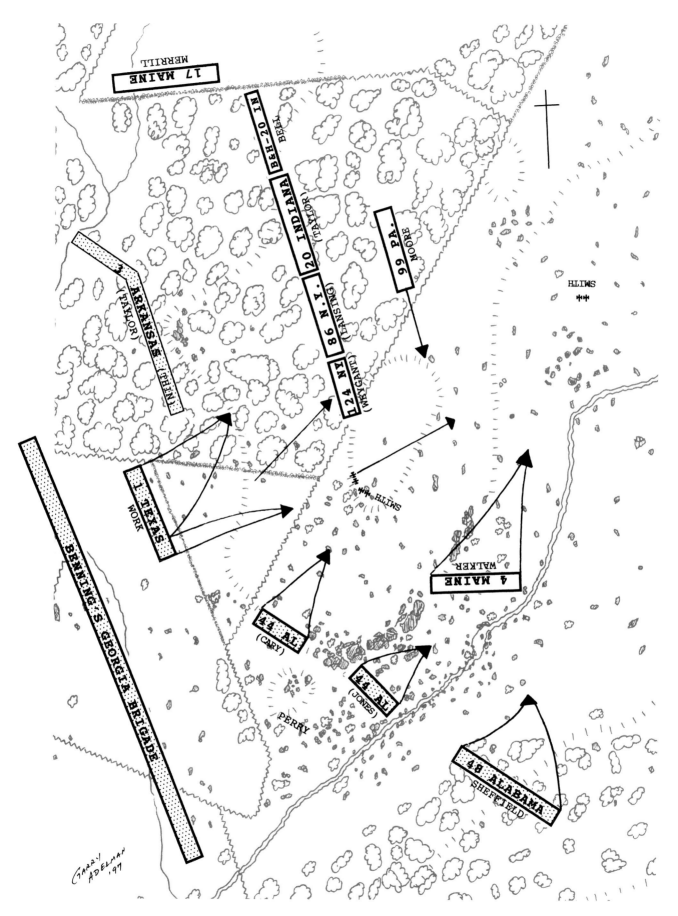

The 44th and 48th Alabama Advance.

beginning gave warning in time for my men to fall flat, and thus largely escape the effect of the main volley."[174]

The rapidly occurring events that followed confused even the most observant of participants. Sharp musketry fire was distracting enough, but the deafening noise, blinding smoke and chaotic nature of the situation rendered the fighting at this area befuddling to all who were there. Perry recalled: "No language can express the intensity of the solicitude with which I surveyed the strange, wild situation which suddenly burst upon my view."[175] Also, the heat was intense, and although the sun was then falling toward the peaks of the South Mountain range, it continued to blaze upon the faces and necks of the troops. All of this was painfully apparent to the commander of the 44th Alabama, who hesitated for an instant to order his men forward. "Such was their extreme exhaustion-having marched without interruption 24 miles to reach the battle-field, and advanced at a double-quick step fully a mile to engage the enemy..."[176] Colonel Perry, who realized that to remain or to retreat were not options, leaped over his prostrate men and futilely shouted the order, "Forward!"[177] He remembered: "It was with the greatest difficulty that I could make myself heard above the din of battle. The order was, however, extended along the line and was promptly obeyed."[178] The men of the 44th, impressed with the spot that fate had chosen for this grapple, unavoidably split into two wings; the right, presumably under the direction of Lieutenant Colonel John A. Jones and the left under Major George W. Cary. "In less than a minute the right wing of the regiment was pouring into the Den—the enemy escaping from the opposite side..."[179] Jones advanced his force slowly from rock to rock through the difficult Plum Run Gorge until they encountered the fire of the 4th Maine positioned in the Valley of Death. Colonel Walker, unimpressed with Jones' force, stated that it was no more than, "a strong skirmish line in the ravine."[180] He was not far off the mark. The 44th's loss of men during the march and in the Gorge, together with the fact that they had split into two wings over difficult ground, rendered the right wing of the 44th little more than a "strong skirmish line."

Meanwhile, twenty-four-year-old Major Cary grabbed the colors with one hand, waved his sword in the other and led the left wing up the south side of the ridge between the Triangular Field and the Den itself.[181] The left of the 44th was fortunate enough to be charging up the hill just as the 124th New York charged down the opposite slope with a dreadfully exposed left flank. The 44th opened an enfilading fire into the already staggered 124th, forced it back, and continued virtually unopposed toward the abandoned guns above the rocks of the Devil's Den.

The 44th Alabama charged across this ground and encountered the exposed flank of the 124th New York.

One of the charging Alabamians was Corporal James L. Forte of Company C. He carried the flag of the 44th, "till [he]... got to the enemy's battery" where he mounted one of Smith's guns and waved the flag defiantly until he "was knocked off by a Yankee with a swab staff." Forte survived the Battle of Gettysburg, but his luck would run out a few months later in Georgia, at a place called Chickamauga.[182]

Additionally, the Alabamians came on far too quickly for Captain George G. Davis and his men of Company F, 4th Maine, perched in the rocks atop the Den. Davis and his 1st Lieutenant were captured and his 2nd Lieutenant was mortally wounded.[183] In addition, 15 of Davis' 23 privates became casualties, with 11 captured, 3 wounded and one killed outright. Among those captured was Sergeant Henry Leach, who had just recovered from his battle with sunstroke.[184]

For young Major Cary, however, standing atop the captured height, life was going quite well. Although Cary could not use the captured Parrott rifles (Smith's men having retired with all of the artillery implements), he proudly went down the hill to show off "an armful of swords" and dozens of prisoners to his colonel.[185] Perry remembered:

> ...the Major found me among the rocks near the foot of the hill, prostrated by heat and excessive exertion...[he] complained that cannon from both sides were playing upon his position....He was ordered to hurry back and withdraw the men from the crest , so that they could find shelter on the sides of the hill.[186]

Cary's exhausted men eagerly obeyed, and pulled back a few rods. Catching their breath, they rested on the slope to await new orders. Colonel Perry, exhausted, and out of the fight for the remainder of the day, gave a compelling account of what he experienced after his disability:

> ...buried in the recesses of the rocks, I could only hear. It is seldom that a soldier in the midst of a great battle, in comparative security and perfect composure, can enjoy the privilege of listening. The incessant roar of small arms, the deadly hiss of Minnie balls, the shouts of the combatants, the booming of cannon, the explosion of shells, and the crash of their fragments among the rocks, all blended together in one dread chorus whose sublimity and terror no power of expression could compass.[187]

Meanwhile the 48th Alabama, advancing beyond the right of the 44th, was detected by the 4th Maine when only 50 yards away.[188] Colonel Walker sent his adjutant to General Ward to report the fact and refused his left to meet this new threat, "making use of the bowlders, which sprinkled the ground, as much as circumstance permitted".[189] During the advance the 48th had become somewhat disorganized and while reforming, they took fire from the Maine men in the valley. Adjutant Sawyer of the 4th remembered "5 to 8 rounds being expended before the enemy returned the fire, which came on our front and left flank."[190] Colonel James L. Sheffield, of the 48th Alabama remembered: "Here the fire of the enemy was severe. Here the men opened fire on the enemy, and for some time continued...."[191] The ground, sprinkled with small trees and boulders, of-fered the men of both sides some protection, but the contest soon took its toll. Major Ebenezer Whitcomb, of the 4th Maine, was wounded. He lingered for over three months before he succumbed to his wounds and earned the distinction of being the highest ranking officer from the state of Maine, killed or mortally wounded at Gettysburg. Walker felt that his unit in this action "christened" the area "for all time" as the "Valley of Death."[192] Accounts of the 48th's actions are few, but Colonel Sheffield reported that "...the left, from the loss of men and their exposed position to a fire from the front and from the mountain on the right, were forced to fall back." Most likely they fell back into the woodline along the slopes of Big Round Top.[193] For the moment, the 44th and 48th Alabama were at a stand-still. Unable to advance with the force at hand and unwilling to retreat, they were content to hold their advanced positions until help arrived.

With the 124th New York reforming in the woods and the 44th Alabama pulled back, the prize of Smith's abandoned guns was too much for the Texans to resist. Advancing up the slope, with their left partially in Rose Woods, the Texans took the crest. General Robertson reported:

> Lieutenant-Colonel Work, with the First Texas Regiment, having pressed forward to the crest of the hill and driven the enemy from his battery, I ordered him to the support of Colonel Manning, directing Major [Frederick Samuel] Bass with two companies to hold the hill, while Colonel Work with the rest of the regiment went to Colonel Manning's relief.[194]

Dead Confederate soldiers at the base of Big Round Top, Gardner, July 1863. This photograph was recorded near the edge of the woods at the Slaughter Pen. (USAMHI)

The Texans either were unaware of the presence of the 44th Alabama or chose to forget their deeds, as they became the second regiment to claim the capture of Smith's guns on July 2nd, 1863. Texan John C. Stinson of Company G mounted a gun, "shook the fragment of his blade and shouted victory."[195]

The crest of the Devil's Den Hill was now held by some 80 men. But the Texans did not remain in their exposed position for long. For the Bluecoats were not yet whipped and there was plenty of courage, spirit and daylight left to prove it.

Ward's Men Retake the Crest

While the fighting on the left of the 4th Maine was very hot, the front of the regiment was confronted with no more than the "strong skirmish line" described by Colonel Walker. But as he moved toward the right of his line the Colonel noticed Rebel soldiers pouring around and through Smith's guns. The "experienced eye of Colonel Walker at once convinced him that the key to the whole position rested at the battery...and once in the possession of the enemy he could rake" the entire length of Ward's line.[196] Without waiting for orders, he seized the initiative and decided to retake the guns. Colonel Walker pulled his men "from the nest of bowlders in the gorge," fell back "about 100 yards" and ordered them to fix bayonets. He would "never forget the 'click' that was made by the fixing of the bayonets, it was as one."[197] He moved his regiment forward "by the right oblique," led it in a charge up and over the top of Houck's Ridge, and drove the enemy from the guns. The ridge, extremely steep and rugged, made this a difficult task. The remnants of the 124th New York moved forward once again and joined the right flank of the boys from Maine.

The encounter was particularly sharp on the left of the 4th, with hand-to-hand fighting, "along the brow of the hill" and "a little to the left of Smith's guns."[198] During the charge, a bullet passed through Colonel Walker's right foot and severed his Achilles tendon. "On foot and Wounded," his sword was wrenched from his hand by a Rebel soldier, and was only recovered with the help of his men, who, after witnessing his predicament, came to his aid.[199]

At this critical moment, the 99th Pennsylvania arrived at the top of Houck's Ridge. They formed in line of battle charging behind and perpendicular to the 4th Maine. Corporal Peter B. Ayars of Company E remembered that the unit fired "one volley, and with a dash... were into the thick of the fight. Above the crack of the rifle, the scream of shell and the cries of the wounded, could be heard the shout for 'Pennsylvania and our homes.'"[200] Major John W.

Corporal Peter B. Ayars, Company E, 99th Pennsylvania.
(G. L. Rogerson Collection, USAMHI)

Moore, commander the 99th, wrote that, "this movement, rapidly executed, placed my command on the brow of a hill, overlooking a deep ravine interspersed with large bowlders of rock."[201] When the charge ended, the men of the 99th were in position atop Devil's Den, facing roughly south and east, and formed nearly a right angle with the rest of the brigade. One soldier of the regiment remembered the "colors resting against one of [Smith's] guns...made it the rallying point, and saved the day."[202] They stood there "as firm as the rocks beneath their feet" and poured volley after volley into the gorge below.[203]

The 4th Maine pulled back and charged up the slope of Houck's Ridge in their bid to recapture Smith's guns.

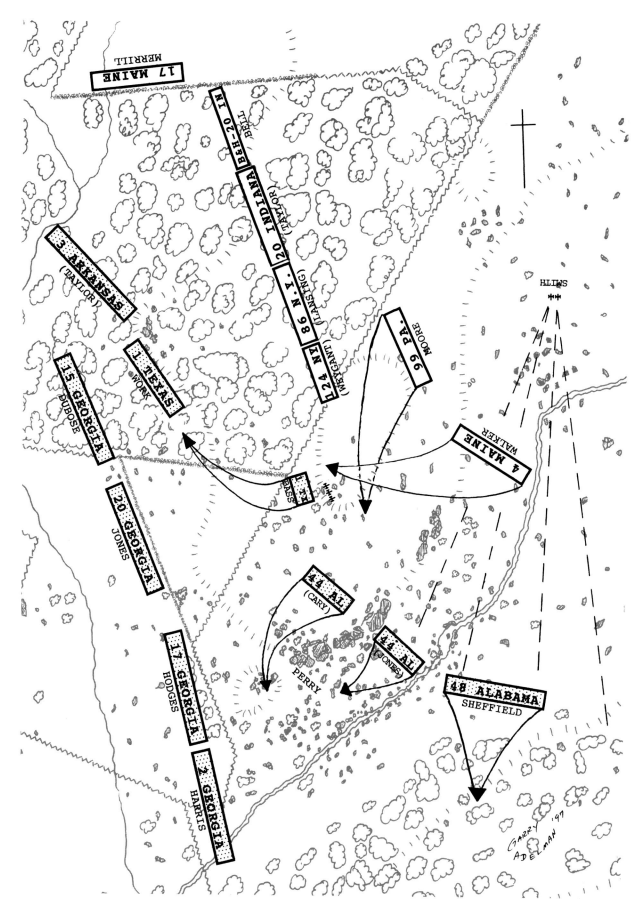

Ward's Men Retake the Crest.

With the 4th Maine no longer blocking the advance of the Alabamians through the Gorge, the Southerners started to work their way into the Plum Run valley. Luckily, Captain James Smith, had "run with all the speed" he could muster to the two guns he had placed on the "hillock," in the rear of his battery. Smith ordered this section to open fire "obliquely through the gully."[204] The enemy was "taken by surprise," and working the guns with "good execution," Smith and his men watched as a Rebel battle flag dropped three times from the effect of their canister.[205] These men, who quickly fell back to the edge of the woods and behind the rocks for protection, were most likely members of the 48th Alabama and possibly the 4th Texas, who, at that time, moved up the slopes of Little Round Top. This deadly fire prevented the Alabamians from exploiting the gap that then existed in the Union lines. It was also about this time that Lieutenant Charles E. Hazlett's Battery D, 5th United States Artillery, which had been hauled to the summit of Little Round Top, began dropping shells into the soldiers around Devil's Den.[206]

At this point, recalled Colonel Walker, "we had it our own way... and could have held the line against double the number that were in our front."[207] Those of the 124th who were not killed or wounded in their ill-fated charge gallantly fought on, reloading and firing down upon the "solid Confederate battle line at the foot of the hill below them." Behind them, and in "plain sight" of all "who chanced to look that way," were the "lifeless remains of Ellis and Cromwell...lying on a huge boulder but a few yards to the rear."[208] In front of the regiment the slope was covered with the carnage of terrible fighting. Captain Charles H. Weygant described in great detail his observations:

Passing down the line, I notice that there is no commissioned officer in command of Company I, and ask, "Where is your plucky new lieutenant?" and the answer comes, "You will find him lying down yonder with four or five of I [Company] beside him." "What!" I answer, "Is he dead?" and I am told that he fell fighting nobly at the head of his company. Reaching Company K, I learn that Lieutenant Finnegan has been borne to the rear wounded in two places. Coming to G, which moved into line that morning with more men than any other company in the regiment, I see a corporal's guard in charge of a corporal, and learn that Captain Nicoll's dead body lies wedged in between two rocks at the farthest point of our advance ... The slope in front was strewn with our dead, and not a few of our severely wounded lay beyond the reach of their unscathed comrades, bleeding, helpless, and some of them dy-

ing. One of their number, who lay farthest away, among the rocks near the body of our truly noble and most esteemed Captain Nicoll, could be seen ever and anon, beneath the continually rising smoke of battle, to raise his arm, and feebly wave a blood covered hand. It was James Scott, of Company B, one of the ten thousand heroes of that great battle.[209]

A. W. Tucker of Company B noted that "there was not more than a strong skirmish line left." The "colors were stuck in the ground and we were ordered to rally on those colors; not a man was to leave them." The regiment had "taken a position" they "were determined to hold as long as there were enough of the 124th left to hold the ground." The men of Company B, on the extreme left of the regiment, became intermingled with the right of the 4th Maine. For a time, the colors of the 124th New York stood side by side with those of Walker's men.[210]

Henry O. Ripley was the Color Sergeant of the 4th Maine, and on that day his "daring and gallantry won him the admiration of all" who witnessed his actions. At one point in the battle, the flag he carried was shot from his hands, the color staff snapping in two. "Before the colors reached the ground...Ripley sprang and caught them and raised them proudly aloft in the storm of bullets," and waved them, "defiantly in the face of the enemy." A staff officer who was riding past "saw the gallant act. He immediately stopped and exclaimed: 'That color bearer of the Maine Fourth ought to be a Major General!'"[2011] By the end of the day that flag was pierced by thirty-two bullets, two pieces of shell, and had part of its staff missing. With the exception of Henry Ripley, who "did not receive a scratch," every member of the color guard was killed or wounded.[212]

The color guard of the 99th Pennsylvania also covered itself with glory that day. Every man in the regiment looked to Color Sergeant Harvey May Munsell, bearer of the United States Flag, as a guide. As men dropped around him like, "leaves fall in Autumn," he remembered:

I mechanically prayed as I never prayed before or since. My heart was in my mouth, or boots, and never to this day have I been able to tell which. My teeth, like those of "poor old Harry Gill, went chatter, chatter, chatter still:" and chatter now when I think of it. Frightened almost to death, and not a soul in the regiment knew it but myself... the members of the 99th, every man of them, looked like ghosts, and it was not until after I made that discovery that I came to the conclusion they thought I was the only man in the regiment not frightened half out of his senses.[213]

The men of the 99th believed that the Devil's Den was now "locked," and they held the "key." As the fighting raged, "the regiment appeared to be elastic, able to contract and expand to any" new development. "They had the guns, the bayonets, the bullets, the pluck, and the courage...not a solitary man of that little band, even for a moment, thought of being driven from the 'Key'."[214]

With the Union lines firmly re-established atop the crest of Houck's Ridge, and converging artillery fire now "playing" upon them from both sides, the Confederates were compelled to withdraw to what Colonel Walker termed "a respectful distance... the enemy taking cover behind the rocks and bowlders and in the Devil's Den."[215] Another critical moment had arrived, but this time for the Southerners. While Colonel Perry and Major Cary of the 44th Alabama "were anxiously discussing the situation" a cry was heard above the din, "There is Benning; we are all right now."[216]

Benning's Assault

Although the arrival of Benning's Georgia Brigade was fortunate for the Texans and Alabamians who were struggling for possession of Devil's Den, it was not in the plans of the Southern commanders. This brigade of 1400 battle-hardened veterans was ordered to support the Alabamians in their advance upon the Union left flank. Benning was directed to keep an interval of 400 yards between his lines and the advancing men of Law's Brigade. Due to the smoke of battle and a sheltering wood, however, they became confused and followed Robertson instead. While Benning's arrival at Devil's Den was the key to capturing the height and three of Smith's guns, it can only be surmised what effect they might have had as a fresh support line in the fight for Little Round Top.

As his unit "swept in from Seminary ridge," General Benning reached "the foot of the peak" and found "part of the 1st Texas, struggling to make the ascent" toward the Union line.[217] Here his men received a withering fire from the Northern troops atop Houck's Ridge. This position was now stronger than it had been all day. The 20th Indiana and the 86th New York held the wooded ridge on the right. The 124th New York and the 4th Maine were well-positioned along the top of the ridge, partially protected by stones and boulders, and the men of the 99th Pennsylvania, along with Smith's rear section of Parrot rifles, were creating such a terrible crossfire in the Gorge, that few dared to pass through it. The Northern line was formidable, and the Southerners were in for a tough fight. But the sheer weight of numbers was now in their favor. The combined Southern force poised at the bottom of the ridge outnumbered the depleted Union force nearly two to one.

"Rock" Benning quickly ordered a general advance and the men from three Southern brigades "commenced ascending the rugged" slopes of Houck's ridge on the left, and crossing the Plum Run Gorge on the right. "The ground was difficult, rocks in many places presenting, by their precipitous sides, insurmountable obstacles, while the fire of the enemy was very heavy and very deadly. The progress was not very rapid, but it was regular and uninterrupted."[218] The 3rd Arkansas anchored the Confederate position and could not move forward until the arrival of reinforcements on its left. The 1st Texas and Benning's 15th Georgia, after "several ineffectual efforts... to separate the men of the two regiments," advanced up the ridge as one.[219] During this initial confusion, Colonel Dudley DuBose of the 15th Georgia was positioned "a little above the foot of a high, wooded, rocky hill."

> At this point my regiment commenced the engagement with the enemy, who occupied the hill. At this point, the nature of the ground was such that I could not see the other portion of our brigade. After fighting the enemy in this position a short time, I saw from the heavy fire of musketry on my right that the other portion of the brigade were hotly engaged trying to carry the hill in their front, which was destitute of trees. I immediately ordered my regiment to...charge that portion of the hill in my front, which order they obeyed willingly and promptly...[220]

When the order came to charge, DuBose's men "raised a deafening yell and went over the rock fence and up the hill shouting and yelling like demons."[221]

While the 15th Georgia and 1st Texas were afforded the protection of trees and rocks as they moved up the slope toward the Union line, the 20th Georgia on their right would have to cross the open, deadly ground of the Triangular Field. This clearing had already claimed the lives of many Texans and New Yorkers. The order to advance was obeyed with "promptness and alacrity and the charge upon the hill and battery...[was] executed courageously."[222] As the Georgians moved up the field, the artillery of both sides indiscriminately threw shells in their ranks. When the 20th was "nearly half way up the hill, one of these shells exploded in front of the regiment, "a fragment of...which glancing from a rock, passed through [the]...brain" of Colonel John A. Jones, killing him instantly. This was a deep shock to the regiment. Their Colonel had "behaved with great coolness and gallantry" all day, and was killed "just as success came in sight."[223]

The advance of the 20th Georgia was stalled by a staggering fire. It fell back, reformed, and advanced again. "In going up the hill," John W. Lokey of Com-

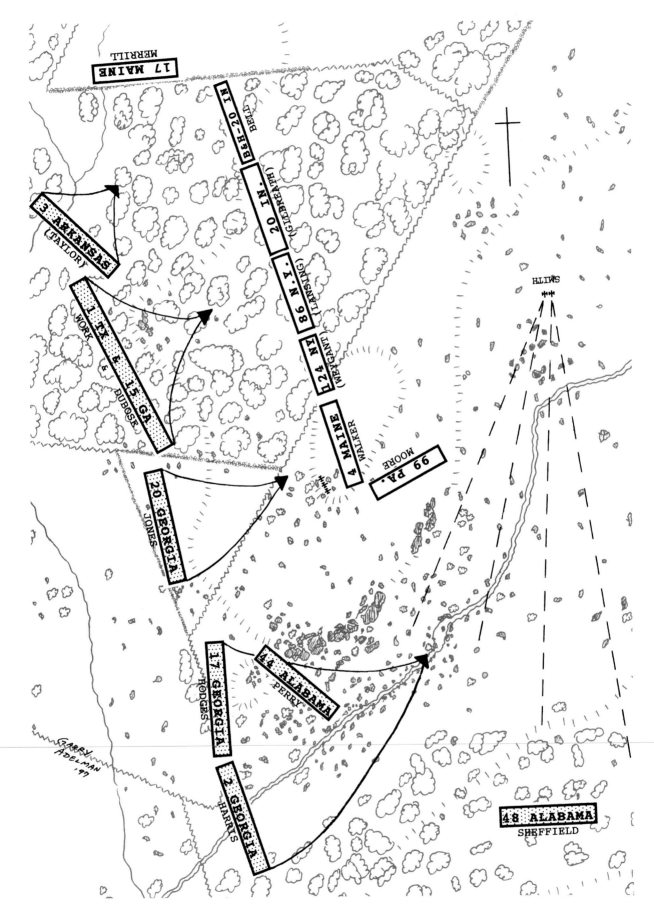

Benning's Assault.

pany B remembered passing Colonel "Jack" Jones. He was "laying on his back with half of his head shot off." He next came upon a man from Company K who was "lying on the ground where he had the protection of the crest of the hill. He was not shooting but lying as close to the ground as he could get." As Lokey passed he shouted, "You better not go up there, you will get shot." Lokey said nothing and moved to the top of the hill. He had thrown up his "old Enfield rifle, and was taking deliberate aim at a Yankee" when a Minie ball passed through his right thigh. "I felt as if lightning had struck me. My gun fell, and I hobbled down the hill." As Lokey limped back, he met the same soldier who had given him advice on the way up. As he passed, the man said, "I told you that you would get shot if you went up there." Lokey's response can only be imagined as he retired to the rear with the wounded.[224]

To the right of the 20th was the 17th Georgia under Colonel Wesley C. Hodges, and the 2nd Georgia under the command of Lieutenant Colonel William Terrell Harris. These two regiments passed through the exhausted Alabamians and took up the assault. Major William S. Shepherd recalled that the regiment was moving:

> ...forward in splendid order until it came to a deep gorge, where the nature of the ground was such that it was impossible to preserve an alignment: but, notwithstanding the rocks, undergrowth, and the deadly fire of the enemy, the officers and men of this regiment moved forward with dauntless courage, driving the enemy before them...[225]

As the right of Benning's Brigade pushed forward through the rock-choked banks of Plum Run, the 99th Pennsylvania and other Union soldiers poured a murderous fire down upon them from the cliffs above. Sergeant William R. Houghton, of Company G, 2nd Georgia returned to the battlefield years later and described the effects of this fire:

> Above us then, [not] quite twenty feet, on the edge of the rock stood a line of blue coated United States regulars firing straight down at our line which had become broken in passing over and around the huge boulders which barred our way. Here fell the gallant [Thomas H.] Muse and Lieutenant [George W.] Mays of my company, shot through the top of the head by the almost vertical fire. Muse fell to his left striking my feet. The government avenue passes directly over the spot where they fell, and just beyond is an iron sign with the words "Devil's Den" on it.[226]

John Maliachi Bowden of Company B, 2nd Georgia, reaffirmed the individual nature of the Devil's Den fighting as, "...Indian fashioned, each man selected a rock or other place of covering for himself. Some even jumped into the creek."[227] Captain John Martin of Company D, 17th Georgia also mentioned this "terrific storm of bullets" from above. "It seemed as if the demons of hell itself were turned loose, so terrific was the onslaught." Martin wrote that this "ravine" was "the bloodiest spot [he]...saw during the war."[228] As the Georgians "plunged through the raking fire that, now more terrific than before, swept

Plum Run Gorge looking northward, Tipton and Myers, 1869 stereo. (Boardman Collection)

Private Isaac H. Beckworth, Company C, 17th Georgia Infantry. (Hazel Clark Collection, USAMHI)

the gorge like a furious torrent" they took cover behind the numerous rocks and fired back. "The enemy, dismayed at such daring, began to break before the fire which was now hurled through his ranks."[229]

Despite the fire to which the Confederates in the Gorge were exposed, an opportunity existed in their front. For a time, it appeared that this force might envelope the left of Ward's Brigade and take Devil's Den in reverse. Only the two guns of Smith's Battery stood between the Georgians and the open valley. Captain Smith recalled that guarding the gap in the Union line was critical. "Every one of those minutes contained sixty seconds and into each second was crowded a lifetime."[230] But once again, due in part to Ward's vigilance at a critical moment, reinforcements arrived.

The 40th New York and 6th New Jersey Arrive

As the situation along his line deteriorated, Ward sent for reinforcements. Division commander General Birney, appreciating the danger, sent two regiments to Ward's left flank. The 200 men of the 6th New Jersey of Burling's Brigade, Humphreys' Division and the 430 soldiers of the 40th New York of DeTrobriand's Brigade, Birney's Division, were called from their positions near the Wheatfield. The deeds of these two regiments are difficult to piece together, for their arrival in the "Valley of Death" was surrounded by peril, courage, sacrifice, and most of all—chaos. Ward's regiments fought atop Devil's Den against overwhelming odds.

Both regiments were ordered into the valley, at the left of Ward's line. For some reason, the 6th New Jersey was sent without a guide. The regiment passed behind Winslow's Battery in the Wheatfield and marched through the woods forming in line along the rail fence atop Houck's Ridge and opened fire upon some distant Southerners.[231] Colonel Stephen R. Gilkyson of the 6th saw the left of Ward's brigade, battling at the Devil's Den Hill amid the three abandoned guns. Although Smith's rear section was still pouring death upon the Southerners, the 6th New Jersey advanced some 200 yards and formed line "directly in front" of the guns, cutting off their fire. Here, Gilkyson's men "secured a fine position, and opened fire with great effect..."[232] The position was indeed a fine one, marked by huge boulders which contributed to a lower casualty rate for the 6th New Jersey. Their left was positioned so that it could easily fire upon any troops who showed themselves in the Plum Run Valley and the men on the right were sheltered by part of Houck's Ridge in their front. This same rise, however, greatly limited

their field of fire. The 6th New Jersey were positioned about 150 yards from the 99th Pennsylvania, whose line ran from the eastern part of Houck's Ridge toward the crest above Devil's Den. Although strongly posted in the left rear of Ward's Brigade, the 6th New Jersey was a small force, insufficient to dislodge any of the Confederates massing in their front. Fortunately for the Yankees, the considerably larger 40th New York was on its way. Colonel Thomas W. Egan of that regiment recalled marching, "across a field of wheat, in front of Captain Winslow's battery, to a position pointed out to [him] by Captain J.C. Briscoe, in a ravine bounded on the left by high hills and upon the right by a gentle ridge."[233]

As the 40th New York went into the valley it passed through the position occupied by Smith's caissons and horses. There Colonel Egan was approached by Smith who begged him, "in beseeching terms" to recapture his three Parrotts atop the ridge. Smith recalled that Egan "promised" to do so and the 40th quickly took position on the left of the 6th New Jersey, who Egan mistook as Ward's left regiment.[234] "These regiments," Captain Smith recalled, "marched down the gully, fighting like tigers, exposed to a terrific fire of musketry...."[235] Lacking the protection of rocks the 40th New York were:

Colonel Thomas Wilberforce Egan, 40th New York Infantry. (USAMHI)

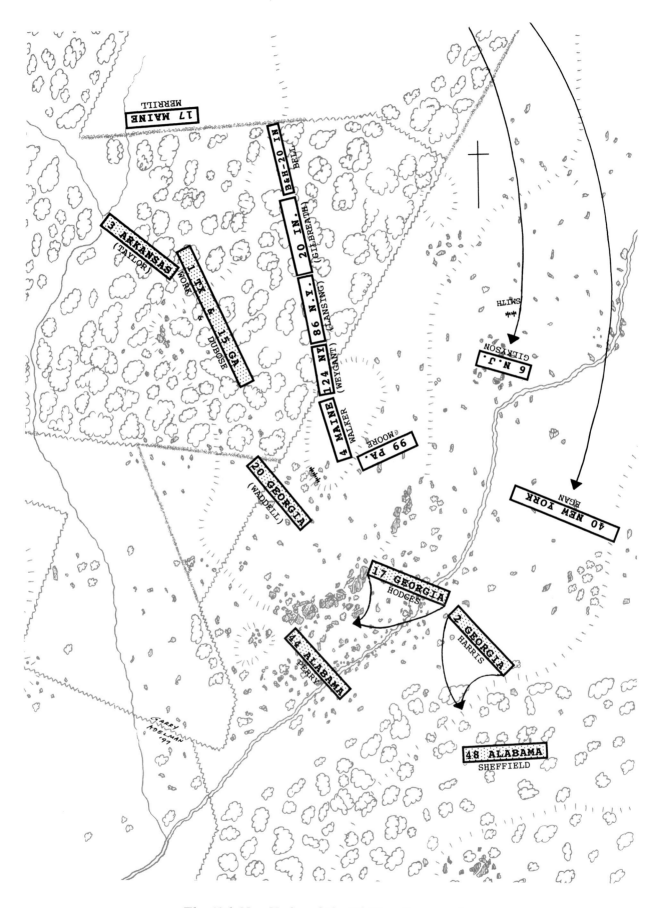

The 40th New York and the 6th New Jersey arrive.

The charge of the 40th New York, c. 1870 John Bachelder engraving. Note Smith's guns depicted along the crest of Houck's Ridge. (Timothy H. Smith Collection)

...under a terrific fire of the enemy's infantry, who were strongly disposed behind the natural defenses of rocks and ridges...[Colonel Egan] immediately ordered...[his] men to charge, when with great alacrity they pushed forward at a double-quick, crossing a marsh up to their knees in mud and water.[236]

As they advanced, straddling Plum Run, the 40th "suffered terribly." Lieutenant Colonel Augustus J. Warner and Captain Madison M. Cannon were wounded. The acting adjutant, twenty-one year old Lieutenant William H. H. Johnson, was killed instantly with a Minie ball through the chest while urging on his men.[237]

At first, the charge of the 40th was successful and inspiring. Egan, wounded in the leg and unhorsed, recalled that, "The enemy fell back upon my advance, but it was attended with no particular advantage to ourselves, for their new position was much stronger than the first."[238] Although disorganized from charging through the Gorge, the 2nd and 17th Georgia and the 44th and 48th Alabama were now posted in the woods and rocks in and around the Slaughter Pen. It is unclear how far into the Gorge the 40th advanced but Major William S. Shepherd, of the 2nd Georgia, wrote that his regiment "repulsed several charges made by the enemy" that day.[239] Colonel Wesley C. Hodges of the 17th Georgia was

less modest claiming they broke the columns of the enemy seven times.[240]

Although the Confederates were close to victory, casualties mounted among the Southerners in the Gorge. The men of the 99th Pennsylvania continued to pour lead onto the Southerners from Houck's Ridge while the 40th New York kept an intense fire in their front. For the men of the 2nd and 17th Georgia the converging fire was horrific. The great number of casualties caused by this crossfire contributed to naming this area the Slaughter Pen. The Georgians, with the aid of the Alabamians, held off the 40th New York but were unable to advance themselves without additional help.

Ward's Retreat

Although the Union force around Devil's Den boasted seven regiments, most of which were in relatively strong positions, the odds against them were simply too great. The Southerners, in addition to having more troops, finally had proper support on their left flank in the form of General George T. Anderson's Georgia Brigade. This unit charged at roughly the same time as Benning's and became engaged in a bloody fight for the southern edge of the Wheatfield. Despite Ward's relentless efforts to defend his line, he realized that it could not hold. For-

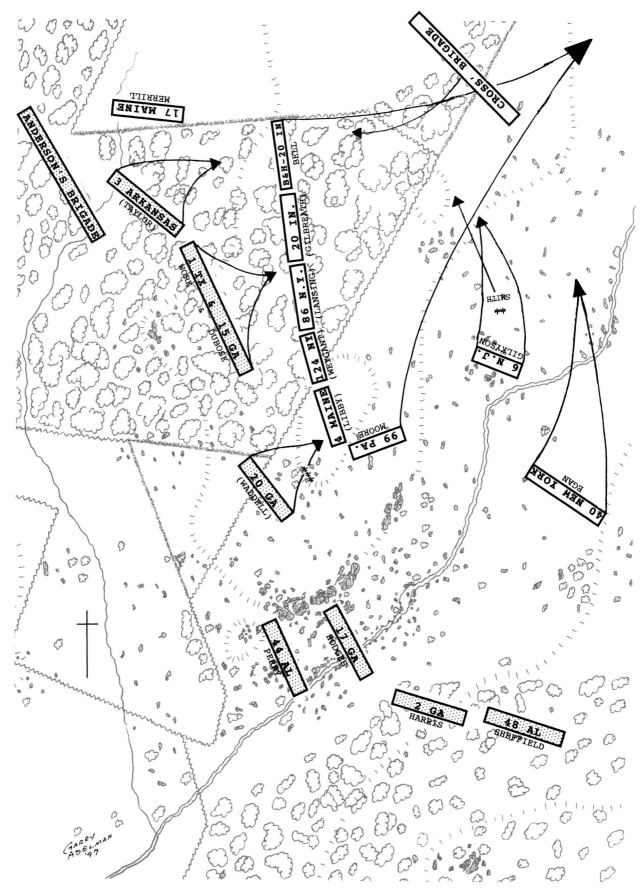

Ward's Retreat.

tunately for the Union, the Devil's Den position was no longer the left flank of the army. The Union force atop Little Round Top was strong and had already held against several Confederate charges. Furthermore, reinforcements were on the way. Caldwell's Division of the Second Corps and Ayres' Division of the Fifth Corps arrived shortly upon the scene, though further to the right of Ward's men.

As General Ward realized that a retreat was imminent, the Southerners sensed that victory was at hand. The men of the 20th Georgia, along with the 1st Texas and 15th Georgia, now operating together, made a final assault against the weary Union troops atop the hill. As General Benning remembered it, "The advance continued, and at length they [the enemy] were driven completely from the peak..."[241] Lieutenant Colonel Work of the 1st Texas reported of his advance with the 15th Georgia, "...both regiments, thus commingled, moved forward and occupied the crest of the hill..."[242]

It is certain that the Yankees were compelled to leave the crest of Devil's Den, yet it is also clear that Ward ordered his men to retreat. Every one of his commanders who survived specifically reported having received such an order from Ward.[243] As they retired, most of Ward's men felt that they were being "relieved" by men of the 2nd or 5th Corps. This was just the case with the 20th Indiana, for the Hoosiers were replaced by the 5th New Hampshire of Cross' Brigade of the 2nd Corps.[244] Lieutenant Ramsdell of the 124th New York remembered the reinforcements:

> I never shall forget the appearance of the Lt. Col. Commanding, who had a long red beard, but the regiment marched with a beautiful straight front that came out to our line in passing over us, taking our position when we retired. Captain Sillaman [sic], being exhausted with the heat, rode my horse to the rear while regiment after regiment of the 6th Corps came out and occupied the ground that been held so well by the 86th, 40th and 124th N.Y., but our losses had been heavy many being killed and wounded, although we succeeded in carrying back with us the bodies of the Colonel and Major.[245]

The left flank of these Union reinforcements rested in Rose Woods and did not extend across Houck's Ridge to Devil's Den. The bulk of Ward's Brigade was not relieved and was forced to retire under the fire of the advancing Confederates. Scores of soldiers from Ward's Brigade were captured as they retreated. The brigade retired from the crest of Houck's Ridge from right to left, with the units directly above the Den the last to leave. The largest number of prisoners came from the 4th Maine who

lost more men captured than all of the Union regiments who fought around the Den combined.[246] When Colonel Walker gave the order to fall back he was unable to walk, owing to his earlier wound. He was saved from capture, "and possibly death," by Sergeant Edgar L. Mowry of Company B and Freeman M. Roberts of Company F, who "wrested" the colonel from the foe and assisted him to the rear.[247]

Another prize that eluded capture was the regimental flag of the 99th Pennsylvania. One member of the color guard, George Broadbent of Lancaster, was an eighteen-year-old boy of fair complexion who was "always kind and gentle, and nicknamed on that account, 'The Lady'." He and Charles W. Herbster of the color guard had presentiments of death a few hours before the battle. Color Sergeant Munsell, the bearer of the United States Flag, recalled the scene:

> They told everybody so, and made all their plans to die. I talked with them about the matter, and tried to ridicule the idea, but all to no purpose. "The Lady" had fired away nearly all his ammunition at the enemy in our front, and had just asked me what we would do after our last cartridges were gone, when a bullet from the enemy struck him square in the temple, right before my eyes, killing him instantly. He fell to the earth, the blood squirting out of the bullet hole over his battle begrimed face. Charles Herbster saw him fall, and was by his side in an instant, took out his handkerchief, wiped the blood from his dead comrades face, kissed him, and said, "Poor Lady is dead!" On his knees, behind the body, Herbster planted himself, and again commenced loading and firing at the enemy in close company with George Setley, another one of my color guard, from Lancaster, Pa. When we were compelled to abandon our position and go to the rear, I tried to get Herbster and Setley to go with us, as they were the only two of the color guard, out of 8, not killed or wounded. Nothing could move them. There they were, riveted to the ground, avenging the lives of their comrades, and there we left them. Setley was frothing at the mouth with excitement and anger, and Herbster taking it as cool as a cucumber. Both were the best shots in the regiment, and both had done great execution. The next day we found Herbster's body lying on top, and square across "the Lady's" and both were completely riddled with bullets. Setley had been wounded, was taken prisoner, and subsequently died in captivity.[248]

Munsell, "with colors riddled, and eleven bulletholes in [his] clothes" commenced to retreat with the regiment. He had gone "a few hundred yards," when a shell landed near him. The blast stunned him and he pitched forward into the hole caused by the explosion, falling on his beloved flag. There he remained and played dead until Union troops of the 6th Corps surged back and charged the enemy. Munsell quickly hopped up and returned to his comrades, who had supposed him dead.[249] Others were not so lucky. Amos Casey, the bearer of the Regimental or State flag, besides being wounded, also suffered the loss of his twin brother that day. As the 99th began its retreat, Corporal James Casey of Company K "industriously applied himself to breaking the guns that strewed the ground to prevent them falling into the hands of the rebels. He found one that was loaded, and remarking to Major Moore that he was going to have another shot, he fired, and at the same moment was himself struck," shot through the body. "Major Moore and Sergeant Graham attempted to bring him from the field, but he bravely told them to lay him down and save themselves." Lieutenant Thomas Kelly of Company K assisted Casey to the rear to get help but Casey died in the process and was left on the field.[250] 1st Lieutenant John R. Nice, of Company H was wounded in the abdomen during the fight and "died a few hours afterwards."[251] Nice was the only officer of the 99th to be killed at Gettysburg. For his family, the loss was tragic. Corporal Henry Nice, John's brother, was also killed at Gettysburg in the fight for Culp's Hill while serving with the 147th Pennsylvania.[252]

The crest now clear of Union resistance, the Texans completed their final advance to the top of the rocky height, and once again reached Smith's abandoned guns. With bullets filling the air, many Texans were shot near the silent pieces.[253] Two men of Company L, "took hold of the trail of one of the captured guns and turned it around with the muzzle pointed toward the enemy" but no ammunition or implements to work the cannons were to be had. George A. Branard, the color bearer, glorified himself when he found, "the highest and largest rock on the crest" and "planted the adored standard of the Texans, adorned with the Lone Star, shining far off to friend and foe, with the effulgence of its glory." Soon after, a Union shell came in and "broke the flagstaff and hurled the hero unconscious down the slope of the mountain."[254]

Another brave soul positioned on a rock atop the crest was Private Wilson J. Barbee of the 1st Texas who served as a courier on General Hood's staff. After Hood's wounding, Barbee rode to the scene of the fight, his horse shot on the way. He grabbed a dropped musket and entered the fray. Reaching the crest of Devil's Den, he mounted a large boulder and fired shot after shot before being hit himself in the right leg. One Texan recalled the remainder of this memorable scene:

George Branard, color bearer of the 1st Texas Infantry. (Hill College Collection, USAMHI)

Climbing instantly back, he again commenced shooting. In less than two minutes he was tumbled off the rock by a ball in the other leg. Still unsatisfied, he crawled back a second time, but there was not more than a minute before, being wounded in the body, he again fell, this time dropping on his back between the rock that had been his perch, and that which was my shelter. Too seriously wounded this time to extricate himself from the narrow passageway, he called for help, and the last time I saw him that day, he was lying there, crying and cursing because the boys would not come to his relief and help him back on to the rock.[255]

It was quite lively atop the crest with batteries from both sides firing on the position and bullets hissing through the air and going "spat as they struck rock." The Texans hid behind boulders and weathered the man-made storm as best they could.

Advancing to the crest on the right of the Texans was the 20th Georgia, who became yet the third regiment to claim the capture of Smith's guns. A dispute over this soon began. Apparently, Benning heard the arguments and quieted his men saying, "Ah, boys, those Texans had captured this battery before you were in a quarter mile of here."[256] This is true. The Texans, although they did so after the

44th Alabama, had briefly held the guns after the 124th New York retired from their heroic charge. Benning was slightly more generous to his men in his official report giving credit to his 20th and 17th regiments as well as the Texans. This is also valid, for without the assistance of the Georgians, not only would the Texans not have captured the guns, they most likely would have been whipped. It is clear that all of the Southern regiments, from the 3rd Arkansas on the left, to the 2nd Georgia on the right contributed significantly to the capture of Smith's three Parrott rifles.

With Ward's withdrawal, the Georgians in the Gorge were treated to "the music of the unmistakable Confederate yell from atop the crest."[257] The 2nd and 17th Georgia, as well as the 44th Alabama, now moved to confront the Union soldiers in their front. This time it was the Union men who received the relentless fire from atop the Devil's Den and it was far too intense for them to handle. The 40th New York and 6th New Jersey held on long enough to effect Ward's retreat and then fell back themselves. A lieutenant in the 6th New Jersey later wrote, "We remained there until our line of battle gave way on our right flank, and the Rebs gave us flank fire. With one in front and flank it was too hot for us..."[258] The 40th New York, in their exposed position, received by far the worst of this fire. Colonel Egan discovered, "that they [the enemy] had gained ground upon my right, which threatened a flank movement, the regiments on my right having fallen to the rear and exposed us to a cross-fire, I was compelled to fall back, rallying my men upon the ridge over which I passed."[259] As these two regiments retired, Captain Smith followed suit with his remaining guns. He recalled that Benning's Georgians were about to take his remaining guns, which were now devoid of infantry support. But, at that moment, he limbered up and retired up Houck's ridge. Smith took the feeble remainder of his battery to the Wheatfield but got there just as Winslow's Battery was retiring.[260]

At this point, both Caldwell's Second Corps Division and Ayres' United States Regulars began a new phase of the battle which focused around the bloody Wheatfield. Benning's Georgians, posted around the Den, spent the remainder of the evening giving flank fire to the Union troops who charged across the Valley of Death.[261] One Texas private recalled that Benning was present when he heard some of the Yankee officers order a charge. Benning exclaimed, "No, boys, hold your fire until they come right up. Then pour a volley into them, and if they don't stop, run your bayonets into their bellies."[262] The bayonet was not necessary, and the South could rightly claim the capture of Devil's Den—from which the Rebels poured death into the Union ranks on Little Round Top and the adjacent areas for the next twenty-two hours.

The Attack Loses Momentum

After hours of bloody and intense fighting, the Confederates finally controlled the Devil's Den area. With the Union occupation of Little Round Top, however, the Den was transformed from the exposed left flank of the Army of the Potomac, to a place where Southerners could merely form for an attack upon the newer and much stronger Union position 500 yards to the east. As strong and impressive as Little Round Top appears today, it was more so for the worn out Rebels who looked in awe of the formidable "mountain" in their front. Thousands of Yankees and several cannon belched iron and lead upon them from the smoke-obscured crest of Little Round Top. Worn out Texans and Alabamians, were already bloodied from several attempts to capture the height, and almost every Southerner who wrote of the fighting in this vicinity alluded to the impregnable nature of the position. For the men of Benning's Brigade, especially those in the valley, it was particularly notable. For it was these Georgians who were next in line to take up the assault. General Benning himself explained the problems of making such an attack.

> ...I was then much in advance of every other part of our line of battle, and the second line of the enemy on the mountain itself was in a position which seemed to me almost impregnable to any merely frontal attack even with fresh men.[263]

At least one man was not intimidated by the sight of Little Round Top. Lieutenant Colonel Harris, after having advanced through the Gorge, tried to lead his 2nd Georgia in an attack against the rocky height.

> He crossed the creek, but few if any of his men crossed with him, they seeing that it was impossible to climb the mountain up which he was endeavoring to charge under the terrific fire of the enemy. At this point, still about 20 yds. in advance of his Command, he fell, pierced by the enemy's bullets.[264]

One of the bullets pierced his heart. At nightfall, four Georgians crossed Plum Run and removed the corpse from the field.[265] Harris' premonition of earlier that day had come true.

A private of the 2nd Georgia wrote just five days after the fight: "We fell back under a heavy fire from the enemy who were posted in the strongest position I ever saw. It was a steep rocky hill on which there were three lines of fortification which was impregnable."[266] Yet another Georgian recalled: "The inaccessible mountain still lay before [us]..., but the steep and rocky sides were beyond the ability of man

"Little Round Top and the Valley of Death." Gallon, 1993. In this scene the Georgians have just overrun Houck's Ridge and are threatening the flank of the 40th New York in the valley below. General Benning (far left) is contemplating an attack on what he called "the mountain." (Courtesy of Dale Gallon Historical Art)

to carry, under the awful hail storm that came like a torrent from its summit."[267] Under these circumstances and the threat of Union counterattack, Benning decided not to assault Little Round Top.

The fight for the Devil's Den was perhaps the most confusing, strange and intense fights of July 2, 1863, a day of so many individual struggles. The heat, the breakdown of the Southern command structure, the peculiarities of the terrain and the short time in which so many events elapsed made the Devil's Den fight one to be remembered. The sheer intensity of the battle made both sides exaggerate the opposition. General Robertson reported of the fight on his left: "For an hour and upward, these two regiments maintained one of the hottest contests, against five or six times their number, that I have ever witnessed."[268] General Ward was even less modest, reporting that, "For nearly two hours my brigade was opposed to at least 10,000 of the enemy, in line and en masse."[269]

It is difficult to make sense of the fighting around Devil's Den. It was a confused nightmare to many. One Texan, Val C. Giles, who fought through the Devil's Kitchen and attacked Little Round Top, described the chaotic nature of the fight on that part of the battlefield:

> Regiments overlapped each other and when we reached the woods and climbed the mountains as far as we could go, we were a badly mixed crowd. Confusion reigned supreme everywhere. Nearly all our officers were gone....By this time order and discipline were gone. Every fellow was his own general. Private soldiers gave commands as loud as officers—nobody paying attention to either.... Officers were cross to the men, and the men were equally cross to the officers. It was the same way with the enemy. We could hear the Yankee officer on the crest of the ridge in front of us cursing the men by platoons, and the men telling [him] to go to a country not very far from them just at that time....A little red paint and a few eagle feathers were all that was necessary to make the crowd on both sides the most veritable savages on earth. 'White-winged Peace' did not roost on Little Round Top that night. There was not a man there who cared a snap for the Golden Rule or that could have remembered one line of the Lord's Prayer. Both sides were whipped and all were mad about it.[270]

Perhaps Captain William C. Robbins of the 4th Alabama said it best: "We whipped the Devil in his Den, but Round Top ran up too much toward the heavens, and we didn't seem to make quite as good progress in that direction."[271]

The Devil's Den, After its Capture

Although the fighting for Devil's Den was over, it was a macabre and uncomfortable place to be on the night of the 2nd and the following morning. For the Confederates, the first order of business was to get their lines of battle straightened out. Companies were reunited, regiments were pieced back together and eventually brigade formation was restored under General Law's direction. About 2:00 a.m., the 1st Texas and 3rd Arkansas were moved from the top of the ridge to the base of Big Round Top where they joined the remainder of Robertson's Brigade who were busy throwing up stone breastworks. Company G of the 1st Texas was actually left among the rocks in Devil's Den on picket duty.[272] A scary and undesirable assignment, it meant standing awake among the blood-stained boulders with dead and dying men covering the Pennsylvania soil.[273]

About an hour later, the 44th and 48th Alabama rejoined Law's Brigade which was to the south of Robertson's and now under the command of Colonel Sheffield. Benning also endeavored to regain organization and soon the Confederates had a nearly unbroken line, by brigades, that stretched from the southwest slopes of Big Round Top to a point in Rose Woods north of the Devil's Den. Shortly after dark, each regiment sent men out on picket duty—a task not received with any enthusiasm by the exhausted and battle-wearied troops. One Texan recalled his experience that evening:

> I stood for two hours on the vidette post between the two armies and listened to the cries of the wounded and dying, and to their pleading for water. One man who lay just in front of me would say, "Oh, pardner, bring me a drink of water, I'll assure you that no one will hurt you. My leg is shot off or I would come to you. I'll give you a dollar for a drink of water. I'll give you all the money I have for a drink of water." To all of which I made no reply, as I had no water to give and could not leave my post for anything. I was so fatigued and overcome with excitement, heat of battle and suffocating smoke that I had to put tobacco in my eyes to prevent myself from going to sleep on post, when I knew it was death to be found asleep at such a time.[274]

Also required was the removal of three of Smith's Parrott rifles. Captain Sam Wilson of Company F, 1st Texas was chosen to supervise the task. Very carefully, he and his party crawled up, "to the cannon, picked out of the path over which the guns were to drawn, all stones and large pebbles, [and] not speaking above a whisper, wrapped the wheels with blankets and brought the guns off so carefully that the noise was not heard 100 yards away."[275] Two pieces were given to Latham's Battery and the other to Reilly's Battery replacing the three guns of Henry's Battalion that were disabled less than ten hours earlier.[276] The removal of the guns and the reorganization of battle lines was made far more difficult and demoralizing by the immense number of casualties sustained in the fighting at Devil's Den. One Georgian wrote immediately following the battle:

> Silence reigned, except the wails of the maimed which rose dismally in the gloom and darkness. What an awful scene it was ... with scarcely a thing visible, except the...mountain which rose darkly on the horizon, among the dead![277]

Private Henry Fluker of the 15th Georgia related the following:

> We began to realize that we were surrounded by death and suffering that no pen can picture. Our deadly determination of a few minutes before to destroy life, had changed to sympathy and sorrow for the suffering ones about us and we went to their relief as whole souled as we had gone at their destruction. The groaning and wailing on this battlefield will never be forgotten by those who were there and heard it, but the cries for water! water! and the peculiar wailing of others which had no semblance of a human cry will ring in our ears until they cease to respond to sound...Lots of our boys, instead of getting what rest they could, spent the night in doing what they could for the suffering. Others spent the night silently digging graves and burying dead comrades; sometimes it chanced to be a dear brother, a loved messmate or officer of their company.[278]

For all of Benning's Brigade, the difficulty in removing the wounded was increased by having only two ambulances available for almost 300 bloodied men. Complaining of this in his official report, Benning remarked that all through the night he could hear the enemy, "throwing up two lines of breastworks, one above the other, on the mountain side" in front of him.[279] This disconcerting sound echoed through the darkness and left a distinct impression upon many of the Southerners who wrote of the fight for Devil's Den.

Although the Yankees fortified their new position, they could not recover many of their dead and wounded comrades who fell around Devil's Den. Sergeant Ransom W. Wood of Co. I, 20th Georgia, happened upon a dead Yankee captain wedged in between two rocks. On him was found a Testament, which the Southerner confiscated. Three days later, the following was found to have been written inside:

> June 21st, 1863
> In case I am killed and my body left upon the field, the finder of this Testament will please send it to my father, John Nicoll, Blooming Grove, Orange County N. York, and confer a great favor on me.
> Isaac Nicoll, Capt. Co. G 124th Regt. N.Y. State.[280]

The book was kindly and promptly sent to Mr. Nicoll. The younger Nicoll was later buried, complete with an inscribed wooden headstone where he fell, by one of his brother officers. His father was successful in getting the body exhumed but it would be some time before transportation could be secured.[281]

Lying near the dead body of Captain Nicoll was the nearly expired James Scott of Company B. From the effects of his five wounds, "Scotty" lay paralyzed on the slope of the Triangular Field for three days, until his eventual removal to a hospital.[282] Also in the area was Corporal Noah B. Kimbark of Company H. Wounded in the chest and both ankles and

Captain Isaac Nicoll, Company G, 124th New York. (Division of Military Affairs N. Y. State Adjutant Generals Office Collection, USAMHI)

remaining in place all night, he was ordered to the rear by a Rebel officer. Unable to move more than a few yards at a time, he endured a terrible day as he searched for a hospital. Luckily, he found one and survived to tell his story.[283]

The long night passed and with the morning sun came the resumption of battle noise. A member of the Pennsylvania Reserves wrote that, "At early dawn the contest opened between the skirmishers, and became brisk, and was kept up nearly all day." Men from all over the south end of the battlefield skirmished with each other. One popular tradition is that of the "Devil's Den sharpshooters." Although there was no organized unit of sharpshooters in any of the Southern regiments that fought around Devil's Den, hardly a visitor can leave Gettysburg without having heard stories of Confederate marksmen perched in the rocks sending bullets into any Union soldier who showed his head on Little Round Top.

That there were such marksmen in both armies is indisputable. Indeed, Robert E. Lee himself had seen a need earlier that year, to separate some Texans for special service in the eastern theater. Unfortunately, Ike N. M. Turner, the man who was to lead this force, was killed a few months prior to the Battle of Gettysburg and the Texas sharpshooter battalion was never organized.[284]

Hundreds of Union soldiers in the area were part of Berdan's Sharpshooters. The Southerners at Gettysburg, however, did not always differentiate between someone who could shoot really well and a "sharpshooter," which by definition is "an expert marksman."[285] It is also an oversimplification to state that the Southerners were firing at the Union line only from the Devil's Den. Undoubtedly, Rebel skirmishers were positioned advantageously along the entire length of their line from the base of Big Round Top, across the Devil's Kitchen, through the Den and into Rose Woods. Of course with its eerie appearance and central location in front of Little Round Top, the Devil's Den attracted the attention of early writers. One soldier of the 22nd Massachusetts, positioned between the Round Tops remembered the stunning accuracy of the Confederates "gathering among the gigantic boulders."

> They were all dead shots, armed mostly with the old-fashioned muzzle-loading Mississippi, or squirrel rifle, carrying a small pea ball that sounded spitefully murderous, as they sharply sang among the cedars and flattened with a dull, ominous thud against the moss-covered boulders that composed our fortifications....much lead was wasted all along the line in an effort to move or silence these murderous fellows.[286]

Michigan men of the 1st United States Sharpshooters "scattered behind the bowlders at the foot of Little Round Top were kept busy exchanging shots" all morning with "Johnies lodged behind bowlders in the vicinity of the den." They were positioned about 300 yards from it "with a marshy interval or swamp intervening."[287] After expending a great deal of ammunition it was determined to stop this harrasing fire that annoyed the artillery and infantrymen along the Union line.

> For this purpose a detail of 20 men was made by Richard W. Tyler, at that time a sergeant of Company K [1st United States Sharpshooters], a gallant soldier who had distinguished himself on previous occasions.... This sortie by our boys (every one of whom would be mentioned if I knew their names) was a most gallant and dangerous undertaking, and it was singular that notwithstanding the brisk fire under which they advanced none were hurt, but narrowly escaped the fast flying bullets, one man being saved by his frying pan (for they carried their cooking kit always), another by his rifle stock, the ball flattening on the barrel, while others "just missed it." But our sharpshooters were fleet travelers—to and fro—and recked not of danger, when the order came to "go." ...With a rush these brave fellows ran across the marsh, and having routed the enemy's pickets in front of the hill, closed in upon them capturing the entire party. There were 20 of them caught in the cave, a number being wounded, and they assured our men that their fire from the Little Round Top had made them prisoners all day. It was made too hot for them to attempt an escape. They were a sorry looking crowd, being very hungry and about famished for want of water.[288]

In the late afternoon of July 3, after the repulse of Longstreet's assault on the Union center, the Confederates on the south end of the battlefield pulled back from their advanced positions. Before this occurred, however, part of Hood's Division repulsed a charge of elements of Farnsworth's Brigade of Yankee cavalry south of the Slyder farm.[289]

Also that afternoon, Army of the Potomac Commander General George Gordon Meade and several of his generals gathered in "a rocky pen directly in the line held by the One hundred and forty-sixth" New York on Little Round Top.[290] The commanding general became impatient as, "the sharpshooters of the enemy" atop Devil's Den and Houck's Ridge "had occupied every available rock and tree and cover, and were keeping up a persistant and fatal fire on the Little Round Top. Men who exposed themselves for a moment were at once shot down."[291] Thus, General Meade ordered the woods in his front cleared of the enemy.

Through a misunderstanding of orders which originated with General Law and went through General Benning, the 15th Georgia was ordered to an isolated position in Rose Woods just as the greatly superior force of Yankees (which Meade had ordered forward) from the Fifth and Sixth Corps advanced to clear the area of Rebels.[292] In the meantime, the mistake in orders was realized and Benning's three other regiments were sent to the rear, but too late to recall the 15th. Colonel DuBose of that regiment skillfully effected its withdrawal but lost over 100 of his men, most of them captured, before joining the remainder of the Georgians on Seminary Ridge. The event left DuBose wondering how any of them escaped at all and embarrassed Benning sufficiently to justify his actions in his official report.[293] The heavy fighting south of town essentially ended with this debacle.

The Aftermath

The morning of "the fourth of July, bathed in calm, refreshing sunlight, dawned as if in joyous commemoration of the old freedom and in bright recognition of the nation's new birth of liberty...." The 118th Pennsylvania was one of the regiments in position on the western face of Big Round Top. "Immediately in front for some half mile was thick timber, concealing the rocks, stones, caves and boulders that made up the well-named, weird, forsaken and desolate Devil's Den."[294] Years later, the historian of the unit recorded their experiences.

About ten o'clock [on the morning of July 4th] the brigade moved out to feel and develop the enemy. At the foot of the hill and in the gorge there were thrilling, horrifying scenes of blood and carnage. The dead lay in all shapes and in every direction, some upon their faces, others on their backs, while others were twisted and knotted in painful contortions. The progress of the advance was much impeded in the effort to tread without stepping upon the bodies. Some kneeling behind the rocks had met their death where they dropped for shelter. The men gave way at times instinctively from the muzzles of muskets resting upon rocks and stones, down the barrels of which the sightless glassy eyes still gazed and the guards of which were grasped by hands convulsed in death. Seeking shelter in kneeling to aim they had fallen in the act of firing. Numbers of the enemy lay in a shallow trench they had dug, evidently to avoid the unerring fire of some expert skirmishers. They had torn and twisted leaves and grass in their agonies and their mouths filled with soil—they had literally bitten the dust.[295]

The area into which the regiment had advanced was shortly nicknamed the "Slaughter Pen." Among the earliest visitors to the site following the battle, the men of the 118th were horrified by the scenes they encountered. In graphic detail their historian wrote:

At one spot, a point either of desperate resistance or formation for an assault, thirty-seven dead bodies lay in line, side by side. In Confederate clothing, their uniforms were bet-

The Slaughter Pen, Gardner, July 1863.
(Courtesy of William A. Frassanito, Gettysburg: A Journey In Time*)*

A stereo view of one of the nameless corpses that lie bloating in the rocks around Devil's Den after the battle, Gardner, July 1863. Sights such as these shocked and horrified early visitors. (GNMP)

ter than usual, and all had new black slouched hats, doubtless from the stock of some neighboring dealer. In front of these bodies lay that of an officer of fine proportions, manly physique and remarkably handsome features. His head rested upon a stone; his limbs were straightened, his hands folded; he had evidently been prepared for decent sepulture. A letter, through which the ball had passed that penetrated his heart, identified him as Captain William A. Dunklin, of the 44th Alabama.[296]

A Northern soldier who claimed to visit the Den on July 4 was A. P. Chase of the 146th New York. He "...found those rocky crevices full of dead Rebel sharpshooters, most of them still grasping their rifles. Behind one short low ridge of rock lay a row of eighteen dead who had been tallied out one by one by our sharpshooters."[297] During the afternoon of the 4th it rained, not a light drizzle, but a heavy downpour that lasted for many hours. The already disfigured unburied dead were drenched, many bloated beyond recognition. It is uncertain exactly how long after the battle bodies of Confederate dead remained unburied in the area around Devil's Den. At least one account, written by a newspaper correspondent on July 11, 1863, gives a general time frame.

The last of the rebel dead on the battlefield were buried only yesterday [July 10]. They were principally found near the foot of Round Top Ridge, where some of the most terrible fighting of the battle took place.... The bodies numbered in all, about fifty.... Decomposition had progressed so far as to render it

impossible to handle the bodies at all, and graves were necessarily dug close by the side of them, and they simply turned over into them.[298]

J. Howard Wert, a local resident and later a battlefield guide, was one of the first civilians to visit the area after the battle. In several publications written years after the war he described the scenes he witnessed in the days following the battle.

...the dead of both armies, as a general rule, were interred with as much care as circumstances would permit. Yet, at the best, the burials of the battlefield must seem shocking and sacreligious as compared with the respect paid to the dead in our own homes. But where the Confederate dead fell thick in the valley between the Round Tops, there was a special pathos in the mode of their interment. A large tract here is entirely destitute of surface soil. It is a massive bed of round, syenitic stones of various sizes. The dead bodies were collected in groups of three or four and stones, sometimes intermingled with brushwood, thrown upon them until a little mound had been formed which, often, only partially concealed the decomposing corpses beneath. At one point, just south-west [actually south-east] of the Devil's Den, Plum Run leaves the surface, its waters being visible here and there beneath the heterogeneously piled, irregular and massive rocks which form a bridge across it of precarious footing. In charging across these piles of rocks, numbers of dead and wounded men fell in the chasms between. The heavy rains which followed the battle, washed down and lodged in these labyrinths other corpses from positions higher up the flat. These bodies were never recovered, but rapidly decomposed by the action of the elements, whilst the bones were washed away or covered with rubbish. More than a month after the battle, in one of these chasms, was presented the hideous spectacle of the remains of five Confederate soldiers piled upon each other, just as they had fallen, in a place from which it would have been impossible to extricate the bodies. It was a hideous and revolting spectacle, but war is replete with horrors. Whenever the writer views these rocks around the Devil's Den, where so many brave men yielded up life, his mind reverts to a black-haried, handsome youth of an Alabama regiment, who, after the battle, lay for weeks in the hospital of the Second Army Corps, moaning with pain. Much of the time he was partially delirious from the fever and suffering induced by a shattered leg, the amputation of which had been too long delayed. In all his raving the prominent subject was those "Awful, awful rocks." He had fallen near this point and those weird surroundings, so different from his Southern home, were ever foremost in his mind through all his weeks of suffering, till death came to his relief...[299]

On the afternoon of July 6, 1863, Wyman S. White of the 2nd United States Sharpshooters walked over the field and "took a look at the Devil's Den where a Rebel's body was down in the cleft of the big rocks and was so bound in between the stones that it was impossible to get it out." At another place he noticed "a Rebel's body standing up almost straight beside a big rock. His rifle lay over on top of the rock. From appearances...he was about to fire when he was hit and instantly killed, falling forward onto the stone and as his body swelled, it straightened up so as to be in a standing position."[300] That same day, a citizen of Gettysburg named Daniel Skelly traveled out to "Round Top" to visit the scene of carnage.

One of the saddest sights of the day's visit on the field I witnessed near the Devil's Den, on the low ground in that vicinity. There were twenty-six Confederate officers, ranking from a colonel to lieutenants, laid side by side in a row for burial. At the head of each was a board giving their names, ranks and commands to which they belonged. A short distance away was another group of thirteen arranged in the same way. They had evidently been prepared for burial by their Confederate companions before they had fallen back, so that their identity would be preserved, and they would receive a respectable burial.[301]

On July 7, Jacob Hoke along with some other citizens of Chambersburg rode over the battlefield to examine the human wreckage first hand. As the party reached the "huge boulders" of Devil's Den, they came upon "unburied confederates. They were

Dead Confederate soldiers in the woods near the Slaughter Pen, Gardner, July 1863. (USAMHI)

black and bloated, eyes open and glaring, and corruption running from their mouths." Hoke "had seen similar sights" a year earlier "upon the field of South Mountain," but those of the party who had not "were shocked and horrified."[302] A correspondent for the *Daily Patriot and Union* of Harrisburg, Pennsylvania visited the field on July 9 and made some interesting comments concerning the appearance of the Gorge in front of Devil's Den.

> Any one anxious about the definition of the word glory will find the answer in the valley in front of Round Top, where numbers of bodies lie bleaching in the sun on the gray granite rocks, in every stage of decomposition, doomed to lie there exposed to the elements in every conceivable position that men killed outright will assume in their fall. Their anxious friends will never even know the horrible condition that death left them in....[There] a scene presented itself which we shall never forget. The bottom of the valley is composed of granite rocks piled on top of each other. These are covered with the Rebel dead, no less then seventy bodies being scattered over perhaps an acre. We hurried over the spot...the ground everywhere presenting indications of the fearful havoc of war.[303]

This was the scene that greeted the first cameramen to the field. In this atmosphere Alexander Gardner and his associates James Gibson and Timothy O'Sullivan would be responsible for recording some of the most vivid and horrifying scenes ever photographed. In his 1866 sketch book Gardner described his thoughts as he walked the death-strewn battlefield.

> ...it was, indeed, a "harvest of death" that was presented; hundreds and thousands of torn Union and rebel soldiers—although many of the former were already interred—strewed the now quiet fighting ground, soaked by the rain, which for two days had drenched the country with its fitful showers. A battle has been often the subject of elaborate description; but it can be described in one simple word, devilish! and the distorted dead recall the ancient legends of men torn in pieces by the savage wantonness of fiends. Swept down without preparation, the shattered bodies fall in all conceivable positions....Some of the dead presented an aspect which showed that they had suffered severely just previous to dissolution, but these were few in number compared with those who wore a calm and reigned expression, as though they had passed away in the act of prayer. Others had a smile on their faces, and looked as if they were in the act of

speaking. Some lay stretched on their backs, as if friendly hands had prepared them for burial. Some were still resting on one knee, their hands grasping their muskets. In some instances the cartridge remained between the teeth, or the musket was held in one hand, and the other was uplifted as though to ward a blow, or appealing to heaven. The faces of all were pale, as though cut in marble, and as the wind swept across the battle-field it waved the hair, and gave the bodies such an appearance of life that a spectator could hardly help thinking they were about to rise and continue the fight.[304]

Some of Gardner's most poignant views were recorded in the immediate vicinity of Devil's Den where the burial crews had not yet completed their work. One deceased Confederate became a particularly intriguing subject for Gardner and his men. They exposed six negatives of this lone corpse and actually dragged the body to a more desirable location.[305] In his scrapbook Gardner told his story of the "Sharpshooter."

> The artist, in passing over the scene of the...engagements, found in a lonely place the covert of a rebel sharpshooter, and photographed the scene....The Confederate soldier had built up between two huge rocks, a stone wall, from the crevices of which he had directed his shots, and in comparative security, picked off our officers. The side of the rock on the left show, by the little white spots, how our sharpshooters and infantry had endeavored to dislodge him. The trees in the vicinity were splintered, and their branches cut off, while the front of the wall looked as if just recovering from an attack of geological smallpox. The sharpshooter had evidently been wounded in the head by a fragment of shell which had exploded over him, and had laid down upon his blanket to await death. There was no means of judging how long he had lived after receiving his wound, but the disordered clothing shows that his sufferings must have been intense. Was he delirious with agony, or did death come slowly to his relief, while memories of home grew dearer as the field of carnage faded before him? What visions, of loved ones far away, may have hovered above his stony pillow! What familiar voices may he not have heard, like whispers beneath the roar of battle, as his eyes grew heavy in their long, last sleep! ...How many skeletons of such men are bleaching to-day in out of the way places no one can tell. Now and then the visitor to a battle-field finds the bones of some

man shot as this one was, but there are hundreds that will never be known of, and will moulder into nothingness among the rocks.[306]

Though official accounts suggest that the burial of the dead was completed shortly after the battle, there is evidence that this was not the case in all instances. David McConaughy, an attorney in Gettysburg, wrote on November 12, 1863, that "There were nearly 40 Rebel bodies in [the] Slaughter pen which were never actually buried, but wrapped in blankets & covered with a few stones & their remains [still] lie scattered about."[307] Michael Jacobs, professor of science and mathematics at Pennsylvania College was one of the earliest historians of the battle. In an article written in 1864, he also described the appearance of the fields around Gettysburg, and the unburied Confederates in Devil's Den.

In front of Little Round Top, amongst huge rocks, lay all summer long the decaying bodies of half a dozen or more of rebels, who had probably belonged to Hood's division, and having been wounded on July 2, in their desperate effort to take Little Round Top, may have crept into the open spaces between these rocks for shelter or for water. There they died undiscovered, and when found they were so far gone in decomposition that they could not be removed. And such also was the position in which they lay that it was impossible to cover them with earth.[308]

Reverend Andrew Cross of the Christian Commission visited the area of Devil's Den several times during the months following the battle and corroborated the accounts given by Jacobs and McConaughy. He described the Den as:

...a mass of huge rocks, of very singular formation, in a hollow, through which Plum run passes. This stream runs among and through these rocks. Between them are crevices of 10 to 15 [feet] deep, and about 1 1/2 to 2 feet wide. In the pursuit of our men, many of their men were wounded and killed on these rocks, who fell into the crevices, from which, if wounded, they could not well escape, and if killed, it would be with difficulty they could be found, and almost impossible to get them out. This whole neighborhood was rocky. When burying the many that were slain here, it was difficult to get earth to bury them, and in a few places they had to be covered with stone. In the latter part of August and first of September [1863], when passing over this ground, in company with Rev. Dr. Junkin, we found some of these men still unburied. It is

generally supposed that these were all Rebels; but in several cases we found the bodies wrapped in the overcoats of our men.[309]

Francis M. Stoke, a Pennsylvania soldier assigned to Camp Letterman Hospital after the battle, journeyed over the Gettysburg battlefield in October 1863. In a letter written to his brother shortly afterward, he gives us one of the best early accounts of the area, and also the first documentable usage of the term "Devil's Den."

Along the middle of this swamp there is a chain of the largest rocks I ever saw; it seems as though nature in some wild freak had forgotten herself and piled great rocks in mad confusion together. This place is known as the Devil's Den. The Rebels in passing over the rocks were shot and fell down between the rocks into the stagnant water and blue mud. And many, I have no doubt, were wounded and fell into the water below and strangled to death. When I visited this place in company with Wm. French, I clambered down to these miserable looking beings. I almost strangled from the effects of the smell caused partly by the decomposed bodies. The crevice is from ten to fifteen feet deep. It is dangerous to pass over these rocks.. Some skeletons of late have been hooked up with iron hooks attached to long poles. You will remember the Rebels buried their own dead here. Scarcely any graves were dug here. They dragged them to where they could throw them into some crevices and tumbled them in and threw a few stones on them and thus left them. The visitor is shocked at every step while passing over this vast charnel house. As soon as the bodies began to decay the stones began falling down among the skeletons thus exposing all that each grave contains. It is not pleasant to the finer feelings of the human breast to see the frames of men (if they are enemies) in every position conceivable. Here all the arms and legs that were shot off were not gathered and buried, but are lying about among the rocks. I saw in a circle of one rod, four legs lying with shoes and stockings on. Whole hands lay withering in the sun.[310]

Another soldier stationed at Camp Letterman General Hospital after the battle was Jacob Shenkel of Company L, 62nd Pennsylvania. On November 11, 1863, he and several other soldiers accompanied a photographer to Devil's Den. Several views were recorded of Stoke and his comrades; some had the men posed as dead. These photographs were then sold at the dedication of the Soldiers' National Cemetery on November 19, 1863.[311] It is not known whether the cameramen were actually trying to fool anyone into believing that the men in the photographs were actually dead, but over the years the existence of these "posed views" has caused much confusion in histories written of the battle. Regardless of the story surrounding their origin, these photographs are important in another respect. Among the scenes recorded were the first views of the wall of rocks that today is known as Devil's Den.[312]

On November 11, 1863, Peter Weaver recorded a series of views at Devil's Den. Among them were the first photographs to highlight the massive wall of boulders. (ACHS)

Post-Battle History

As the Gettysburg battlefield and Devil's Den in particular grew in popularity over the next fifty years, many individuals played a role in its preservation, monumentation, commercialization, and exploitation. Some of what occurred was unprecedented in the annals of American history—motivated by an unselfishness that exemplifies Americans values. Other things that occurred, however, were driven purely by greed, and did little to honor the memory of the fallen heroes "who here gave their last full measure of devotion."

Within months of the battle it was local citizens, led by David McConaughy (a prominent Gettysburg attorney), who first preserved part of the ground that is today the Gettysburg National Military Park. Many townspeople soon made their living by providing services to the great throngs of tourists that began to flock to the battlefield every summer. Hotels, boarding houses, and restaurants sprang up throughout the town. Livery stables flourished, and young men as well as old offered their services to guide parties over the battlefield. Stories told by these early guides would have a lasting impact on the way the public perceived and still perceives the Devil's Den. As the years went by and the grounds of the Gettysburg Battlefield Memorial Association (GBMA) grew, veterans gatherings and regimental reunions became commonplace. Monuments were erected all over the field. By the 1890s Gettysburg had one of the largest outdoor collections of bronze and granite statues anywhere in the world, and had established itself as a "Mecca" for future generations of Americans interested in the heritage of their great country. In 1895 the GBMA turned over its holdings to the Federal government and the Gettysburg National Military Park was established.

But there is a dark side to the story. At the time the national park was formed, a struggle was taking place to determine whether Gettysburg would become a great historic shrine or a giant amusement park. By 1895 there were at least three properties on the field which were nothing more than theme parks. In 1884 a railroad spur was constructed from the town, directly across the field of "Pickett's Charge," so that tourists could be transported to the largest of these parks on the eastern slope of Little Round Top. By 1894 an electric trolley ran over the most sacred parts of the field allowing travelers to stop and visit other parks. Although the railroad, the trolley, and the amusement parks were located on private property at the edge of battlefield land, they were situated on sensitive areas of the field, and in some instances, within feet of newly erected monuments. In the haste to construct these so-called "improvements," much historic ground was irreparably destroyed. Words were exchanged between veterans and local businessmen. Tempers boiled and lawsuits were filed. In the end, this issue would not be decided until arguments were heard in the United States Supreme Court. With the popularity of Devil's Den well established at an early date, it is no coincidence that the area was caught in the middle of this confrontation between preservation and commercialization. This chapter examines some of the specific events that for good or bad came together to make Devil's Den one of the most popular tourist attractions to emerge from the American Civil War.

The Lore of the Sharpshooter

When reading the descriptions of early visitors to the field during the years following the battle, it becomes obvious that one of the highlights of any tour was a visit to Devil's Den. Although some accounts are repetitive, they are presented in order to provide the reader with an understanding of how stories of the Den quickly became ingrained into the history of the battle. Even before the Civil War was over, visitors flocked to Gettysburg to see what was already considered to be the great battlefield of the war. Early on there was a great demand for knowledgeable persons to take these "tourists" over the field and explain the movements of the armies during the three days of fighting: thus the Gettysburg battlefield guide was born. The stories told by these early guides would have a lasting effect on the writ-

An early guided tour at Devil's Den.
(Timothy H. Smith Collection)

ings of many visitors for years to come. In October 1864 Isaac Moorhead of Erie, Pennsylvania, toured the field with John Frey, one such local guide. Moorhead wrote of his visit:

As we approached Round Top it was at once evident that it was the key of the whole position—that point lost and all was lost. Driving our carriage down the rocky lane that leads from the turnpike to Round Top, we soon reached the base. Dismounting among the rocks, we saw some bones of a rebel, with shreds of his "butternut" clothing. We passed through the woods filled with rocks, and ascended the Round Top. The summit is clear of trees, but they are scattered on the sides. On a large rock near the summit is chiseled the inscription; "Col. Strong Vincent fell here com'g 3rd, Brig. 1st div. 5th corps, July 2d, 1863." Standing on the rock and looking down into the valley, Mr. Frey called my attention to the "Devil's Den," which consisted of two immense rocks standing up side by side, with a small but convenient opening between them. Across the top was another immense rock. The opening was in such a position that neither shot nor shell, although freely thrown at the rebel sharp-shooter occupying this place, could reach him. The story goes (and I deem it an exceedingly plausible one, and Mr. Frey says he does not doubt it), that Col. Vincent was hit by this sharp-shooter in the "Devil's Den." After repeated efforts to dislodge him, two of Berdan's sharpshooters were called up and the locality of the fellow pointed out to them. One of them slipped down to the friendly cover of a large Whitewood tree, to the right of the Vincent rock, and flanking the opening of the "Devil's Den." Here waiting until the rebel

reloaded his gun, and coming cautiously to the end of the rock, he took deliberate aim and sent the rebel to his long home. This [Berdan] sharp-shooter has been at Gettysburg since the battle, and went with Mr. Frey to all these localities. The rebels grave is just at the mouth of the den, and his boots I saw lying just within the den.

...Passing down to the vast rocks, scattered about in the valley at the foot of the mountain, which afforded such excellent lurking spots for the enemy's sharp-shooters, we were told by our guide that many wounded rebels had crawled under these rocks for safety. After the battle heavy rains set in and drowned many of them, and the current of water brought them to view. Others there were undiscovered until the flesh had fallen from their bones. Here, in a secluded spot among the rocks, I found the bones of a rebel just as he had fallen. Picking up one of his shoes to remove the string, to tie together some little trees, the bones of his foot tumbled out. It was a "Georgia state shoe" made from canvas, with leather tips and heel stiffeners. From among his ribs I picked up a battered minie ball which doubtless caused his death. Moving aside a flat stone, Mr. Frey showed us the grinning face and skull of a rebel. Some of them in this rocky part of the field have very shallow graves.[1]

In June 1865 another visitor wrote of his trip to the Den. This account is unusual, for the writer actually tries to describe the fighting that occurred there instead of the sharpshooter action.

Between the two Round Tops is a ragged ravine, a rough wilderness of huge rocks, piled up in uncouth wildness; this is Devil's "Den," and the sounds of Hell echoed there when McLaws Division of Longstreet's Corps attempted to pierce our line by passing up the ravine. They were dreadfully cut up by a cross fire on either Round Top, and for weeks thereafter the stench from putrefying bodies of dead rebels, lying on those rocks, was something dreadful. Devil's Den is quiet enough now, and when I looked over into it yesterday, a striped squirrel was running blithely over the ledges flecked with the quivering shadows of the young birches.[2]

In July 1865, the laying of the cornerstone for the Soldiers Monument in the National Cemetery attracted a large crowd of visitors to Gettysburg. A few of the reporters covering the event took this opportunity to visit the battlefield, and of course visit the Den. Lorenzo L. Crounse of the New York *Times* wrote:

In front of [Little Round Top] is the little valley, rendered moist by a stagnant brook: the "Devil's Den," a remarkable upheaval of enormous rocks, forming a cavern a hundred feet long, and large enough to admit a man; through this runs a trickling stream, and here our poor wounded men crawled during the battle for water and safety, only to meet their death by drowning when the rains of the night suddenly swelled this stream to a torrent from which there was no escape. A dozen bodies were afterward taken from a huge crevice, where they had been left by the receding waters.[3]

In November 1865, George Gross, in a party of Philadelphians, was taken over the field by Captain Adolphus F. Cavada, who had served on General Andrew A. Humphreys' staff at Gettysburg. The events of his tour were recorded in an article for the *Philadelphia Press*. In Gross' version of the story, the already-famous Rebel sharpshooter survives.

The remarkable ledge of rocks known as "Devil's Den," directly opposite Round Top, was occupied by the enemy's sharpshooters, one of whom had a perfectly safe position within the cleft, and picked off our men with fatal accuracy. The face of the boulder behind which he lay is still covered with the marks of the Minies sent at him. One "went for him" clean through the crevice, but missed. He was finally dislodged by a charge, and escaped through an opening to the rear. Seven rifles, it is said, were found in his hiding-place. There is room enough for fifty. On the slope in front of this den lie bleaching the bones of rebel dead, washed out by the rains.[4]

In June 1866, the Congressional Committee on Military Affairs, headed by Robert Cummings Schenck, journeyed to Gettysburg for a visit of the battlefield. Their guide was none other than John Bachelder himself, who gave many such tours. One of the party was Brevet Brigadier General Henry V. Boynton. He wrote in great detail of his tour and described the Devil's Den as "a low, abrupt ridge, with great walls of loose stone masses." While there Bachelder told the party that "the rebel sharpshooters" occupied the Den while "our forces were on Little Round Top, and large numbers of our men were killed by them." Boynton described that the Gorge was "the scene of fierce fighting," and marks of the "bloody story" could still be seen. "Dented into these enduring rocks" the party could plainly see "the marks of shell, the black rays of their explosion, and the scars of the glancing shot." While in the Den one of the men made a gruesome discovery, "a perfect skeleton, which the rains had washed out of its shallow bed."[5]

The residue of lead from bullets can clearly be seen in many early views of the Den including this stereo entitled "Signal Rock at Round Top," Mumper & Co., c. 1878 stereo. (Fields of Glory)

Other visitors made use of the tourbooks that were starting to be sold around town as guides to the field. Such was the case with John Watts De Peyster, who visited the field in the spring of 1867. His impressions of the southern end of the battlefield are very interesting.

...Little Round Top, [is] 280 feet high; just to the North of this is a still more remarkable exhibition of Volcanic agencies. The two hills were perfect forts covering our left flank. Jutting out from Little Round Top, toward the East, is thrust forth that accumulation of syenite boulders, which, in certain places, seem as if piled up, in others as if tossed about in sport by the hands of giants. At its foot is the "Slaughter Pen," so named from the numbers of Rebels who perished and were buried there....The Eastern slope of the Round Tops sinks to a little stream or thread of water known as Plum Run. Beyond this is the Devils Den, even more remarkable than the Granite Spur. Within musket range of life and cultivation, it is an absolute solitude which excites in the beholder a feeling of awe. No gorge of the wildest mountains is more striking in its romantic peculiarities. Across this run Crawford's Division made their brilliant charge. From the Devils Den the Rebel sharpshooters sped so ma[n]y fatal bullets into our lines, and numerous shallow graves and even scattered bones mark the spot where they met with a just retribution. In one nook of the

Den a vast scooping mass of primitive rock recalls to the observer who has traveled in Italy, the idea of an enormous antique tassa of syenite hollowed by a Cyclopian chisel. Within its circular rim of dark syenite, the turf is unusually green and luxuriant.[6]

In most early accounts of Devil's Den the one thing that seems to be missing is the actual fighting on July 2. The accounts focus on the appearance of the Den, and of course, on the action of the sharpshooters after it was captured, a relatively minor incident considering all that occurred there. Also, many accounts generically refer to all Confederate dead in the area as rebel sharpshooters. As years went by, the aura surrounding the Devil's Den sharpshooter grew. Examination of early guide and tour books of the battlefield from the late 19th and early 20th century reveals how the stories grew. An 1898 tourbook gives the following information:

This curious upheaval of massive boulders lies a good rifle-shot from Little Round Top. It was occupied by Confederate sharpshooters during the second day's fight, whose fire was most disastrous to the federals upon Little Round Top. When by superhuman efforts Hazlett's battery had been lifted over the boulders to the summit of that eminence, its guns could not be effectively used for this sharp fire. Then it was that eight companies of Berdan's Sharpshooters were brought to their aid, and so reduced the Confederate fire that the artillery could be used to shell their position at the Devil's Den. After the fight the dead bodies of sixty-eight Confederates were taken form the crevices of these boulders.[7]

It is not known when the use of the number "sixty-eight" first appeared, or from what source that particular figure was derived. It appears, however, in many tourbooks printed around the turn of the century. Another book gives a higher number of dead taken from the Den.

The Devil's Den, a mass of jagged and picturesque rock, was a favorite retreat for riflemen during the battle. Among the crevices of the rock they would lie in wait and pick off the enemy at will with their long range rifles. At last they became so harassing to the enemy that a whole battery of artillery, loaded with grape shot, was turned on the rocky eminence and their rifles silenced forever. After the battle over a hundred dead riflemen were found in these rocky crevices.[8]

In the early years of battlefield tours a new aspect was added to the already famous sharpshooter story, one we like to call "death by concussion." Us-ing first-hand knowledge of how history is created, the following has been prepared.

The first recorded reference located for the story comes from the 25th anniversary of the battle in 1888. Ex-Senator Warner Mills was asked by a reporter about a walking cane he was using that was inscribed "Devil's Den - July 1, 2, 3, 1863."[9] He replied that he had gotten it on a recent trip to Gettysburg where he had toured the battlefield in company with several others, including General James Longstreet. He stated that "the Devil's Den was a rocky place on the field of battle." During his visit he was told "They found One confederate soldier dead in a hole among those rocks, who had'nt a wound upon him. It is supposed that he was killed by concussion of a passing cannon ball." In 1899, an article appeared in the Gettysburg *Compiler*, giving an eyewitness account of the battle by Augustus P. Martin, commander of the Union Fifth Corps Artillery at Gettysburg. The article was actually an interview with Martin written by battlefield guide Luther Minnigh. It is impossible to say how much influence Minnigh had on Martin's account, but the story sounds strangely familiar.

Among the interesting incidents that occurred on Little Round Top was the summary way in which a sharpshooter was disposed of in rear of the Devil's Den. He had concealed himself behind a stone wall between two boulders and for a long time we were annoyed by shots from that direction, one of which actually combed my hair over my left ear and passed through the shoulder of a man a little taller than myself who was standing behind me for a cover. At last we were able to locate the spot, by the use of a field glass, from whence the shots came by little puffs of smoke that preceded the whizzing of the bullets that passed our heads. We then loaded one of our guns with a percussion shell, taking careful and accurate aim. When the shot was fired the shell struck and exploded on the face of one of the boulders. We supposed the shot had frightened him away, as we were no longer troubled with shots from that location. When the battle was ended we rode over to the Devil's Den and found behind the wall a dead Confederate soldier lying upon his back and, so far as we could see, did not have a mark upon his body, and from that fact became convinced that he was killed by the concussion of the shell when it exploded on the face of the boulder.[10]

This makes an interesting story, but there are a few problems. It sounds as if the location referred to is the home of the Rebel sharpshooter above the

Luther Minnigh (1849-1905), battlefield guide. (Timothy H. Smith Collection)

Devil's Den. This is almost certainly a perversion of the story of the dead sharpshooter originally told by Alexander Gardner in his scrapbook published in 1866. Gardner stated, however, that "The sharpshooter had evidently been wounded in the head by a fragment of shell which had exploded over him..." There was no mention of death by concussion. Of course there is also the problem that Gardner had moved the body to that location, and unless Martin was referring to another body that had been taken away and buried previously, none would have been in that position when he "rode over to the Devil's Den" after the battle.[11] Since Minnigh was a popular battlefield guide and the article was published in Gettysburg, it gained great notoriety and the story of "death by concussion" was retold time and time again. A 1910 postcard of "The Devil's Den" sold in Gettysburg provides slightly more detail.

One of the natural landmarks that attract attention of tourists is the immense ledge of rocks in front of Round Top. It furnished shelter for Confederate sharpshooters who were picking off the gunners at the batteries on Little Round Top. The barricade of one is yet pointed out in the rear. He had been killed by

the concussion of a shell, which exploded at the crevice of the rock against which his head was leaning, and when found there was not a mark on his body.[12]

There is no doubt, given the above information from the back of the postcard, that most guides were familiar with Gardner's photograph and pointed out the spot of the sharpshooter's demise regularly on tours. There is also no doubt that they were telling people that he died by the concussion of a shell. Another account of an apparently different soldier was being told in 1938 during the 75th anniversary.

...the body of one man was found in a half-kneeling position in the cup of a peculiarly shaped rock. No mark upon him furnished a means of designating the manner in which he was killed. There was not a scar on his body; he had fallen against the side of the rock while in the act of firing. His rifle lay across the top of the stone, the butt against his shoulder, one arm extended along the barrel, while the other arm, crooked, with finger on trigger, was still in position. Officials asserted that a shell exploding nearby or over head had caused concussion, resulting in his death. Similar other incidents are told.[13]

"Similar other incidents" were in fact told. Over the years, the concussion story would transcend the lone sharpshooter in Devil's Den and would be applied to many, and in a few cases, all of the dead found in that area after the battle. Evidence for this statement occurs in a 1911 history of the battle entitled: *Gettysburg: The Pivotal Battle Of The Civil War*. This is also an in-depth account of the entire sharpshooter episode and for that reason has been reproduced in its entirety.

We have had occasion heretofore to speak of the expert marksmanship of the Confederate soldiers, but on no field of the war did they exhibit greater skill in that capacity than at this time and place. The rocks of Devil's Den are certainly five hundred yards, and probably more, from the summit of Little Round Top; but across the yawning chasm of Plum Run they made life uncertain for the Union soldiers who guarded it. The Confederates, however, had one great advantage over their opponents. They were shooting upward, and the boulders of Little Round Top were aglow with the rays of the setting sun. The Union soldiers stood out against the sky clear and distinct to their eyes, a shining mark for their dexterity; while the superior quality of their powder must also be taken into consideration.

On the other hand, the Union soldiers were looking downward, into an abyss, as it were, with the dazzling sunshine in their eyes, and the marks at which they directed their shots indistinct, within the shadow of overhanging rocks. Nevertheless a company or two of Berdan's sharpshooters were hastily distributed among the rocks and crevices, and they soon returned the Confederate fire with satisfactory effect; and as the sun went down behind the South Mountain, giving to each party of distant combatants a fair and equal chance, the Union artillery was brought into play upon their rocky stronghold, with the result that, when the battle was over, many a Georgian, and many an Alabamian, was found among the rocks of Devil's Den who never retreated, not a few bearing no mark of ball or shell, but killed by the concussion of shell or solid-shot against the rocks upon which they depended for protection.[14]

Notice that "not a few" Georgians and Alabamians were killed by concussion. One can only imagine what is meant by "not a few." As time went on the retelling of the story only reaffirmed its accuracy. A 1978 publication stated that "Union cannon...sent round after round hissing over the meadows into Devil's Den. Wounded or dying men dragged themselves into rocky crevices for shelter against the intense bombardment. Later, some bodies were discovered with no visible wounds, evidence of death by concussion from the terrible cannonading."[15] Another 1970s tourbook has probably the most exaggerated rendition of the story.

> The burial committee of the Civil War pulled out 20 men from the cracks and crevices of these big boulders who did not have a mark on their bodies, but were undoubtedly dead. The men apparently sought shelter here during the height of the battle and thought they were safe, but little did they know, that when a cannon ball exploded near one of those boulders, the noise and echoes were loud enough to cause any man to have a concussion. These 20 men died of concussion.[16]

The idea that the burial committee of the Civil War (as if there was such a thing) examined each of the bodies dragged from the rocks of the Den to find the locations of their wounds is simply preposterous. Although it is possible that a few men at the battle did suffer "death by concussion," the story concerning bodies dragged from the Den seems to have little basis in fact. And yet, this story is one that is still commonly repeated today. It is interesting to note just how deeply the story of the sharpshooters has become ingrained in the story of the battle itself. On September 10, 1978 during the Middle East Peace Summit, President Carter paid a visit to Gettysburg in company with Menachem Begin and Anwar Sadat. One of the stops planned for their tour was Little Round Top. In preparation for this historic event, an NPS memorandum noted that Devil's Den was used by sharpshooters during the battle to pick off high ranking officers on Little Round Top. It warned that the Secret Service should secure that area, in an effort to guard against another such occurrence.[17]

Myth and Legend: Stories of Devil's Den

With the popularity of Devil's Den and its surroundings it was inevitable that, over the years, other stories and legends would become popular. Affectionately know as "old guide stories," some of these tales were a mixture of half-truths, embellishments and downright fiction. Today, the Association of Licensed Battlefield Guides is made up of over 100 individuals from all walks of life. As a group, none in the world can touch their knowledge of the battle and battlefield. This, however, was not always the case. Actual licensing of guides did not come about until 1915, and up until that point it was impossible for anyone to control the information being distributed by ill-informed individuals.[18] There were some who took their job very seriously, and today these guides are considered early historians of the battle. But, because of the great demand to see the field, there were three times as many "hackdrivers," whose purpose it was to get the party around the field and take their money, occasionally throwing in stories that they had heard over the years. Early newspapers (especially out of town newspapers), are filled with comments on tours to Gettysburg. In 1888, a reporter for the New York *Times* gave one of the harshest accounts. In an article entitled "Never Mind The Guide," he wrote:

> [When arriving to Gettysburg the visitor]...is furnished with a guide, a horse and buggy. Then his troubles begin. The guide was born at Gettysburg. He was nine years old when the battle was fought, and for three days he and the other members of the family lived in a cellar. On the fourth day he hovered on the outskirts of the battle, and following the example of his elders, picked up everything that was movable and stored it in the cellar. As soon as the army had moved on and visitors began pouring into Gettysburg he became a guide. He knew nothing about the battle except what had been told to him by his father, who had maintained a deter-

Tourists at Devil's Den, Tipton, c. 1895. (GNMP)

mined condition of masterful inactivity in the cellar until the fight was over. For years, on an average of twice a day, he hears an authoritative history of the battle. His gray matter becomes impregnated with certain striking bits of each history. He dovetails these bits together and learns them by heart. He takes a visitor over the battlefield and tells his story of the battle... Nothing can induce him to modify his story, and if the visitor is satisfied that inaccuracies are hurled at him and protests, the guide may be silenced, but he cannot be induced to retract. He was born on the ground and has been a guide ever since he was old enough to hold the reins. He lived through the battle and if he does not know how the battle of Gettysburg was fought, who does?[19]

Many considered this to be a serious problem. A map of the battlefield published by the GBMA in 1888 contained a notice to the visitor printed in bold letters. "IMPORTANT: Visitors who come to Gettysburg to see the battlefield. DO NOT allow yourselves to be picked up by irresponsible guides who infest our streets and depots."[20]

It was in this atmosphere that some of the interesting myths and legends of the battlefield were cre-

ated. Much has undoubtedly been lost or forgotten over the years, but some still survives. William D. Holtzworth, a veteran of the Civil War, and one of the earliest guides, often told a story of how in 1884 he found "a silver watch hidden under a boulder near Devil's Den." He had the mainspring repaired and he wore it on his tours of the field. It supposedly kept perfect time.[21] He also told the popular story of how wounded soldiers helped each other to get water.

A number of wounded soldiers lay between the lines in front of the Round Top, in the heat of the day, in their agony for water they "pieced up," to use their own term, and the man with two legs but no arms carried the man with two arms and no legs, together with the canteens to the spring at Devil's Den, and thus obtained water.[22]

Another story near and dear to the hearts of battlefield romanticists is "Bloody Run." The term "Valley of Death" was heavily used by visitors and guides by the 1880s, but the term "Bloody Run" is conspicuously absent from all early accounts and tourbooks. If the story existed at the turn of the century, it would have appeared in one of the numerous publications which contain such stories.

Since this is not the case, it seems to be a story that evolved over the years. An 1893 reporter for *Harper's Weekly* wrote that the Valley of Death "won its sanguine name honestly. Plum Run ran red with blood, and the turf was carpeted with the bodies of the slain, blue and gray, that lay side by side where death had found them in the struggle."[23] The earliest written reference to "Bloody Run" thus far uncovered comes from a 1927 book entitled *Human Interest Stories of the Three Days' Battles at Gettysburg.*

> Bloody Run in the Valley of Death...acquired its name during the second day's engagement at Gettysburg...."Bloody Run" was literally filled with bodies of men from both armies. Its waters, until then flowing in peaceful fashion along its course, turned red from the blood spilled by these gallant soldiers. Its outlet spread the discouraging and silent message to other sections of the field. For days after the battle the hospital corps diligently struggled to give Christian burial to these bodies piled two, three and in some places four deep in the blood soaked banks of the small stream. Their task was a mammoth one. Most of the bodies were beyond recognition. Others had been trampled to a mash...."Bloody Run" flows on. It is shallow now. Its banks are overgrown with brush, but its name lives on.[24]

This legend is popular today and is fully endorsed by the National Park Service who recite it several times daily in their official orientation to the battlefield: the Electric Map. A book published during the centennial of the battle in 1963 tells the story in a similar manner:

> When the regulars swarmed towards the wheat field they passed Plum Run, the meandering stream in front of lower Cemetery Ridge, and they saw an incredible sight: the water was running red with the blood of wounded soldiers. One of the severest side effects of a wound is drastic dehydration, and badly hurt Federals had dragged themselves to Plum Run to get a drink. Many simply fell over and died in the water or along the banks, and Plum Run was rechristened during the afternoon of July 2 to "Bloody Run."[25]

Much of the legend and lore of the Den revolves around the other aspects of its history, whether it be geological or natural. An 1880s visitor to the Den came away with the impression that it was known as the "Devil's Trap."

> There is utter dreariness in this ravine. The trees squat. Cedars that on the two hills near by grow to the height of the royal lombard become stumpy bushes as they approach the Devil's Trap which frowns and gives an ac-

Looking across Plum Run to Devil's Den, Tipton, c. 1880s. (ACHS)

tual grimace over the thistles in its maw. From the great crevice of the pile of rocks there were once pulled the bodies of seven sharpshooters, who wore gray and rested, until found, upon beds of mullein, soft sister of the cactus. A little, spotted green snake curled himself up in a crack that was made by a projectile, and around which were white spots made by bullets. But the desolation of the Devil's Trap is revealed in all other parts of the battleground.[26]

Another legend concerns the impact that the battle had on the vulture population in this area. Undisputably, there is an unusually large population of these avian scavengers on the Gettysburg battlefield. Studies conducted by Penn State University and the Virginia Polytechnic Institute in the early 1980s showed that "approximately 150 black and 300 turkey vultures roost at Devil's Den in the winter."[27] Although some of these birds migrate south to as far as southern Florida, most of the them can be observed year-round, "riding the rising air currents" above Big Round Top" or "sunning in the trees along Crawford Avenue."[28]

Over the years, many have suggested that the large number of vultures on the battlefield today are a direct result of the battle. "Attracted to the Gettysburg area by the thousands of dead horses left after the battle in July 1863," they have made this their home. Until recently some have even suggested "that the vultures at Gettysburg today are the same birds present in 1863." As late as 1978 rangers at the National Park were informing visitors that the vultures lived to be 118 years old, and it was possible that some of them were living witnesses to the battle. In reality, the maximum recorded longevity of a turkey vulture is about 17 years, so the story of the 100 year old vulture is a little difficult to believe.[29] An 1885 tourbook published by the Gettysburg & Harrisburg Railroad Company does mention that "MULTITUDES of buzzards, that filthiest of birds, swarmed over the battle-field, both during and after the battle."[30] The *1886 History Of Adams County* also mentions the existence of turkey vultures as part of the local fauna, and in 1895 problems arose when they began "roosting on the observation tower on Big Round Top."[31] During a interview published in 1915, Samuel Bushman (son of Emanuel) made some very interesting comments on the subject.

You might think the buzzards would have swarmed to the battlefield, and we used to have a popular guide here who declared that they gathered from the four corners of the earth to prey on the dead. He described how, when they rose from their horrid feast, they darkened the sky. Some one asked him why he told such a yarn as that. "Oh, well!" he says, "it amuses the people. They want things made exciting." Really, there were no buzzards here, probably because they were frightened away by the smell of the powder and the noise of the cannonading. They never made their appearance till several months later.[32]

Another popular guide story concerning a bird appeared in the Gettysburg *Compiler* in 1902.

York tourists at Gettysburg yesterday became interested in a flock of crows near Devil's Den, when they discovered among the flock an albino, with pink beak and pink eyes. Guide R. Frank Lott stated that the white crow is not a stranger to the battlefield. With his somber companions the bird visits the Field year after year. This season he has been observed more frequently than at any previous time. His haunt seems to be near the Devil's Den, as he is seldom seen in any other locality. From time to time local ornithologists have tried to capture the bird, but he is too cunning for them. It appears that his black brethren stand sentinel, never failing to give warning of danger. The superstitious advance many curious theories regarding the presence of the white-mantled bird. Some of them convince themselves that in the bird dwells the spirit of the many men who fell in the terrible conflict in the Devil's Den, while others see him an omen of perpetual peace.[33]

Although stories like that of the vultures and the crow were believed, other stories were beyond fiction, and for that reason have died out because they were not retold. One example supposedly occurred, not at the Den, but in the woods nearby on the slopes of Big Round Top.

You don't need to believe this one if you don't want to. It was told by a former battlefield guide. It seems that this guide was driving a truck-load of veterans around the battlefield some years ago. As they were passing Big Round Top a Union veteran jumped up in the back of the truck and shouted: "Over there's the rock I was hiding behind trying to pick off a Confederate during the battle." Up popped a Southerner saying: "Yes, and I'm the guy you were shooting at." The former guide then related the story as it unfolded. These two men were hiding behind rocks attempting to shoot each other. After about 12 shots they became disgusted and by mutual agreement stacked their rifles against the rocks and walked out to the middle to find out why they were getting no results. They concluded that both were shooting so accurately that the bullets were meeting in mid-air and falling to the ground.[34]

Another tale of sharpshooting in the woods on Big Round Top was written by John T. Campbell in 1908. A few weeks after the battle he traveled to Gettysburg to care for his brother, Joseph A. Campbell of Battery C, 4th U.S. Artillery, who was wounded in the battle. Unfortunately, his brother died on July 20 and was buried before he arrived.[35] During his visit he spent much time going over the battlefield, and while on Round Top he heard the following story.

On the north side of Big Round Top and near the summit I saw the whitening bones of a Johnny who had killed and wounded 17 of our men during the night. He rolled a rock as big as a bushel basket ahead of him, while he crawled behind it. He could see our men toward the sky, while they could only see the flash of his gun, which they shot at all night. At the dawn he could not retreat and our boys "got him." They could not dig a grave there. They cut brush and laid it across him head down hill, and carried dirt and weighted down the ends of the brush. His head had rolled down hill some 10 feet: his shoes with the bones of his feet had fallen sidewise and lay there. A soldier (convalescent) of the Pennsylvania Reserves, who was on the top that night, and whose brother was killed by this rebel, showed me and explained as above.[36]

Some tales relating to Devil's Den made good newspaper copy and great tour stories, and for that reason were publicized. A good example is an 1890 article which appeared in the Gettysburg *Star and Sentinel* entitled "Hidden At Gettysburg."

When going into the battle of Gettysburg, Lee Mason gave his friend John Ambrose a package to deliver to his wife when the war was over, as he felt a presentiment that he would not outlive the engagement. He was killed in the battle. Ambrose too, was shot in the fierce fighting at Devil's Den, and while helpless among the rocks bethought him of the packet for his friend's widow. Fearing the Confederates might get it from his body, he concealed it between the rocks. Ambrose was taken to the hospital unconscious, and lost a leg there. After the war he wandered out west. He is now living in Westmoreland County. Recently he learned that Mrs. Mason was living in McKeesport, and that reminded him of the packet. He went to Gettysburg and found the package. It contained $500 in gold and some papers. The gold was intact, but the papers had rotted. Sunday the property was turned over to Mrs. Mason.[37]

At first glance this appears to be an incredible story; $500 hidden in the Den for almost 30 years. The problem is verification of the facts involved in this account. First of all, there are only three men named Mason who are known to have been killed or mortally wounded at Gettysburg, none are named Lee, and none fought in the Devil's Den area. Secondly, there is no John Ambrose who fought in the Den area. There is a John Ambrose from Westmoreland County, Pennsylvania who was wounded at Gettysburg, and seems to fit the man in the article, but this soldier was in Co. E of the 11th

Battlefield guide Charles Sheads and party of visitors at the actual Devil's Den, Williams, c. 1900. Notice the flask in the guide's hand. (ACHS)

Pennsylvania Infantry which fought on Oak Ridge during the first day.[38] Either the names in the article are incorrect, or the incident did not occur in the fashion that it appears in print. A more humorous incident that occurred at Devil's Den between an early visitor and a guide was printed in a newspaper around the turn of the century.

> There are drivers who are all additions to the satisfaction of the visitor, some of whom have been old soldiers. With one of these an amusing incident occurred. He was describing how the Rebel sharpshooters were shelled out of Devil's Den, and while trying to escape, got [stuck] fast in the mud around the spring, where the Union soldiers shot them. There was a southern woman in the party this old soldier had in charge, and she asked.
> "Did You shot any of those poor men stuck in the mud?"
> "I did, Ma'am," said he.
> "You miserable, cold-blooded murderer!" she exclaimed, "to shoot those poor men when they couldn't run," and she charged on him with her umbrella, knocking off his hat, and him chasing around an adjacent monument.[39]

A good example of exaggerated oral history appears in the Gettysburg *Times* in 1938. It does not pertain to Devil's Den but to nearby Little Round Top and is included here only because of its amusing nature. This classic article was entitled "Baltimorean Says 'Little' Round Top Named for Her Great-Grandfather."

> A great many Gettysburgians who have lived these many years under the delusion that Little Round Top was so named because of its proximity to a larger hill of similar shape are set aright about the matter by Mrs. Lily N. Neary, Baltimore, who calmly asserts that hill was named for her great-grandfather—Peter Little—the same person for whom Littlestown was named.[40]

This is an interesting assertion. If only we could identify the "Big" family that the other Round Top must be named for, we would have it all sorted out. Oddly enough, Lily N. Neary was, in fact the daughter of Gettysburg native Ephraim Hanaway Little whose grandfather was none other than Ephraim Hanaway, the man who did own the western slopes of Little Round Top at the time of the battle.[41] It just goes to show that a shred of truth can be found in every myth.

The casual observer might, at this point, get the impression that the era of battlefield lore and legend is in the past, and now historians can get down to the real business of sorting out fact from fiction.

But this is not the case at all. At present the battlefield and particularly the Devil's Den are targets for a new barrage of stories—spine-tingling tales of ghosts on the battlefield. The eerie appearance of the Den contributes much to the public's willingness to accept these recent tales at face value. But ask any long-time resident their opinion on the current ghost craze. A 1972 interview with Emily Grace Rosensteel, a long time resident of the Gettysburg battlefield, makes reference to there being "surprisingly few" ghost stories told of the battlefield. In reference to Devil's Den, she said "they always claim there's a ghost down there," but she never believed it. "My husband never believed in it either. And he said if there would have been they'd have sure seen or heard him because they say he was in and around up and under those rocks."[42]

It cannot be stressed enough that the ghost stories now being told are a relatively new addition to the battlefield. The forward to Jack McLaughlin's 1963 *Gettysburg: The Long Encampment*, even goes so far as to make the remark: "Ghosts? No one has ever seen one at Gettysburg."[43] The first of these recent ghost stories associated with the Den appeared in *Blue and Gray Magazine* in 1986, and at present there are about 15 different stories concerning ghosts or unusual occurrences at the Den which appear in several different publications.[44] The lore of the battlefield has also made its way into the tabloids sold in many grocery stores. The *Weekly World News* ran an article in 1992 concerning two children who lived at Gettysburg during the battle, and were transported "through a time warp" from 1863 to the present.[45] It is unclear what impact these new stories will have on the way Americans perceive the Devil's Den. But one thing is certain: the heavy fighting that occurred there on July 2 will continue to take a backseat to the myth, lore, legend and fiction that surrounds it.

Memorialization

Within weeks of the battle, a local attorney named David McConaughy purchased some of the land on which the battle was fought in order to preserve its historical integrity. He, along with a group of other citizens founded the Gettysburg Battlefield Memorial Association (GBMA), and on April 30, 1864 this organization was incorporated by the state of Pennsylvania.[46] During the first few years of this association, the sections of the field that were protected included parts of Culp's Hill, East Cemetery Hill and Little Round Top.[47] Consisting mostly of local citizens, the organization had a sincere desire to see the ground on which the battle was fought preserved, but little else was done during the first fifteen years of GBMA's existence. In the summer of

1878 all that changed during an encampment of the Pennsylvania Grand Army of the Republic on East Cemetery Hill. "The scope and possibility of the Memorial Association" and "the apparent apathy or inactivity of those controlling it" attracted the attention of John M. Vanderslice of Philadelphia, the Assistant Adjutant-General of the department, and he determined to have the G.A.R. take a more active role. "Circulars were issued to all the Posts and letters were written to personal friends throughout the state." In a short time the GBMA was revitalized, and under this new leadership the era of monumentation and memorialization began. During the next twenty years, the battlefield as it is today was created.[48]

The land around Devil's Den, however, was never part of the GBMA's holdings, and its preservation is more interesting and complicated. Houck's Ridge was a popular place for the quarrying of "Gettysburg granite." On one of his visits to Gettysburg General Samuel W. Crawford "noticed a stone-cutter blasting away one of the rocks in the Valley of Death for building purposes." Crawford had a special feeling for the battlefield, and was "aroused to anger at seeing any one cutting off the limb of a tree for a cane or interfering in any way with its natural beauty... especially to this spot" which "he held so sacred.... Looking upon this as desecration, he negotiated..." with its owner, John Houck, and on December 13, 1872, gained possession of the ground.[49] A week later the Gettysburg *Compiler* publicized the transaction.

> Gen. S. W. Crawford, of the U.S. Army has purchased of John Houck about 47 acres of land immediately west of Little Round Top, at $500. The Pennsylvania Reserves, commanded by Gen. Crawford charged over this ground on the second day of the Battle of Gettysburg, and includes the collection of rocks known as "Devil's Den." The site would be a good one for buildings for a summer resort, and the General may have such use of it in view.[50]

For the next two decades this 47 acre tract of land would be known as Crawford Park. In the summer of 1878, one of the first monuments on the entire battlefield was erected on his land. Dedicated to the memory of Charles Frederick Taylor, colonel of the 13th Pennsylvania Reserves who was killed in the action on the evening of July 2, 1863, this tablet has since been relocated to a more accurate location and replaced by a more substantial monument.[51] In 1880 Crawford became a director of the newly reorganized GBMA, a post which he held until his death on November 3, 1892.[52] Concerned about the preservation of his land, Crawford, in a letter to historian John Bachelder, voiced his concerns about

General Samuel Wiley Crawford (1829-1892). (GNMP)

the "reckless placing of monuments" on the field. He further stated that as far as his property was concerned it would not be permitted, unless authorized by some authority that he recognized.[53]

In 1884 the 124th New York became the first regimental organization from that state to erect a monument on the field of Gettysburg. Built by the St. Johnsbury Granite Company of Vermont, and surmounted by a statue of Colonel Augustus Van Horne Ellis, it was erected on the crest of Houck's Ridge in Crawford Park, where it still stands today. The dedication ceremony was held on July 2, 1884, at 10 o'clock in the morning. A "prayer was offered by Rev. James C. Dennison, who was formerly a lieutenant in the regiment and wounded in the battle." The oration of the day was given by General Stewart L. Woodford of New York, but Colonel John Bachelder also gave "an interesting account of the second day's battle on that portion of the line."[54] Within weeks of the dedication, however, "some scoundrel" broke several inches off the tip of Colonel Ellis' sword. It was the first serious incident of vandalism reported to have occurred to a monument anywhere on the field.[55]

In October 1884, Colonel John Bachelder initiated a conference of veterans in Gettysburg to discuss the construction of a new avenue, "to start

Crawford Park, Tipton, 1880s stereo. The monument to Colonel Taylor of the 13th Pennsylvania Reserves can be seen in the foreground. (Timothy H. Smith Collection)

in the vicinity of Devil's Den, passing through the woods west of the Ellis monument and crossing the Wheatfield toward the peach orchard." Many veterans felt this avenue would "open up a very important part of the field, and a large number of regimental associations" contemplated the erection of monuments along its path. General Crawford, on whose property the road would start, was not so convinced, and wrote to Bachelder that he was "very anxious" in regard to the "new road" being used by guides and tourists across his property. "I fear that it will ruin the 'Devil's Den' & if so, my interest then will cease."[56] In the end, the avenue was laid out and on October 28, 1885, the 20th Indiana formally dedicated their monument nearby. "Captain J. B. Brown fully described the part taken by the regiment in the contest on the afternoon of July 2nd." The monument was placed where several color-bearers of the regiment fell, and near the spot where Colonel John Wheeler was killed.[57]

On May 24, 1886, Washington M. Worrell and Amos W. Bachman of the 99th Pennsylvania visited Devil's Den and located the position for their regimental monument.[58] The monument was formally dedicated at 4:30 pm on July 1, 1886, with Charles Fasnact the keynote speaker. Among the veterans in the crowd that day was a welcome but unexpected visitor, Daniel Edgar Sickles.[59] In 1887 the Com-

Photograph of the New Jersey National Guard encampment in the Wheatfield during the dedication of their monuments, Tipton, July, 1888. (ACHS)

monwealth of Pennsylvania allocated $1500 dollars to each of its regiments that fought in the battle so that each might erect a suitable memorial.[60] A few regimental associations (such as the 99th's) had erected monuments already. These units either improved their existing monuments, or erected new ones in their place, relocating the older ones to a secondary position occupied by the regiment during the battle. The 99th, adopting the latter course, took this opportunity to move their first monument to a location near the High Water Mark. The new monument, which stands atop Devil's Den today, was dedicated on "Pennsylvania Day," September 11, 1889.[61] The colors were held proudly aloft by Amos Casey who had been wounded carrying them during the battle. The monument was unveiled by Chantilla Setley, the daughter of Abram Setley, who named her after the battlefield upon which the beloved General Philip Kearny gave his life.[62] The keynote address was given by Captain Albert Magnin and on that day he made a prophecy that has more than proven itself true.

> Here in the years to come, as in the years since those terrible days in July, 1863, this battlefield shall be the "Mecca," and this monument one of the shrines at which patriotism shall come to offer her devotions. Here our children and our children's children and the children of unborn generations shall come to pay tribute to undying valor and heroism.[63]

The year 1888 marked the 25th anniversary of the battle and a busy year for monumentation at Devil's Den. On June 30, the 6th New Jersey Monument was dedicated during an encampment of the New Jersey National Guard, during which over 1,600 people tented in the famous Wheatfield. On July 2, dozens of New York regiments dedicated monuments, including the 40th and 86th, as well as the 4th New York Artillery.[64] The 40th New York placed their monument in the "Valley of Death," and dedicated it to the memory of its comrades that were killed "in the grand endeavor for the betterment of mankind." Corporal James Tanner remarked to the crowd that "When you and I have long been dust and ashes, this insensate stone, until it shall by the action of time be reduced to the elements, will tell to all people the story of those who held life so cheap and country so dear that they cheerfully flung away life for country."[65] Charles H. McMaster gave the address at the dedication of 86th New York Monument. He felt that the monument marked "one of the critical points of the critical day of the great battle," and described how, in that "wood, and across the Devil's Den, the heel of the Third Corps caught, and by gallant fighting, Ward's Brigade kept the whole army from falling."[66] Appropriately enough, at the monument to

the 4th New York Independent Battery, Captain James Smith gave the dedicatory remarks. The site upon which the monument was located was chosen by James R. Hill and Frederick W. Watkins in April 1888. Although both men were veterans of the battery and both were wounded at Gettysburg, their selection for the site of the monument was one that to this day has caused problems in our interpretation of the battle for Houck's Ridge.[67] On October 31, 1888, Smith wrote to the board of New York Commissioners of Gettysburg Monuments and "respectfully petitioned to change the location of the monument." Unfortunately, the move was never effected.[68]

The 4th Maine Monument was also to be dedicated on July 2, 1888, but owing to delays the monument was not ready on time. On October 10, 1888, Elijah Walker addressed a crowd in which "Only a few survivors of the command were present."[69] In the weeks that followed, flank markers were placed near the monument without the "consent or knowledge" of Walker, which faced the regiment in a more westerly than southern direction. This led to a formal protest by Colonel Walker and eventually the flank markers were adjusted to their desired position where they rest today.[70]

Although Samuel W. Crawford held title to the land around Devil's Den for twenty years and frequently "assured the other members of the GBMA that it would be handed over to the association at his death," no arrangements were ever made for that organization to acquire the property.[71] Crawford often disagreed with the GBMA on how his land was to be memorialized. When the state of Pennsylvania in 1887 provided funding for each of its units to erect a memorial, "The conclusion of the reserve association was that if monuments were erected for each regiment at Gettysburg they would be lost in the wilderness of monuments on the battlefield."[72] Therefore, it was decided to pool their money and erect a "Memorial Hall on Little Round Top Mountain, to commemorate the achievements of the Reserve Corps in the great battle fought there...."[73]

"The grand idea of a 'Memorial Hall' originated in the mind of the great and glorious war governor, Andrew G. Curtin...." A bill was drafted in Harrisburg, which if approved, would have resulted in the construction of a hall that would "overshadow any and everything erected by other states on the battlefield of Gettysburg." The bill asked for an additional $11,500 to be added to the $13,500 already allocated to the reserves for the construction of separate monuments. The building was to be 120 feet long, constructed of granite, iron and glass, and would have included tablets on its wall to honor each and every organization from the state of Pennsylvania engaged in the battle. The building would also

Looking across Crawford Park from Little Round Top. Harper's Weekly, *July 7, 1888.*
(Timothy H. Smith Collection)

The Devil's Den, Tipton, c. 1888. Under magnification, the sign on the tree in the
middle of the view reads "Crawford Park, Notice..." (ACHS)

include "fire-proof rooms for the preservation of records and relics" pertaining to the reserves.[74] The bill was passed by the state legislature but was vetoed by Governor James A. Beaver "for constitutional reasons."[75] It seems that the veterans of other regiments did not want to see a memorial to one unit overshadow all others around it, and this project was not supported by the GBMA. According to the Gettysburg *Star and Sentinel* "General S. Wiley Crawford, commander of the reserves, was so incensed at the refusal to build a memorial building that he will not allow any monument to be located on his ground."[76] These actions so upset some of the Pennsylvania Reserves that they were not in favor of the erection of their regimental monuments at all, and at Pennsylvania Reserve Day on the Gettysburg Battlefield held on September 2, 1890, some were still calling for the state of Pennsylvania and the GBMA to support the Memorial Hall concept.[77] Crawford also still hoped that the state would allocate the funds for the Memorial Hall, which could be erected on his land, and thereby circumvent GBMA approval.[78] It is unclear whether his bitterness over Memorial Hall or his feeble condition affected his decision making during the last year of his life, but on November 3, 1892 when Samuel Crawford died, there was no provision to turn over his ground to the GBMA and his property became part of his estate.[79] When asked about it later General Daniel Sickles stated that it was "of course, unfortunate that General Crawford did not give the property...over to the Battle-field Association, as he promised to do." Crawford had often told Sickles "that it was his intention to deed that property to the Battlefield Association in his will. He should have given it to the association before his death. He became by reason of his wounds, weakened in intellect, and undoubtedly never carried out his intention on account of that weakness."[80] This was not the only unusual thing that Crawford did during the last year of his life. His actions in December of 1891 would have a lasting effect on the battlefield for generations.

Commercialization

In the spring of 1884, the Gettysburg and Harrisburg Railroad completed construction of a line that linked Gettysburg with the state capital. Shortly afterward, it developed an excursion line across the battlefield. This line passed over the fields of "Pickett's Charge," crossed GBMA holdings near the present location of the monument to Father William Corby and ran through the woods to a station established on the east side of Little Round Top.[81] Construction on the "Round Top Branch" began on April 24, 1884 and was completed in early June of that year.[82] "Dynamite ...accomplished wonders in splitting and moving granite, in one instance throwing a rock estimated at nine tons several hundred feet."[83] At the terminus of the tracks, 13 acres of land were purchased from Lewis A. Bushman and developed into a park to provide a destination for visitors over this new route. Improvements to the tract included "a spacious pavilion, a kitchen with range, two wells of water with pumps and all necessary buildings."[84] When it opened, "Round Top Park" became an overnight success. On July 4, 1884, Colonel John H. McClellan held an "Ox Roast" at the new park to celebrate its opening. Admission was free and the Colonel provided a "massive beef" weighing over 1,300 pounds. It was estimated that between five and six thousand people attended.[85]

The town sent out more than half of its population, the surrounding county contributed all who could be spared from the harvest, and the railroad brought in their hundreds, the new road having two trains of fourteen cars. Round-Top may have had as large a crowd twenty-one years ago but certainly not as happy....The grounds are large, and well shaded by thrifty oaks and hickories; the buildings are ample and at the proper points; two artesian wells furnish cool and delicious water; seats and tables dot the entire park, and well-made walks lead in every direction....The dancing pavilion was occupied all day, the Springs Hotel Orchestra furnishing excellent music....How many partook of the beef it is impossible to say, but all who desired were liberally served, with an abundance of sandwiches, hot coffee, &c., thrown in. Truly it was a rare feast—a fitting feature of the celebration of our National Anniversary, and of the completion of the new Gettysburg and Harrisburg Railroad.[86]

Early on, problems developed with the large amount of people at the park pouring out onto the grounds of the GBMA. Some felt that the railroad was turning the battlefield into a huge playground. The Gettysburg & Harrisburg Railroad Company even tried to get permission from the GBMA to construct a path to the top of Little Round Top where, it was announced, an observatory 60 feet high would be erected for the benefit of the excursionists, since the one on Big Round Top was too difficult to reach.[87] Less than a month after its opening the GBMA was already issuing warnings against visitors to Round Top Park.

The Battlefield Memorial Association have expended a good deal of money in the purchase and preservation of the grove in and around Round-Top. It is their desire to keep

The ox roast at Round Top Park on July 4, 1884, Tipton, 1884. The man standing in front of the table in the center of the view is Colonel John H. McClellan. (ACHS)

it open for the accommodation of visitors and the public generally. But it must be borne in mind that it is private property, just as much so as if owned by private individuals, and cannot be used for pic-nic purposes without the assent of the Association; and then only on condition that no damage be done to growing timber. A good deal of the timber has already been damaged by persons hitching horses to trees. It may not be generally known that, under the charter of the Association, any barking of trees or injury to shrubbery, fencing or monuments or indications, renders the party offending liable to a fine of $50. It is the interest of the public, as well as the Association, to have the groves in and around the Round-Tops kept in best possible condition. If unwarranted trespassing continues it will become necessary to enforce the law, and to exclude horses and vehicles from stopping in any portion of the park.[88]

Regardless of the GBMA's reaction to the park, in the next few years its popularity surged as excursionists from Baltimore, Washington, Philadelphia, New York, and Pittsburg arrived in ever-growing numbers. It was no longer necessary to enter the town of Gettysburg and hire a hack driver to reach the southern portions of the field (many had long complained about the exorbitant prices charged by some early battlefield guides). It was now possible to travel from one of these cities by train directly to Little Round Top. It was advertised that tickets to Gettysburg were to be had at all stations of the Pennsylvania and other railroads via Harrisburg: tickets were $1.60, regular fare, one way, "Harrisburg to Gettysburg, and return, including guide to the battlefield and carriage, $3.00" (sold in groups of five

only).[89] An 1885 advertisement gave the following description of the park.

To make the Gettysburg and Harrisburg Railroad more complete, a spur has been built from Gettysburg to Round Top, three miles, in the same careful and splendid manner as the main line. Indeed, the construction of the Gettysburg and Harrisburg Railroad is of the highest standard, and justifies the great credit given to the best American railroad-work. The spur road ends on the side of Little Round Top itself, within a good stone's-throw of the summit made so famous by the patriot blood of Vincent and his brothers-in-arms. The track ends in a choicely laid-out park. Here have been gathered with lavish hand every comfort and convenience that can make happy the life of the picnicker or excursionist. Dining-rooms, a dancing pavilion, rooms for rest and recreation, shady seats and lounging-places under the great trees, kitchens, baggage-rooms, places for your bundles and baskets, spring-water in abundance, the choicest of breezes, the perfume of a carpet of wild flowers, and a natural awning of leaves to check the sun's rays, should they become too ardent, are the fittings of this Paradise.[90]

In 1886, the Rosensteel family purchased 2 acres of land (at the modern intersection of Sedgwick Avenue and Wheatfield Road) adjacent to Round Top Park and set up a refreshment stand. One of their early notices advertised "Sandwiches, ice cream, cakes, pop, ginger ale, cigars and tobacco...boarding and lodging...meals at all hours" and stabling for horses.

"Remember the place where the avenue joins Round Top Park."[91] Over the years this was expanded into "Rosensteel's Pavilion" where thousands were entertained each summer. A few relics found on the field by the family were put on display and in the decades that followed this collection was expanded to become one of the largest of its kind in the country. Today, that collection is the backbone of the GNMP collection, a percentage of which is on display at the museum.[92] Another attraction that sprang up at the park was a photographic studio. In the summer of 1884 it was William H. Tipton who established a "Tin-type" and "battlefield bazaar gallery at Round Top Park," erecting the first photographic establishment directly on the battlefield. Today, examples of tintypes taken at the Park are very rare.[93]

Newspapers in Gettysburg during the 1880s and early 1890s are filled with announcements of sum-

Tintype produced at Round Top Park, Tipton, c. 1888. This view was recorded within feet of the Henry Stewart portrait. (Timothy H. Smith Collection)

Tintype of Henry Stewart, Tipton, c. 1888. This image was produced near William Tipton's gallery at Round Top Park. Henry was employed there during the summer of 1888. The proximity of the studio, and thus a portion of Round Top Park, was established by the authors when they located the large boulder in the background of this view. It must be kept in mind, however, that a tintype is a reverse image. (ACHS)

mer picnics on Round Top. One popular annual event was the St. Francis Xavier Catholic Church Picnic. Activities included competitions at the fish pond, shooting gallery and the very popular knife and cane ringing contests.[94] For a time the park even included a merry-go-round complete with organ.[95] A little community developed around the park and a school house was built for the children who lived in the area.[96]

At some point, the railroad abandoned its park on the eastern slopes of Little Round Top because it simply "did not pay," and on August 29, 1896, it sold its property to the Gettysburg National Military Park Commission.[97] The railroad spur remained open however, and the other attractions that had grown up around the park, such as Rosensteel's, continued to be popular with visitors through the early decades of the 20th century. With the advent of the automobile, popularity of the railroad waned and gradually the atmosphere of the park changed. By 1913 a casino had been added.[98] In 1918 conditions were so bad that an officer inspecting nearby Camp Colt, complained:

Colonel John P. Nicholson, Chairman of the Gettysburg Battlefield Commission, stated to me that he has been trying to get conditions on Little Round Top corrected; for this purpose he had an item in the sundry civil bill for $5,000 with which to purchase and thus control the privately controlled grounds now used as a dance house and general resort, but that it was stricken out; as a result the resort is continued on privately owned property that lies just beyond, but immediately adjacent to his jurisdiction and likewise just beyond the jurisdiction of the military authorities. The condition described to me by Col. Nicholson is certainly very deplorable. He says that this resort is frequented by prostitutes, not only from Gettysburg, but who come in excursions from the neighboring towns of York, Harrisburg, Chambersburg and Emmitsburg. These excursions bring in with them quantities of beer and whiskey which they give or sell to the soldiers. As a result of this debauchery the grounds, the immediate surroundings of the resort itself, part of them lying with the Battlefield reservations, are used for association purposes. On a single evening over 50-couples were detected and driven from hiding places behind the tablets, monuments, rocks and trees of the reservation. On one occasion his officers found over 300 empty beer bottles scattered around their various hiding places. Colonel Nicholson further stated that he found it impossible to properly police this point.[99]

In 1939 the tracks of the excursion train which had fallen into disrepair were finally removed, and the ground was purchased by the Government. Round Top Museum, the pavilions and the dance hall were eventually torn down. Today, very little can be seen of the actual park but traces of the railroad bed through the woods along the eastern edge of Little Round Top. A few houses from the community which developed around the station, and "Round Top Schoolhouse" are also still there. With the excitement created by the opening of "Round Top Park" in 1884 and so many excursions at Little Round Top each weekend, it is not surprising that Devil's Den, with its close proximity, was also destined to become a popular tourist attraction.

Some were amazed at the popularity of the Den. One Gettysburgian even claimed that, among visitors, "The Devil's Den is preferable to Little Round Top....It is the natural curiosity of the Den that makes it interesting to people - not the historical part of it." Another resident explained that "The Devil's Den is an objective point. There is something about the name that every man, woman and child seems to know, and read about, and they all want to go there; there is no question about that."[100] In 1885, Sarah Mumper, purchased the five acre tract of land just southeast of Plum Run at Devil's Den that had been owned by John Musser at the time of the battle.[101] Sarah's husband was Levi Mumper, a veteran of the Civil War who was born in 1843. His unit, the 127th Pennsylvania, saw action at the battle of Fredericksburg on December 13, 1862 and following his discharge, he returned to Gettysburg where he learned the art of photography from the Tyson Brothers. In 1865, he married Sallie S. Shaffer and started his own gallery. In the years following the Civil War he established a thriving business in Adams County, and fathered nine children, most of which helped with the family business at one time or another.[102]

With the purchase of the property adjacent to Devil's Den, a temporary structure was soon erected and during the summer months a souvenir stand and gallery was operated. By 1888, a permanent building was erected on the grounds and used interchangeably as a small restaurant, dark room, and souvenir stand. Levi put in a well, a "water closet...a sort of stable" and a dancing floor which was described as some boards laid onto the ground.[103] In no time at all the Mumpers began to reap the rewards of having a gallery on the battlefield within close proximity to Devil's Den and Round Top Park. Levi stated that "for a man doing work on the battlefield a dark room where he can change plates is very valuable."[104] Although the Mumpers had the ability to record outdoor group portraits, most of the business performed at the stand focused on the making of tintypes, selling tourbooks, souvenirs, and stereo cards. While working at the gallery during the summer of 1888, Levi's son, Jacob I. Mumper, had an unusual experience. The Gettysburg *Star and Sentinel* ran the following article on July 17, 1888.

On last Thursday Jacob Mumper discovered and unearthed the remains of a soldier, near the Devil's Den. Mr. Mumper was showing the beauty of the den to a tourist and when walking over the pathway, north of it, annually frequented by thousands of visitors, he discovered a human bone and commenced an investigation, and, after going down about a foot, found the skeleton in good condition of a large man. All the bones were there but those of the right arm. In the superficial grave were found two or three Alabama buttons, some US buttons, a light gold ring, engraved in diamond shaped form. Nothing found conclu-

Mumper's Gallery at Devil's Den, Mumper, c. 1888. The man seated to the right is Jacob Mumper. (ACHS)

Big Round Top from the 6th New Jersey Monument, Mumper & Co., c. 1888. Mumper's Gallery is visible at the right-as is the Devil's Kitchen on the hill above. (ACHS)

sively indicated to which army the soldier belonged. As the den was occupied by Confederate sharpshooters, the probability is that he was one of them, and the theory is corroborated by the finding of the Southern buttons. On the other hand the engraving of the ring might indicate that he belonged to our army, as the diamond was the Third Corps badge. No vestige of his uniform remained.[105]

The Gettysburg *Compiler* also reported the incident but stated that "with the bones were found U.S. and Georgia buttons, a gold ring, and more than a dozen bullets," and added that recent heavy rains were responsible for uncovering the bones.[106]

Jacob, who worked at the stand for his father, wanted to go into the photography business on his own and asked his father if he would be willing to sell the Devil's Den studio to him. Thus, on March 8, 1889 Levi Mumper and his wife sold their five acre tract and "photographic gallery near Round Top" to their son Jacob I. Mumper, and a business partner, W. Harvey Gelbach for the sum of $1000.[107] This partnership, however, would be short-lived, and as it dissolved Levi tried to purchase back his son's half interest in the business, but "of course that didn't suit Mr. Gelbach." On January 2, 1890, Jacob conveyed his half interest in the tract over to Gelbach. Apparently Gelbach's unwillingness to have Jacob's half interest sold back to his father had something to do with a third party interested in the gallery. On June 23, 1890, Harvey Gelbach conveyed the half interest he had gotten from Jacob Mumper to none other than William H. Tipton, who would soon have grandiose plans for the property at Devil's Den.[108]

William Tipton and the Gettysburg Electric Railway

For any student of Gettysburg history, and the development of Gettysburg National Military Park, the name William H. Tipton is hard to avoid. With little schooling as a youth, Tipton boasted that he "graduated with honors from the school of Hard Knocks." He began his photographic career at the age of twelve as an apprentice to the Tyson brothers of Gettysburg. Tipton later regarded his "three years apprenticeship as the most valuable" years of his life.[109] In 1866 when the Tyson brothers' partnership dissolved he became the manager of the gallery under the ownership of C. J. Tyson. In 1868, together with Robert A. Myers, one of his employees, he purchased the studio and conducted it under the name of "Tipton and Myers." In 1873, C. J. Tyson bought out Myers' interest in the studio and it was conducted under the name W. H. Tipton and Co., until 1880 when Tipton became its sole owner.[110]

Over the years, his operation grew and by the 1890s he was one of the most respected businessmen in town. Tipton dabbled in politics, was elected as town burgess in 1884, and served several terms. He also served on the town council, for a time as president, and in 1897-98 even served a term in the Pennsylvania State Legislature. These exploits earned him the nickname "Boss Tipton."[111] His accomplishments as a photographer are well known, but it is the interaction between his political career and his personal interests that is the least understood aspect of his life.

William Tipton, resting in center foreground, and a group of early battlefield hackdrivers, or guides, at Devil's Den, Tipton, c. 1888. (ACHS)

In May 1889, an act of the Pennsylvania Legislature provided for the incorporation of street railway companies, and during the next few years trolley companies were formed all over the state. On July 28, 1892, letters of incorporation were granted to the Gettysburg Electric Railway Company. From the outset, the proposal of this railway in Gettysburg was controversial.[112] Within a week, the town council, of which William Tipton was a member, passed an ordinance that gave the railway company the right of way "through the best streets of the town," and amazingly enough, the town received no compensation in return.[113] Early on, it was obvious that the true intention of the promoters was not to bring mass transportation to Gettysburg, but to use the town as the base for a system of tracks that would weave all over the battlefield, and generate substantial revenue for its investors. The president of the railway and its principal investor was Edward M. Hoffer of Hummelstown, Pennsylvania.[114] After securing the use of the streets of Gettysburg, Hoffer somehow managed to acquire the consent of the Cumberland Township supervisors for the use of the Taneytown Road and the Baltimore Pike.[115] His next step was to send a proposal to the GBMA, in which he asked to extend his lines over the battlefield along Hancock Avenue, from the Taneytown Road to Little Round Top, and across the Wheatfield and Peach Orchard to the Emmitsburg Road. He also requested access to the first day's field, Culp's Hill, and even the summit of Big Round Top. He assured the GBMA that no cuts or embankments would be constructed and the railway would be kept in good repair. Again, no compensation was offered for the use of the land. At the board of directors meeting held in late August 1891, the GBMA, puzzled that someone would make such a request, rejected the proposal with but one dissenting vote.[116] For the time being the trolley was stalled, and for most involved the issue seems to have been forgotten. But if Hoffer could not get the permission of the GBMA to use their land, he was determined to find another route. At that time, the park's holdings consisted of no more than six hundred acres and much historically sensitive land was still in private hands, especially on the southern end of the battlefield. In September 1891 the Gettysburg *Star and Sentinel* warned that "Negotiations for the right of way for this company are being conducted but with great secrecy."[117] Over the next few months, announcements were slowly published in the local papers that the railway company was securing the rights-of-way on important pieces of land bordering the battlefield. The Codori, Wible, and Timber's farms were all mentioned.[118]

During this period Tipton did not remain idle. There is direct evidence that he negotiated for the trolley company on several occasions to gain access

to key pieces of property. His most important contribution came in December 1891 when he used his influence to secure from General Samuel W. Crawford a right-of-way across his land in the Valley of Death for the sum of $1.00. At the same meeting Crawford also gave Tipton "the exclusive right to take photographs on his land" at Devil's Den. Crawford died less than a year later, and would never see the implication of this "right-of-way."[119] When construction of the trolley started across this land in the spring of 1893, many who knew the general were mystified that such a deal had been made. Officials of the GBMA argued that the sale rested on Crawford's "imperfect knowledge of the facts," and the act was "inconsistent with every promise or purpose he had ever before had." All of General Crawford's immediate family and friends plainly asserted that "in this matter he was, in his feeble condition, misled and overborne by parties who had a strong personal interest in securing this grant."[120]

Few had more of a "strong personal interest" in the project than William H. Tipton, the man who secured the grant from Crawford. On April 2, 1892, he acquired sole ownership in the gallery at Devil's Den by purchasing Harvey Gelbach's half-interest for $600 dollars. On the same day he also acquired title to an adjacent tract of ground from Ella R. Sherfy for $503.12.[121] Tipton now owned about 13 acres of land just east of Devil's Den: land he would shortly develop into an attraction every bit as popular as "Round Top Park." He knew the electric railway would be passing over this land and it is likely that he made arrangements with Mr. Hoffer to make his park a designated stop along the trolley line even before he had acquired title to the property. As early as March 1892, the route of the proposed trolley had leaked out and was described by a Philadelphia newspaper:

> It will start from the square in Gettysburg, run out the Baltimore pike, pass Cemetery hill, encircle the National Cemetery, thence along the Emmitsburg road to the Peach Orchard, through the Wheatfield to Devil's Den, and through the Valley of Death to Little Round Top Park. The return will be made via the Bloody Angle and Hancock avenue to Gettysburg.[122]

Coincidentally, it was during this same period that a bill was being created in Congress for the establishment of a national military park at Gettysburg. The bill was in committee, and still had a long way to go, but already some people were predicting that the Gettysburg Electric Railway and the Gettysburg National Military Park were on a collision course.[123] In April 1892, the Gettysburg *Star and Sentinel*, which was keeping tabs on the progress of the railway company, stated that it was resisting "these steps of madness to the best of its ability but its warnings fell on leaden ears." The "only escape" left was "in some way, to break the entanglement" that the town council, the Cumberland Township supervisors, and a few local citizens had now gotten them into.[124] Although the citizens of Gettysburg knew exactly what was going on with the railway, it seems the country at large was not concerned with what most considered a less than serious proposal of a small trolley company. After all, the GBMA had already refused to allow the use of its holdings in the project. It was not until the actual construction began that the public at large fully understood what the editor of the *Star and Sentinel* had been warning them about for the past two years.[125]

On April 17 and 18, 1893 "a gang of Italians arrived from Baltimore." Shanties were erected "on the lot belonging to Mr. Wm. H. Tipton near Devil's Den," and work began on the Round Top end of the electric railway.[126] During the next few days the sound of dynamite blasting rocks on Tipton's land was heard in town more and more frequently.[127] In no time at all, the eyes and ears of the entire country turned on the work being done at Gettysburg and by May 9, 1893 the word "vandalism" was used by observers to describe the work being done. One eyewitness described that:

All along the line, in the vicinity of Devil's Den, there is heavy blasting and digging and filling; and great havoc is played with the face of the landscape. Huge masses of rock are displaced, great boulders are moved, the valley is to be filled the width and height of a track from the bridge over Plum Run in front of Round Top to the north end of the Valley, and a wholly new appearance will be given to the famous field of carnage.[128]

For the next few weeks, veterans and concerned citizens watched in disbelief as the trolley company cut a thirty-foot-wide path through some of the most sacred ground on American soil. Historic trees were felled, streams were forded, and rocks that still showed the scars of battle were forever blasted from the face of the earth. In some instances, the trolley roadbed passed within feet of monuments that had been dedicated just a few years before. Public outcry was immediate and in some cases very bitter. Newspapers around the country demanded an explanation for this "infamous outrage." The New York *Times* described the trolley construction as "ruthless vandalism."[129] Veterans from Philadelphia complained that they could not "find words in the English language severe enough to censure the authorities of the city of Gettysburg in allowing money-making vandals to mar the sacredness, the beauty and ro-

The "Howard" at Devil's Den. Other trolley cars were named Sedgwick, Slocum, Sickles, Hancock and Reynolds.
(ACHS)

mantic features of the place."[130] General Daniel Sickles also voiced his outrage and was particularly upset with the route of destruction.

[The Trolley]...then makes its way circuitously to Round Top by blasting and leveling rocks and cutting the trees through the Devil's Den region, robbing it of its mystery and jungle wildness. These made the place interesting, independent of its association, and gave a peculiar character to the battle which was fought at and from this point.[131]

The Harrisburg *Telegraph* pointedly stated that "Gettysburg will be made a show, a circus, simply to put money into the purse of a petty, private corporation, unless something is done to prevent it."[132] On May 23, the Gettysburg *Star and Sentinel* reported that "the vandalism of the trolley company and the stupidity or greed of the Gettysburg councilmen [Tipton and friends] is the subject of discussion wherever a group of survivors of that battle meet."[133] John Bachelder was sent to Gettysburg in June to make a preliminary report to the secretary of war on the work being done by the railway company. On arriving at Devil's Den, he noticed not only the "wanton destruction of an important landmark of the field," but also the so-called improvements that were being made by William Tipton to his park.

The boulders which covered the combatants in the desperate engagement between the Fourth Maine and the Fortieth New-York of the Union Army and the Forty-fourth Alabama and the right of Benning's Brigade of the Confederate Army are already blasted, and the fragments broken under the hammer are covered with earth to form a roadbed. And it is this locality which has been turned into a park to which cheap excursions are to be run from Baltimore and other cities. This is the most wild and picturesque section of the field. For the distance of over one mile before reaching this locality, the road cuts ruthlessly through the scene of some of the most desperate encounters of the battle...[134]

The outrage reached a fever pitch during the summer of 1893 when veterans traveled to the battlefield and witnessed the destruction firsthand. One article printed in *Harper's Weekly* not only described the "desecration," but provided photographs as proof of what was actually going on.[135] This was important. For people who had not been to Gettysburg themselves there was conflicting information, and some did not know who to believe. Those in favor of the trolley's construction, mostly those who had some personal interest in it, made the claim that the accusations were un-

founded and that "instead of mutilating and destroying natural formations, such as 'The Devil's Den' it has most carefully avoided any destruction" by going around them.[136] The *Hummelstown Sun*, Hoffer's hometown newspaper, described the allegations of vandalism as "exaggerated, untrue and slanderous statements."[137] William T. Ziegler, a member of the state legislature from Gettysburg, repeatedly stated that "these stories about the field being desecrated...are not true in any particular." It is more than coincidental that Ziegler had just sold a lot in town to the railway company on which its power plant was being erected.[138] William H. Tipton, by this time president of the town council, even traveled to Philadelphia as an agent for the trolley company and tried to settle a dispute with the veterans of the 72nd Pennsylvania, who owned part of the ground near the Angle on which the trolley was intending to pass over. In an interview with a paper from that city, Tipton stated that "if any vandalism had been committed, it was done by the Battlefield Association."[139] He further stated:

...All right thinking people...heartily desire the road to be built, that the reports of the condition of the field since the work on the road began were maliciously exaggerated, and he even asserted that, the pictures printed were untrue. Colonel Bachelder did not escape his condemnation and was said to be allied to the land company in trying to squeeze money out of the trolley people.[140]

On July 1-3, 1893, "New York Day" was held on the Gettysburg Battlefield. In the weeks leading up to the event, there was some serious talk among the veterans of that state to take matters into their own hands and tear the tracks up themselves. Violence was averted only when General Daniel Sickles appealed to the veterans to instead find a peaceable solution to the problem by boycotting the trolley.[141] An amusing incident occurred, however, on July 3, just after the dedication of the 44th New York Monument at Little Round Top, when William H. Tipton arrived to take some photographs of the veterans in front of their new monument. Unfortunately for Tipton, his role in the railway's construction was well-known to the party, and an angry crowd of veterans turned on him. After a short altercation, his camera was knocked over and broken, and he was sent on his way. Tipton held Generals Sickles and Butterfield responsible and later pressed charges against Sickles for the incident.[142]

Everyone who was opposed to the trolley looked for an early solution to the problem, but things would not be so easy. By the time the general public was fully informed as to what was really going on, construction was well under way and Mr. Hoffer had absolutely no intention of stopping. The executive committee of GBMA met on May 19, 1893 and called for Secretary of War Daniel Lamont to intervene and stop the "needless desecration," and "preserve the Battlefield for posterity."[143] The War Department, which on March 3, 1893 had been appropriated $25,000 "to preserve and mark the lines of battle at Gettysburg," decided to look into the matter. Major George W. Davis of the Judge Advocate General's Department was asked to visit Gettysburg, investigate the "report that great damage was being done," and to examine appropriate legal options.[144] Davis assessed the situation and concluded that there was little the federal government could do but start condemnation proceedings. He suggested that the Attorney General of Pennsylvania had the authority to step in, examine their charter, and make sure the proper procedures were followed in getting approvals and rights-of-way.[145] As a result, on July 8, 1893, a petition was sent to the Attorney General of the Commonwealth William U. Hensel. Drawn by Edward McPherson and thirty-nine other citizens of Gettysburg and Cumberland Township, the petition asked Hensel to take a look at the matter and give a "preliminary injunction" to stop work on the trolley road.[146]

As soon as the three-man Gettysburg Park Commission set up by the sundry bill of March 3 was assembled, it was sent to Gettysburg to investigate the damage and strike a deal with Hoffer to stop the excavation. Negotiations failed and to the outrage of many, the railway company kept right on grading.[147] On July 21, the United States government notified the electric railway company of its intention to condemn their land and requested that work be suspended at once.[148] At this point it looked as if the end was near for Hoffer and friends, but things were about to take an unexpected twist. On August 7, the Attorney General of Pennsylvania announced that he would not interfere with the trolley as requested by the people of Gettysburg. In an "elaborate opinion" that was said to "closely resemble" a brief filed by the trolley company, he went so far as to say that the trolley company had carefully avoided destroying natural formations by going around them.[149] The only hope now for stopping the trolley was with the slow moving wheels of justice. The battle that raged in the courts for the next two and a half years is complicated.

At first, it was decided to condemn strips of land across the trolley's route for the purpose of building roads to mark the lines of battle. This would cut up the trolley and put it out of business.[150] In the meantime, the GBMA and the Park Commission tried desperately to get Hoffer to change the route and use the Wheatfield Road over to Little Round Top, instead of looping through the Rose Woods, past Devil's Den, and across the Valley of Death. After continuous delaying tactics, Hoffer again would not budge, and demanded $60,000 in return for the abandonment of what he felt was the more scenic and profitable route.[151]

On May 15, 1894, arguments were finally heard at Philadelphia in U.S. District Court and on May 29, 1894, Judge Dallas ruled in favor of the trolley and dismissed the case. He pointed out that in the sundry bill passed by Congress on March 3, 1893, which gave the government power to mark the lines of battle, there was "no expressed intent to acquire real estate."[152]

Just one week later, on June 7, President Grover Cleveland approved a joint resolution of Congress giving the secretary of war the power to condemn lands at Gettysburg, thereby correcting the difficulties that Judge Dallas pointed out.[153] New condemnation proceedings immediately began. One of the most important and time consuming issues was the establishment of a value for the land the government intended to condemn.[154] After considerable delay, Judge Dallas again ruled in favor of the trolley on April 23, 1895. This time, he ruled on the grounds that "the acquisition of property for park purposes was not a public necessity, which alone could justify the use of the power of eminent domain."[155] Eventually, the case reached the Supreme Court of the United States and on January 27, 1896, Judge Peckham ruled in favor of the government, reversed the decision of Judge Dallas, and ruled that "this condemnation was a legitimate public use of land."[156]

As it turned out, the trolley continued to operate for another twenty years before the tracks were finally dismantled. In December 1894, Hoffer sold the trolley to J. L. Murphy of Chicago.[157] The new owners were much less belligerent than Hoffer and willing to make concessions to the Park Commission.[158] Seemingly secure in the fact that it won the right to condemn, the commissioners had more important projects and controversies that required their attention.

Meanwhile, the destructive nature of the trolley's construction was forgotten by most and it became a popular way to tour the battlefield. The Gettysburg Electric Railway officially began operation on July 13, 1893. During the first summer of its existence the line was only partially completed and the tracks stopped short of Tipton's park at Devil's Den.[159] To enhance visitation during its first season the trolley company therefore constructed "Wheatfield Park," (also referred to as "Wible's Grove," or "Wible's Woods"). This small park was established in the Rose woods just south of the Wheatfield on the land then owned by William Wible.[160] Improvements

The trolley at Devil's Den, Tipton, c. 1895. (GNMP)

"At Tipton Park," Tipton, c. 1895. The boulder that the group is sitting on can still be found, very close to the location of the photographic gallery. Notice also the spring in the foreground. (GNMP)

made to the grounds included: a dancing pavilion, 70 by 75 feet, two eating stands, 30 x 30 feet, two cedar water pumps, tables and benches. Picnics were held there on weekends to draw excursionists out onto the trolley, and an agreement was made with Wible calling for a payment of $5 per excursion.[161] As an example, the annual picnic of St. Francis Xavier Church was held "at Wible's Grove" on August 16, 1893. A pleasant day was spent in the woods, with music provided by a first class orchestra. Refreshments and supper were served in abundance, while dancing, target shooting and other innocent amusements were provided. Admission was 25 cents.[162]

With the completion of the trolley line around Devil's Den and through the Valley of Death to Little Round Top in May 1894, visitors could travel from town all the way to "Round Top Park" and back. With the popularity of Devil's Den, "Tipton Park" quickly became "the principle stopping place for excursionists" on the trolley line.[163] It was recorded that during the first month of the 1894 season alone 15,427 fares were collected by the railway.[164] One visitor recalled: "The town of Gettysburg is given over to the battlefield. That is almost the only business, and furnishes substantially the only occupation of the greater part of its people. The 3,600 inhabitants of the little shire are mostly hotel keepers, photographers, guides, and carriage drivers."[165] It is true that with the popularity of the trolley growing, many profited, and many became critical of the park commission's continuing efforts to condemn the trolley. Emanuel Bushman said the following in the summer of 1894.

> We have the electric car and we are going to keep it. The people want it. Strangers want it. What a pleasure it is to ride out to Round-Top a hot evening! A healthy, invigorating ride. We won't allow a dictator or two to tell us we shall not have it. It is the biggest humbug in the world to say the electric road is desecrating the battlefield. That, too, after making twenty miles of wagon roads all through and all over the battlefield. Now, gentlemen, just leave the trolley alone.[166]

During the next ten years the roughly thirteen-acre Tipton Park would enjoy heavy visitation during the summer months. As the years went by, Tipton made many "improvements" to the property. He converted the building originally erected by Mumper into a restaurant. He constructed a separate dark room for the development of plates and storage of his equipment. He also erected a dancing pavilion 40 by 50 feet with a 10 by 12 foot bandstand, two water closets (gentlemen's and ladies), sheds for stabling or sheltering horses, and a few swings for the

children to play on. Besides the tintype gallery and photographic business, Tipton Park also supplied souvenirs, relics, lunches and refreshments, and catered large parties for families, excursionists and Sunday school groups.[167] Mary E. Tipton (William's wife) ran the restaurant and among the most popular items served were ham sandwiches, soup, soft drinks, lemonade, ice cream, and cigars. Year after year, business at the park steadily increased and she recalled "that during the summer as many as 2000 to 3000 people [would] visit the park in one day in busy seasons."[168] The 1890s Gettysburg newspapers are filled with notices of picnics and excursions to "Tipton Park." Although they must have been plentiful, photographs (mostly tintypes) taken on the grounds of Tipton Park are rarely seen today. With Devil's Den close at hand, and his exclusive contract with Crawford, most of his business was probably done there.[169]

Although many enjoyed the festivities at the park, others accused Tipton of permitting "it to be the scene of revelries which many right-minded people consider[ed] a desecration of the ground con-

Although thousands of tintypes must have been produced at the Devil's Den gallery by both Mumper and Tipton, this is the only known tintype thus far positively identified. Because of its distinctive markings, the rock that the woman is sitting on can easily be found today. (Timothy H. Smith Collection)

secrated by the blood of hundreds of heroes and patriots."[170] According to a Tipton descendant years later, "the main feature of the stand was the selling of gin. On more than one occasion tourist excursion members got a little much and caused bloody fights and riots. Several were known to have lost arms or legs due to falls under the moving trolley, while they were nowhere near the state of sobriety."[171] In 1901 condemnation proceedings were approved by the secretary of war, and on May 7-9 of that year a hearing was held to decide the land's fate. The jury visited the grounds of the park and heard testimony concerning its value. The central issue was its close proximity to "Devil's Den" and how that fact greatly increased the worth of the property. Estimates of its value ranged from $3,000 to $30,000, depending on whose side the witness was testifying.[172] On May 17th the jury awarded Tipton the sum of $6,150. Initially Tipton appealed the case, and another hearing was scheduled, but in the first week of December 1901, he withdrew his appeal and accepted the money.[173]

On March 6, 1902 Tipton's land was turned over to the government, and by August, the last of the park was dismantled, the restaurant building "being rolled bodily several hundred yards up the new Warren" Avenue to the base of Little Round Top where it was leased to David Weikert.[174] "Blind

Davy," as he was called, lost his sight in "a premature blast" during the construction of the Round Top Extension of the Gettysburg & Harrisburg Railroad in May of 1884. "On account of his misfortune", Mr. Weikert was given permission to conduct a stand at that point by the GBMA, and this liberty was continued by the Commission. The new stand replaced one that was taken down in the spring of 1901. Weikert ran the stand and sold refreshments, relics and souvenirs until 1919, during the years becoming a familiar sight to thousands of visitors to the field.[175]

The trolley that ran across Tipton Park remained in operation for a number of years afterwards. By that time the automobile was coming into its own and the popularity of the trolley was waning. In May 1917 the trolley was made a thing of the past. The government finally appropriated the $30,000 needed to purchase the land of the trolley line, and the tracks were ripped up.[176] Ironically, the same townspeople who urged the trolley to be built in Gettysburg were now happy to see it go. The Gettysburg *Compiler* (once the voice of the proponents for the trolley) reported that "The quicker our streets are free from tracks not used the better will the town streets be for the service of the thousands of autos that flock here from every direction. The passing of the trolley is a happy event for which

"Blind Davey's" Souvenir Stand, Tipton, 1902. This building was originally used by Mumper, remodeled by Tipton and later moved to a location along Warren Avenue. (GNMP)

The Philiadelphia Brewers Association at Devil's Den, Tipton, May 28, 1887. A wooden ladder appears in several views, suggesting that it was used to place members of the parties in hard-to-reach places. Notice the large amount of graffiti upon the rocks. (ACHS)

Cabinet card of party in front of the "Table Rock," Tipton c. 1892. The "Devil's Den" sign, also seen in the previous view, can be useful in establishing the date for photographs taken in the area. Under magnification the sign below can be discerned as an advertisement for Luther Minnigh's guidebook. (Boardman Collection)

incensed Tipton that he began using some creative advertising of his own. One such notice read:

Caution—to Visitors of the Battlefield!!! By a ruling of the Battlefield Commission, permits to make photographic groups on the lands of the U.S. have been granted to all applicants, hence are neither certificates of experience or ability. So called battlefield photographers have been button-holing the visitors at every prominent point until it has become an intolerable nuisance. And now the commissioners in their efforts to correct this have allowed special places or points to each, changing them every week. My operators from Monday morning Aug. 17, till Monday morning August 24, will be located on Little Round Top and under this ruling cannot make any plates at East Cemetery Hill or Devil's Den during this time-but plates will be made at other points if special arrangements are made at the studio or with my operators....Visitors are cautioned that all photographers on the field are not my operators, and to be sure that my name is on every receipt and is signed by my representative.[186]

There was some credence to Tipton's statement, since Williams did have problems concerning his business practices while on park ground. For a while the commissioners talked of revoking his license.[187]

Interest has been generated in these photographs for many reasons. Virtually every monument dedication on the field was captured by one of these photographers. Many of the views contain famous figures who at one time visited the field. And of course many are collected because of their importance as cultural documents of their period. The views invariably show parties in their Sunday best, with ladies showing off the latest fashions. In later years it became an opportunity for a proud motorist to have his picture taken alongside his new automobile. One of the most appealing aspects of these photographs is the information unintentionally provided in the background, such as rock carvings, or moved monuments.

Examples of these group portraits can be found in local flea markets and antique shops in great quantities. Along with a number of other Gettysburg souvenirs, they have become popular collectors items.[188] They range in size from 3 1/2x5 inch post card size views to extra large 20x24 inch views mounted on heavy bevelled panels (the most common size being 8x10 inches). Between the 1880s and 1930s at least nine local photographic firms are known to have been active in their production (W. H. Tipton, 1884-1929, Mumper & Co., c. 1884-1895; Mumper and Gelbach, 1889; J. I. Mumper, c. 1895-1911; Levi Mumper, 1897-1909; Mumper Studios, 1911-1948; M. F. Williams, c. 1895-1929; Ira Williams, c. 1929-1960s; and the Battlefield Photo Co., c. 1907-1912). For a short period (1907-1909), five of these firms were active at the same time.[189] From a study of negative numbers and dates on the existing examples of their works, it can be ascertained that during this period at least 60,000 views were taken of groups on the field by professional Gettysburg photographers.[190] The following infor-

Eddie Plank and Connie Mack at Devil's Den, Tipton, November 6, 1913. Plank, a pitcher and member of the Baseball Hall of Fame, was born in Adams County. Two months before this photograph was taken, he was named the Most Valuable Player of the World Series. Eddie's team was the Philadelphia Athletics and Connie Mack was its manager. (ACHS)

mation has been collected to help date and identify the group portraits taken on the battlefield in general, and more specifically, at Devil's Den.

William H. Tipton (1850-1929). Tipton was by far the most prolific of the Gettysburg photographers. Active at the time of the battle as an apprentice to the Tyson Brothers, by the 1880s he was firmly established in the Gettysburg area; well equipped and well staffed to handle the demands and rigors of the tourist market.[191] His advertisements in newspapers and early guidebooks are plentiful, lengthy, and sometimes a bit harsh on the competition. One of his 1886 advertisements boasted:

> We do not pretend to offer these views in competition with the worthless photographs made by parties with no reputation at stake, but claim they are as fine as any series of photographs made anywhere, and as fine as an experience of twenty-three years on the field with the best equipment and care can produce. See these Views before Purchasing Inferior Pictures.[192]

William Howard Tipton, c. 1925.
(Timothy H. Smith Collection)

During the 1884 season, coinciding with the opening of his tintype gallery at Round Top Park, he recorded his first group portraits in front of the rocks of Devil's Den. An examination of his 1894 catalog shows that Tipton's firm was very active in Devil's Den during each season (April through October), from 1884 to 1894, the year his catalog was published. At that time the negative numbers on his group views alone had reached 2000.[193] By 1894 he gained sole ownership of the gallery at Devil's Den, established Tipton Park and had arranged for it to be a stop along the Gettysburg Electric Railway. With the galleries at Little Round Top and Devil's Den, it must have been very advantageous for the storage of his outdoor photographic equipment.

An examination of Tipton's work indicates that by 1900 the negative numbers on his group views had reached 6000 and by 1920 were running into the 30,000s. His firm seems to have been active in taking group views on the field until his death in 1929. His mounts vary in color and size, and are embossed with a number of different labels.

Levi Mumper (1843-1916). Like Tipton, the Mumpers were also known to have taken group portraits in front of the rocks of Devil's Den. The story of the Mumpers is confusing, and the records concerning their operation apparently have not survived. Through an examination of newspaper and tourbook advertisements along with surviving examples of group views, it is possible, however, to construct a timeframe for their work. "Mumper & Co." was operated by Levi Mumper, a veteran of the Civil War, born in 1843. Following his discharge he learned the art of photography from the Tysons. In 1865 he married Sallie S. Shaffer, and started his own gallery. In the years following the Civil War, he established a thriving business and by the 1880's was William Tipton's only real competition in the Gettysburg area. Also during that time he fathered nine children.[194] It was Levi Mumper who built the small gallery at Devil's Den which W. H. Tipton acquired and used to great advantage. Levi also dabbled in the furniture business with his son Charles, and in 1895 sold his photographic gallery and equipment to his eldest son Jacob I. Mumper. His interest in the furniture business was short-lived. In 1897 he received permission to record group views on the battlefield from the park commission and in 1899 he opened a new studio at his residence on Stratton Street, which he continued to operate until 1909, when he finally retired.[195] "Mumper & Co., Battlefield Photographers, Gettysburg Pa." imprints on group portraits dating from the early 1890s are known, but are rare. By 1896, Jacob was using his own imprint on the bottom of his views. Adding to the confusion however, are a few J. I. Mumper imprints that seem to predate 1895, and a few Mumper

& Co. imprints are dated as late as 1899. "L. Mumper, 7 Stratton St., Gettysburg, Pa." imprints are more common, but as a rule are undated and absent of negative numbers. Since a catalog has not surfaced for either Mumper & Co. or L. Mumper it is not known exactly how many group photos that Levi recorded during the many years he operated his Gettysburg studios. Several "L. Mumper" and "Mumper & Co." group portraits taken at Devil's Den are preserved in the collections of the ACHS.

Jacob I. Mumper (1867-1923). In 1889, Jacob Mumper and his partner W. Harvey Gelbach purchased Levi Mumper's studio at Devil's Den. The partnership lasted less than a year, and in 1890 Jacob sold his half-interest in the gallery to Gelbach, who shortly afterward went into partnership with W. H. Tipton.[196] Today, examples of their work are very rare and the few mounts the authors have examined are imprinted "Mumper & Gelbach, Gettysburg, Pa., Battlefield Photographers At Devil's Den." All views bearing this label were undoubtedly taken during the 1889 season. It is unclear whether Jacob spent the following five years in business for himself or working with his father, but in 1895 he took over Levi's studio. Shortly, the Mumper & Co. imprint was replaced with "J. I. Mumper, 29 Baltimore Street., Gettysburg, Pa." Mumper appears on the rotating schedule set up by the Gettysburg National Military Park Commission in 1895. Much to Tipton's chagrin, J. I. Mumper also referred to himself as "Official Battlefield Photographer."[197] A study of his negative numbers indicates that by 1900 he had reached 3,000, by September of 1902 he had reached 6800, by July of 1904 he had reached 7100, and by June of 1906 he had reached 8600. During the years he operated the Baltimore Street studio, the negative numbers on his group views must have exceeded 10,000. He was very active in recording group portraits on the battlefield until 1911 when he sold his business to his brother Clyde Mumper (1879-1967). The same year Jacob became the manager and sole owner of a souvenir business located in the Jennie Wade Museum. In 1913, Clyde sold the studio to his brother John A. Mumper (1874-1957), but remained on as his assistant. In 1919 Clyde bought back the business, operating the gallery until his retirement in 1948.[198] Thus ended a family business that had been active in Adams County for over eighty years. During Clyde and John's ownership photographs were simply imprinted "Mumper Studios, Gettysburg, Pa." Views taken at Devil's Den bearing this imprint are quite common, and negative numbers from this series are known to run to about 3700.

M. F. Williams (1867-1929). Marion F. Williams Jr. was born in 1867, the son of a Civil War veteran. Better known as "Max," he began his photographic career in about 1890, probably working for one of the already established firms in town. There is no evidence that he recorded any views under his own

A party of visitors at the Devil's Bath, Levi Mumper, 1907. (ACHS)

Charles Sheads with a party at the Den, Williams, c. 1905. The vehicle appears to be a 1904 or 1905 Cadillac. Many of these group views have become collector's items because of the automobiles that appear in them. (ACHS)

name prior to the formation of the Gettysburg National Military Park in 1895. Along with W. H. Tipton, and J. I. Mumper, Williams was placed on the rotation of battlefield photographers in 1895.[199] Early examples of Williams' work are embossed with "M. F. Williams, National Park Photographer" (five examples can be seen at the ACHS). Being a novice at the trade, Williams' career started off on shaky ground with the park commissioners, but as the years passed M. F. Williams became firmly established in the story of Gettysburg photography. In 1903 he opened a photographic studio on High Street in Gettysburg. A 1906 advertisement boasted of "special attention given to photographing tourist parties and reunions. Having made thousands of plates, we insure satisfaction." One of his business cards bragged that his "expert operators" were "always at Devil's Den." He was quite active in the taking of group views from 1895 until his death in 1929. His obituary stated that "for many years he took pictures of parties on the battlefield, being located at Devil's Den."[200] His views are generally undated, and a timeframe for each photograph can only be established by the type of mount, label, or through internal evidence. Examples of his work exist with negative numbers as low as 357 and as high as 9991.

Upon Max's death in 1929, his son, Ira L. Williams, took over his Gettysburg studio and ran it until his death in 1977. According to Ira's obituary he was "best known for the pictures he took of elementary classes."[201] And his favorite backdrop for hundreds of these photos taken during the 1940s and 50s was Devil's Den. Over 2,000 of Ira Williams' negatives are preserved at the ACHS.

The Battlefield Photo Company. Although more than a few examples of this firm's work exist, little is known concerning its ownership or activities. The Battlefield Photo Company is known to have been active on the battlefield from at least 1909 to 1912, but no firm dates have thus far been established. A 1909 advertisement stated their "specialty" as "group and view work."[202] Negative numbers from this firm are known to number above 2000.

Rock Carvings

During the preparation of this book, hundreds of group portraits taken in front of the boulders of Devil's Den were examined. And while today, the rocks appear to look just as they did at the time of the battle, it is apparent that at one time, the rocks of the Den were literally covered with carved and painted graffiti. Rock carvings are not unique to Devil's Den; carvings can be found on rocks at Culp's Hill, Spangler's Spring, the Stony Hill, McAllister's Mill, the Weikert Farm, and the summits of Big and Little Round Top. But nowhere else on the field do they appear in such great quantity. Who was responsible for the carvings? When did they first appear on the rocks of the Den? And when, how, and why were the inscriptions removed?

Because some of the photographs taken at Devil's Den by Tipton, Mumper, and Williams are datable, the authors were able to piece together a basic time frame for the growth of this graffiti on those rocks in particular. An examination of the earliest views from C. J. Tyson and the Weavers, indicates that there were few incriptions on the rocks before the 1880s. As Devil's Den grew in popularity over the next few years, the graffiti increased, and by the 25th anniversary of the battle in 1888, portions of the Den were literally covered with names and dates. By 1895 the carvings disappear, and in views taken after that date, large white blotches exist in the places where the inscriptions once appeared.[203] A partial explanation for this mystery was solved by an 1898 tourbook which included a section on Devil's Den. A lengthy caption beneath a photograph of the Table Rock read in part:

> Time and the chisel employed by the United States government have greatly altered the face of these boulders. Since 1837, the earliest date inscribed, it had been common practice to place inscriptions here. Acting upon the argument that what had been done would continue while the suggestion remained, the government had all carefully removed.[204]

Upon a field investigation of areas where rock carvings are known to have existed, it is not difficult to determine the meaning of the term "carefully removed." The white blotches that appear in views of the Den taken after 1895 are actually marks made by a chisel used to obliterate the inscriptions from the rock. These scratches, made over a hundred years ago, consist of short vertical strokes about two inches in length, and are referred to in one early tourbook as "chisel marks."[205] Not only do "scratch-outs" appear in great abundance throughout the Devil's Den area, they have also been found on the rocks of Little and Big Round Top. Once the eye has been trained to recognize these marks, it becomes clear just how great the proliferation of rock carvings once was in the Den area. The greatest single concentration of "scratch-outs" can be found in the passage under the "Table Rock." Along with these chisel marks are still at least six carvings in the area of Devil's Den that have survived. These were either missed, or carved after the park had already removed the others.

There is good evidence that some of the inscriptions actually predate the battle. Because of its sub-

The Table Rock, Tipton, c. 1895. The white blotches which appear on the face of the boulders are chisel marks. (Tim Smith Collection)

sequent removal, the "1837" date for the earliest carving cannot be fully substantiated, but luckily, one carving at the south end of the Plum Run Gorge was missed because of its difficult to reach location. It can still be seen (after a rigorous climb) atop a large boulder and reads: "D. FORNEY 1849." Most of the carvings, however, were not missed by the government chiselers, and it may never be known how many actually predated the battle. The existence of carvings on the rocks of the Den before the battle, and the fact it was the most heavily visited and rockiest area of the field still in private hands during the memorial period (John Houck, 1858-1872 and Crawford Park,1872-1894), must have only aggravated the situation. Because it was private property, visitors were not bound by the rules and regulations that existed on the nearby GBMA grounds.[206] On February 5, 1894, the Gettysburg National Military Park Commission purchased Crawford's land from his heirs. In a short time, the rock carvings disappeared.

No documentation has yet been found in park records or local newspapers that mentions the removal of the graffiti. A William Tipton photograph of "Coxey's Army" however, offers some helpful information. Jacob Sechler Coxey was a self-made businessman whose concern for the unemployed during the depression following the panic of 1893, made him a hero to the poor. In the spring of 1894, he led a group of unemployed citizens on a march from Ohio to Washington D. C., which ended in a violent demonstration on the steps of the Capitol on the 1st of May.[207] A contingent of "Coxey's Army," about 150 men, led by Colonel S. H. Thomas, a Civil War Veteran, visited Gettysburg on July 13, 1894. They were taken to Devil's Den, where Tipton apparently allowed them to encamp at his park. They stayed for three days, and drew quite a crowd of visitors.[208] These men were not well-liked by everyone and were seen by many as an unruly group of troublemakers. One Philadelphia newspaper commented that, "Thirty-one years ago Plum Run ran red with soldiers blood. To-day it runs black from the dirty clothing of a band of tramps."[209] At some point while this group was encamped at his park, Tipton got a few of them together with their colonel, and took a photograph in front of Devil's Den. Although Tipton was probably not concerned with it at the time, he was also recording a view showing the carvings in the process of being chiseled away.

Over the years, many have speculated that most of the carvings were the work of veterans. Because there is no way of determining what the greater majority of these carvings once represented, an examination of the existing photographic record predating their removal is essential. The earliest views of Devil's Den that show a carving on one of its boulders were taken in the 1880s. Between then and 1895 the firms of Tipton and Mumper alone recorded hundreds of group portraits in front of the famous "Table Rock" at Devil's Den. Because it was well-known that these photographs were being taken, It is no coincidence that the boulders appearing in the background of these views quickly became the most

Coxey's Army at Devil's Den, Tipton, May 1894. This extraordinary photograph, which captures carvings in the process of being chiseled, provides us with an approximate time frame for the removal of the graffiti at Devil's Den. (GNMP)

Detail of a Tipton group view dated April 26, 1887. Between 1884 and 1894 carvings appear in great numbers on views taken of the Den. (ACHS)

Maurice Fox, the man whose name is prominently featured on the face of the Table Rock in many views, Tipton, February 22, 1892. (The Horse Soldier)

Carved into a rock atop Devil's Den, "P. Noel" is one of just a few carvings that survived the chisels of the Park Commission.

popular locations to place inscriptions. Of roughly 30 different inscriptions identified in pre-scratch-out photographs (usually names, initials, or symbols), only three in the Devil's Den area (one painted and two carved) were related to the battle. The greater majority of those identified can be attributed directly to local residents, and not veterans. Because these carvings can be seen as historical documents instead of graffiti, some information on the more interesting inscriptions is provided.

The "4th Maine" is one of three inscriptions that can be attributed to veterans and one of the six that can still be located today. This inscription, carved into a rock several feet northeast of the 4th Maine monument, was apparently done by an experienced stonecutter. Little is known concerning when or by whom it was carved, and although it must have been done over a hundred years ago, it was only recently rediscovered. The area around it had for years been overgrown by weeds and underbrush. In the early 1990s a fence was removed from across the Valley of Death and in the fall of 1993 the ground was cleared by a Civil War roundtable. One frosty winter afternoon a couple of months later, the sun was observed glaring off a strange pattern in the rock. Closer examination revealed a carving that had been presumably covered by thorn bushes for decades. Very similar to that of the 4th Maine is a carving for "The 40th N.Y. Vols." This carving is located on a rock just a few feet from the monument for that regiment in the Valley of Death. A circa 1888 photograph of the newly erected monument unintentionally captured the carving also. It is a least possible that both the 4th Maine and 40th New York carvings predate the erection of their respective monuments.

An inscription on a rock near the intersection of Cross and Sickles Avenues once read "Col John Wheeler 20th Ind. Vols. Killed in Action July 2nd, 1863." This inscription was not carved, but painted on the rocks. If it were not for a Tipton photograph in the collection of the ACHS, this inscription would probably have remained unknown. At one time there were apparently many such locations marked around the field, many by numbered stakes that have since deteriorated. Because of the inscription, today this rock has taken on a whole new significance. It is interesting to note that a 1986 NPS plan for the readjustment of park roads called for the widening of the avenues at this intersection. The plan was rejected, but it is quite probable that, had it been adopted, the rock would have been removed or destroyed in the process.

Several non-military carvings have also survived over the years. One of the best examples is "P. Noel." This carving can be seen just a few feet from the left flank marker for Smith's New York Battery atop Devil's Den. Research indicates that the most likely person to have carved this inscription is Park Noel (1868-1942). Park was born in the area, the son of William and Catherine Noel. His obituary mentions that he was "a stone cutter by trade," and that "he aided in the erection of several monuments around the battlefield." Looking at the carving, it is obvious that it was professionally done.[210] In 1888, at the time the 4th New York monument was placed, Park would have been twenty years old. Incidentally, the base of the monument is made of "Gettysburg Granite," indicating that a local contractor was involved in its erection. A humorous anecdote concerning this inscription is included in a recent book entitled *Haunted Gettysburg*, in which the carving is attributed to Pauline Noel, who supposedly died at Devil's Den and whose ghost is responsible for the carving. It cannot be stressed enough that this story, like many of the ghost stories, is an outright fabrication. No one named Pauline Noel ever lived or died near the Den.[211]

"J. Tipton" can be seen scratched atop the large boulders of Devil's Den itself, just south of the bridge across the cavern. J. Tipton could be one of a number of individuals. Most likely it was a relative of William Tipton who helped out at the park. From the fact that so many "scratch-outs" surround this carving, it must have been made after 1894.

The carving "D. Forney 1849" can be seen atop the "Elephant Rock" at the southern edge of the Gorge. It may be the most important of the rock carvings to have survived, for it does indeed predate the war, and gives evidence of the popularity of the Den before the battle. Because of its location, it is easy to understand how it was missed by the government chiselers. Research at the ACHS indicates that D. Forney can only be David S. Forney (1828-1911). David was the son of Samuel and Eliza Forney, and appears in the 1850 census as an "artist." Before the outbreak of the Civil War he moved south and took up residence in Virginia, where he became a painter of some note. There is no evidence that he served in the Confederate army, but he lived in the south during and after the war. He died in Virginia, but was brought home and buried with his family in the Evergreen Cemetery at Gettysburg.[212]

The "Flag Rock" is located south of the Elephant Rock, and has for years been one of the most popular of the carved rocks. On it is inscribed "U. F. S. 1873" along with a small and large American flag. There are several other carvings that are worn away and are not readily discernible. Many are curious as to what U. F. S. may stand for, but as is the case with most initials any identification would be pure speculation.

Through photographs taken in front of the boulders of Devil's Den, many of the inscriptions that were chiseled out by the park commission in 1894 have been identified. Among them appear many local surnames including Myers, Tate, Gulden, Sachs, Wible and Wisotzky. "F. Mumper and J. Mumper" (Frank and, Jacob or John), undoubtedly sons of photographer Levi Mumper, also had their names scratched in the rocks. One of the nicest carvings was that of "G. W. Trostle May the 13th 1876." George William Trostle was the son of Abraham and Catherine Trostle. On July 2, 1863, his family's farm was the scene of bitter fighting as Captain John Bigelow's 9th Massachusetts Battery made a stand a few feet from the house, against the 21st Mississippi of Barksdale's Brigade. After the war, George built a house along the Wheatfield Road, just across from the modern entrance to Ayers Avenue (the house no longer stands, but appears in many postwar photographs).[213] When he carved his name on May 13, 1876, he lived just a half a mile from the Den. In 1879 a veteran of the 53rd Pennsylvania visited Gettysburg and toured the field with Trostle as his guide.

> George W. Trostle will always be kindly remembered for the good care taken of me while I tarried with them. Their house has been built since the battle and stands on the same ground we fought over....I started out early with Mr. Trostle for escort to look over the battlefield between here and Little Round Top. Here the ground is rough, being covered with rocks. Some fifty or seventy-five acres here, including Little Round Top is owned by the Gettysburg Battlefield Association and is left as it was after the battle. As we pass down toward the Devil's Den, I saw a marble block which marks the spot where the Colonel of the 1st Pennsylvania Reserves fell. The Devil's Den is a huge mass of rocks, piled up in all shapes. This place was taken and held by the Rebels some time, but when retaken by our forces we captured a number of prisoners hiding among the rocks.[214]

The inscription most frequently seen in early photographs is "Maurice Fox." Maurice C. Fox (1867-1914) was born in Littlestown, Adams County, Pennsylvania. At the age of two he suffered from severe sunstroke and was permanently paralyzed. During his youth, his family moved to Gettysburg, where he spent the rest of his life as a "terrible cripple." He became "a familiar figure" on the streets of town "in his specially built tricycle." Despite his handicap he worked as a photographer, an insurance salesman, and for years he owned a successful grocery store on Baltimore Street in Gettysburg.[215] It is presumed that at one point, he worked for one of the photographers at the Den. With his disability, it is unlikely that he himself carved or painted his name on the

face of the "Table Rock." It must have been done by one of his friends.

Among the most interesting carvings once adorning the Table Rock was that of "C. M. Young." Charles Morris Young (1869-1964) was born just a few miles from Devil's Den, in a house along the Taneytown Road. His parents were Christopher and Anna Louise Young. When just sixteen years old, Charles went to work for William H. Tipton carving battle scenes on canes. Upon receiving a scholarship, he attended the Pennsylvania Academy of Fine Arts from 1891-1895. After graduation, he traveled to Paris (1897-1898) where he studied under Collorosi. During the next 60 years Young established a worldwide reputation, producing hundreds of portraits and landscapes. Among his personal friends were Monet, Whistler, and Mary Cassatt. Today the works of C. M. Young hang in some of the most respected art galleries in the world including the Pennsylvania Academy of Fine Arts, the Corcoran Gallery in Washington, D.C., the National Gallery in Budapest, Hungary, the National Museum in Santiago, Chile and the Louvre in Paris, France. Many of his early works can be seen locally at the ACHS and Adams County Public Library. For years a large oil painting by Young entitled Gen. Meade's Headquarters hung in the lobby at the Eagle Hotel. Several others are still privately owned in the Gettysburg area including one entitled Devil's Den by Moonlight. Charles Morris Young died at his home in Radnor, Pennsylvania on November 14, 1964.[216] The carving "C. M. Young" first appears in photographs taken in 1886, or about the time he started working for Tipton's gallery (Ira M. Young, a brother to Charles, has his name scratched on the rocks as well). The artistically carved giant hand that appears just below his name, may also be his handiwork. It is somewhat ironic that a piece of graffiti on the boulders of Devil's Den was one of the earliest works of this world-renowned artist.

The Gettysburg National Military Park: 1895 To The Present

As early as the 25th anniversary of the battle in 1888 there was talk of a National Park at Gettysburg. In 1889 the Pennsylvania State Legislature "formally invited the United States to purchase land and occupy the field of Gettysburg" in order to create a park.[217] It was not until March 1892 that the first real bill which proposed the establishment of "The Gettysburg National Park," was introduced into Congress.[218] This bill went through many changes in committee, and finally, on March 3, 1893 was passed as a sundry act appropriating $25,000 to purchase

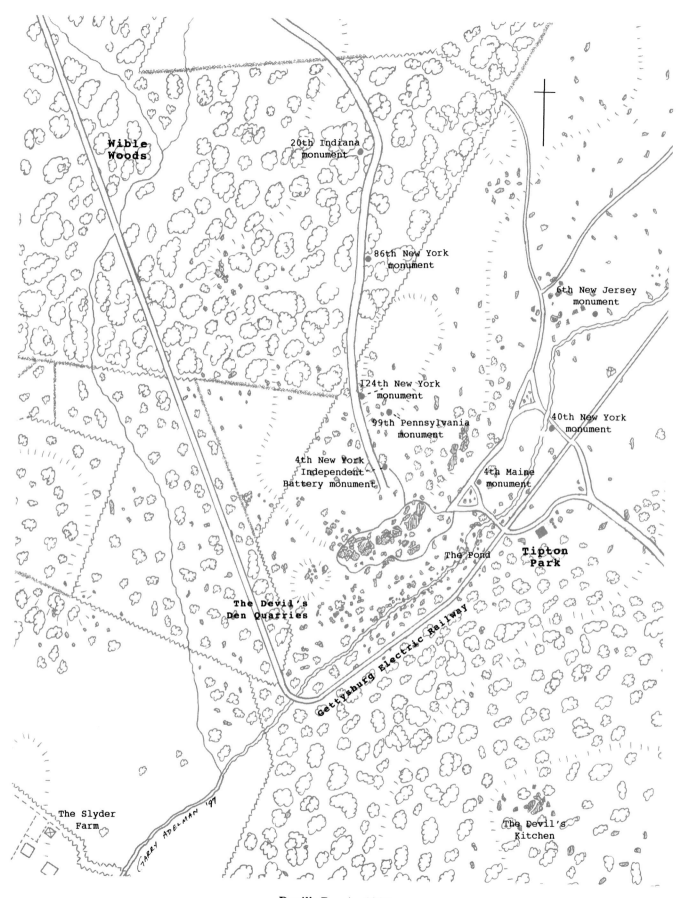

Devil's Den in 1895.

lands in order to "preserve and mark" the lines of Battle at Gettysburg. On May 3, the secretary of war appointed to the three man Gettysburg Park Commission John B. Bachelder of Massachusetts, John P. Nicholson of Pennsylvania, and William H. Forney of Alabama. The Park Commission was appointed by the secretary of war and as a result, the park remained under the jurisdiction of the War Department for the next 40 years (1893-1933).[219]

Immediately upon their organization, the commissioners were embroiled in the controversy concerning the trolley. At their first meeting in Gettysburg on July 1, 1893, an engineer, Colonel Emmor B. Cope, was hired to lay out the avenues, map the battlefield, and supervise the day-to-day activities on the field and in the office.[220] Despite its problems and responsibilities that the commission faced at the outset, it was soon able to acquire significant tracts of land. One of their first major accomplishments was the purchase of the Crawford Tract on February 5, 1894 from the heirs of Samuel Crawford for $700.[221] Upon obtaining ownership, the commissioners took steps to clean up the Den, chiseling off the rock carvings that were by now beginning to proliferate on the face of some of the boulders. To insure that no further damage was done the commission posted notices around its land in the summer of 1894.

> To whom it may concern:
> Notice is hereby given to all persons, that they are forbidden to enter or go upon any grounds or portions of land consisting part of the battlefield of Gettysburg belonging to the United States, in such a way and manner as may disfigure the natural features of the ground, or with a view of exercise thereon of any special or exclusive privilege of any kind claimed by them, or for the purpose of indulging in pic-nics, or merry making of a nature inconsistent with the solemn and sacred associations of this field forever consecrated to patriotism and to the memory of heroes who fought and died here; and all who disregard this notice will be held and treated as trespassers.
> Chairman, John P. Nicholson.[222]

Of course the "exclusive privilege" the commissioners were eliminating was Tipton's agreement with Crawford that he alone had the right to take photographs on the land.

Continuing development pressures convinced many that the creation of the park was vital to the preservation of the field. In 1893 General Daniel Sickles announced "that his express and single purpose in returning in his age to congress" was "to secure the passage of a law making the entire Gettysburg battlefield a National Park."[223] On December 6, 1893, Congressman Sickles led the drive by introducing the bill himself, and on February 11, 1895, Congress passed the act "to establish a National Military Park at Gettysburg."[224] Shortly afterward, a meeting was held by the GBMA and its roughly 600 acres of land and 320 monuments were transferred to the Federal Government.[225]

As far as memorialization is concerned, a few important additions were made during the War Department years. In 1900 the park commission marked the position of Captain Smith's section of guns in the Valley of Death with two ten pounder Parrotts and a "monumental tablet with an appropriate inscription." Smith had died in 1893, and it is not clear how the commission arrived at that location for the guns. It was at this same time that two additional gun carriages mounted with Parrotts were placed on Sickles Avenue near the 4th New York Battery's monument. (See appendix III).[226] Three other monuments were erected near Devil's Den in the subsequent years, all brigade markers. Around 1907, cast iron tablets were placed along Sickles Avenue to mark the advanced positions of Robertson's and Benning's Confederate Brigades.[227] By 1912 a brigade marker had also been placed just inside the Rose Woods to describe the actions of General John Henry Hobart Ward's Union Brigade during the battle.[228]

In the years following its creation, one of the primary goals of the Gettysburg National Military Park was to construct avenues so as to make more areas accessible, and to improve many of the avenues already in existence. Most thought these new avenues a vast improvement over the previous ones. The park commission in 1895 explained that:

> All these avenues have been and are being constructed on the Telford system, which was adopted after full consideration and study of the subject as promising the best results in solidity and durability. The stone used is syenitic granite [actually diabase] and ironstone, very hard and of excellent quality. A foundation pavement is laid of 8-inch wedgelike stones set on edge and well knapped and chinked; on this 4 inches of stone 1 1/2 inches in size; then a slight layer of clay as a binder, and finally a top dressing of 1 or 2 inches of quarter-inch stone screenings; the whole rolled thoroughly with a steam roller weighing 14 tons; side and under drains are placed where needed. The results of the above method and process are roadways smooth and solid and which will last for generations.[229]

Not everyone was impressed by the new avenues. Many had trouble understanding the difference be-

Sickles Avenue, West of Devil's Den, Tipton, 1896. (GNMP)

The hitching rail at Devil's Den, Tipton, 1897. (GNMP)

tween the commission digging, blasting, and disfiguring the battlefield to create roads, and the Electric Railway blasting and digging to create a bed for the trolley. One early tourbook actually openly complained about the "Gettysburg Battlefield Commission" stating how they had "disfigured" areas of the field with these avenues.

> They have also allowed the contractor to hire Italian laborers in express violation of their orders from the War Department, thereby cutting down wages from a dollar and a half a day to ninety cents. They also built a mile of useless avenue from the Weikert House past the Trostle buildings to keep the trolley off the battlefield. The avenues are not properly constructed and do not wear and cost $5.00 per square yard, etc.[230]

In 1887 the GBMA had decided to name all battlefield avenues "after the leading officers who commanded in the various localities," and this rule was pretty well adhered to during the War Department years.[231] In 1896 Sickles avenue was constructed. It runs from the "Emmitsburg road near the Rogers house southeastward, via the Loop and the Wheatfield, to the Devil's Den."[232] In 1897 construction was started on "Crawford avenue which leads from Devil's Den northward through the Valley of Death to the Wheatfield road, including a bridge over Plum Run." At the same time other improvements were made at Devil's Den including hitching rails, for visitors to tie their horses.[233] By 1898 Crawford Avenue had been completed, and Sickles Avenue through the Den was further "beautified" by "Guard Chain and Balls and Paths" running along the western side of the avenue in front of the boulders. It was probably also at this time that the iron sign "Devil's Den," was placed near the av-

enue.[234] In 1902 Warren Avenue was constructed. It runs westward from the saddle between the Round Tops, "along the base of Little Round Top to Plum Run Valley and crossing that run joins Crawford avenue near the Devil's Den." A bridge was constructed across Plum Run at the point on which it crossed.[235] The date for the construction of Warren Avenue was undoubtedly related to the condemnation proceedings of Tipton Park which were finally settled in early 1902. Over the years, many of the avenues originally designed by the Park Commission have been improved or removed. But for the most part, (with the exception of being made one-way), the three avenues (Sickles, Crawford, and Warren) in the Den area have remained unchanged since their construction.[236] It must be remembered, however, that these roads were built between 1896 and 1902, and that the battlefield had been well traveled over for 30 years before these roads were built. Many have, over the years, assumed that the commission avenues were simply built over the beds of roads that already existed. This is not necessarily true, especially in the Devil's Den area, which was never owned by the GBMA.

Through an examination of photographs taken before these roads were built, it becomes clear that when given the choice, the commissioners preferred to create new roads instead of improving existing ones. It appears that the original Crawford Avenue (although not named as such) was actually just west of the modern one. If one examines this area closely, especially during the winter, it is still possible to trace its original route. Before Warren Avenue was put in, there was a road leading from the summit of Little Round Top across the Valley of Death. About halfway down the hill was a "Y" where it branched off into two separate directions. The northern branch crossed Plum Run near the 40th New York

View from Little Round Top showing the early road system around Devil's Den, Tipton, July, 1888. (ACHS)

Monument to hook up with Crawford Avenue. The intersection of these avenues can be clearly seen today. On this road there was no bridge and carriages would just splash through a shallow point in the stream. The southern branch ran down from the hill to a point just east of the trolley line, where it veered toward Tipton Park and crossed Plum Run at the spot now marked by the modern foot bridge. The stone foundation under this bridge reveals that it was originally built for quite a different purpose than delivering a pedestrian to the restrooms. The first documentable bridge at this vicinity was built by William Tipton and friends in the fall of 1892, and was actively used by most traffic to Devil's Den from that time until the construction of Warren Avenue in 1902.[237] The length of the roadbed from Warren Avenue to the footbridge can still be clearly seen, and is presently used by the NPS as a service road.

During the War Department years the park was run much differently than it is today by the National Park Service. One little known fact is that during its administration five guards, who were responsible for the enforcement of park rules, were assigned to different parts of the battlefield. One of them was, at least in daylight hours during the season, stationed at Devil's Den.[238]

One of the original missions of the GBMA, and one that the GNMP Commission tried to honor was "to preserve...the natural and artificial defenses as they were at the time of said battle, and by such perpetuation and such memorial structures as a generous and patriotic people may aid to erect..." Although the care of the monuments sounds like a simple matter, the job of keeping the battlefield looking exactly as it appeared at the time of the battle is not an easy one. In July 1895 it was reported that:

> ...a considerable force is trimming the trees and clearing out the underbrush about the Devil's Den on land formerly owned by Gen. Crawford, greatly improving the general appearance and showing the movements of troops. Mr. Tipton proposes to restore his tract to what it was at the time of the battle.[239]

These projects were very important, but early on there were problems, mainly because few agreed on what certain parts of the field actually looked like in 1863. In 1911, a veteran who fought at Devil's Den wrote to the War Department and complained:

> ...the efforts which are being made to keep the land as it was at the time of the battle are commendable. The particular part of the battlefield in which I was interested is however disappointing in that regard. It is the part where the 124th N.Y. fought on the second day, and the hill on which they fought

was cleared land at the time. Now this ground is grown up with tall underbrush and even trees. Major Richardson [of the Park Commission] promised several years ago to have this part of the field cleared up, but as yet it has not been done. Both the veterans [*sic*] and their friends were greatly disappointed on reaching Gettysburg this time to find that that condition existed. Cannot something be done about it?[240]

The Park only took a few days to answer the veterans of the 124th. The response given by John Nicholson gives some idea of the problems facing the park commission on such matters

> The entire hill was cleared off in 1909, but immediately following the clearing up, two regiments of the Brigade complained that the hill was too bare, and that it did not look like the time of the Battle. Moreover the representatives of Smith's New York Battery complained, so we determined to let it grow again until some uniform conclusion was reached, this where there is nothing but memory to guide, it is difficult to reconcile. Our own judgment is that apart from the few low bushes it is as in 1863, but as it will only require an hour to clean up as the Regiment wishes, it will at once be finished, and the 124th New York and the 99th Penna. may take up the differences of opinion between them.[241]

As continually pointed out by historian William Frassanito, one of the biggest mistakes made by early park historians was in not realizing the potential of dating and examining the views taken by photographers such as Gardner and Brady when trying to determine how the field appeared at the time of the battle. In the case of Houck's Ridge, a Brady photograph taken from the summit of Little Round Top in July 1863 gives us a pretty clear idea of what Houck's Ridge looked like at the time, and the veteran of the 124th New York was right. Its eastern face was denuded of trees, and much clearer than it is today.[242]

In 1933, the National Park Service was established, and the Department of the Interior took over the management and responsibilities of the Gettysburg National Military Park. From the start, many were concerned about how the NPS would run a military park, and feared that it would be run as a natural, instead of historical, park. Over the years this apparent conflict has resulted in many different opinions on how the park should be preserved. Gettysburg is designated a National Park, and as such has a responsibility to protect its natural resources. Under existing guidelines, it not so easy for them to deforest large amounts of land, in order to return them to their pre-battle appearance. There has also been much discussion over what should be used as documentation, to establish how the field should be restored, especially in areas where the first photographs were not taken until the 1880s or 90s.[243] Much to the NPS's credit, there have been several attempts to restore the battlefield, and volunteers can frequently be seen clearing brush from overgrown areas. With the help of historians, perhaps even more can be done to return the park to its 1863 appearance.

Early in the NPS years there were changes made in the vicinity of Devil's Den. In the spring of 1935, as part of a PWA project, A. R. Warner & Son of Waynesboro, Pennsylvania was contracted to build a small stone comfort station just on the east side of Plum Run. A stone wall was built to replace the hitching rails around the parking areas and the cannon balls, chains, and walkways were all removed.[244]

Because of the popularity of Devil's Den, it has always been its own worst enemy. The NPS had long been concerned that the "heavy pedestrian use and inadequate walkways" were resulting in erosion and safety problems around the large boulders in Devil's Den and Houck's Ridge.[245] Traffic problems caused by cars and buses parking in the Devil's Den, and the intrusion this traffic caused on the vista from Little Round Top, added to their concerns. During the 1980s it was decided that something must be done. After studying the problems the park released an alternative, apparently the 5th such plan, in May 1986. The park proposed the complete removal of Crawford, Warren, and part of Sickles Av-

enues. Walking trails would be added or improved for those still wanted access to the Den. At face value the idea did not sound bad, and was presented as an improvement by park officials, but there were strings attached. To help alleviate the traffic problems that the removal of these roads would create, two new roads would have to be constructed, one across the eastern base of Little Round Top, and one along the old trolley roadbed from Cross Avenue to a huge "turnaround" just south of Devil's Den where a parking lot for 24 cars and three buses was to be added.[246] The plan would have resulted in the further destruction of significant features at Devil's Den. The massive parking area would have been located directly on ground where Texans, Alabamians, and Georgians gave their lives in the assault on Devil's Den. It would have moved the parking lot from one side of Devil's Den to the other, and in the process unnecessarily destroyed battlefield land. Concerned citizens, led by some of the battlefield guides, protested vigorously.[247] Only after two years of public pressure, and a change in superintendents, did park officials shelve the idea. But there were compromises. Today, the official NPS tour route no longer passes through Devil's Den, and buses are now forbidden to park on Crawford Avenue, or to drive through the Den.

The problem of how to properly maintain and preserve the park will never be fully resolved, and is an ongoing issue. With each new superintendent and administration, changes occur in how the park is managed and operated. Unfortunately, not all change is good, and many times changes are made

The monument to Smith's Battery after its mysterious accident.

just for the sake of change, without the parties involved clearly understanding the impact their decision will have upon future generations of visitors to the battlefield.[248] Such was the case with Devil's Den in 1986.

Among the problems most prevalent at Devil's Den today is vandalism. It is not a new problem. The first major incident of vandalism to any monument in the park occurred to the 124th New York Monument in 1884. One of the worst cases happened on March 3 or 4, 1913. Someone took a hammer "and mutilated nine monuments" on the southern end of the field, including the 40th New York. A $500 reward was offered for any information leading to the arrest of this individual. The damaged monuments were repaired, and today, were it not for a file at the National Archives that tells of the incident, it might be forgotten.[249] More recent cases of vandalism include the collapse of the statue for the 4th New York Battery above the Den. On February 18, 1995, the statue was knocked off the monument and onto the ground beside it, with no explanation of how it got there.

There are many kinds of vandalism, some worse than others, some intentional and some accidental. Every Saturday during the season, dozens of people picnic on the rocks of the Den, and invariably, a large amount of trash is left behind, thrown between the cracks and crevices, just as the Confederate bodies once were.

Another example of unintentional damage at Devil's Den, was the filming of the movie "Gettysburg." While in production during the summer of 1993, a few of the scenes were filmed on the battlefield. On the entire battlefield, however, the only area in which a combat scene was filmed at the actual location on which it occurred was the Triangular Field at Devil's Den. Colonel Ellis of the 124th leads a charge down across the field, reels in his saddle and falls, as the 1st Texas charges over the wall to capture Smith's Battery. It took two days to film this scene, during which Devil's Den was closed to visitors. When the public was allowed to return to the area the next day, many were not amused to see the appearance of the stone wall atop the Triangular Field. In filming the movie a hole was smashed through it and it has not yet been restored. Although the wall is probably not original, and has been restacked many times over the years, it is hard not to see this as vandalism.

Of course, every once in a while, someone brings a spray can to Devil's Den and paints "I love Angie" or some such garbage on one of its boulders. Such modern graffiti reflects back to the hundreds of townspeople who must have chiseled and painted their names on the rocks during the Crawford Park years. With this, it should be remembered that while Devil's Den is always changing, some things will always remain the same.

The damage to the fence atop the Triangular Field during the filming of the movie Gettysburg.

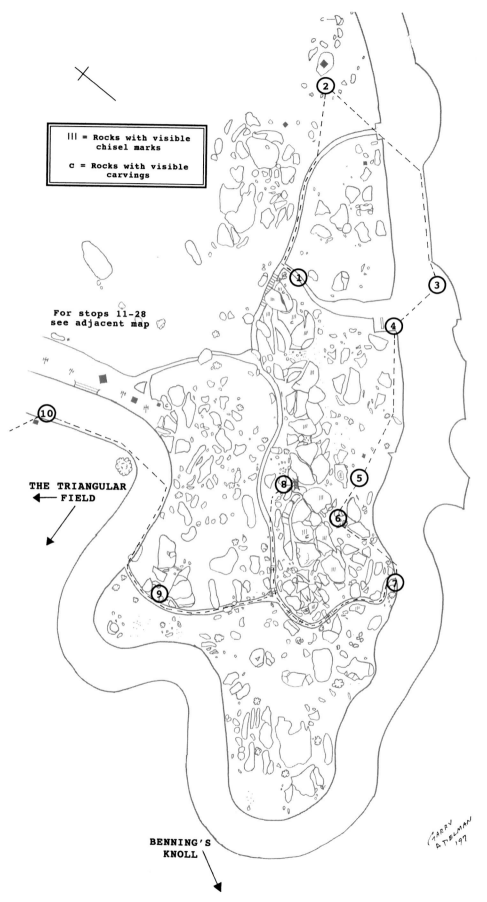

III = Rocks with visible
chisel marks

c = Rocks with visible
carvings

For stops 11-28
see adjacent map

THE
SLAUGHTER
PEN

THE TRIANGULAR
← FIELD

BENNING'S
KNOLL

A Tour of Devil's Den (Stops 1-10).

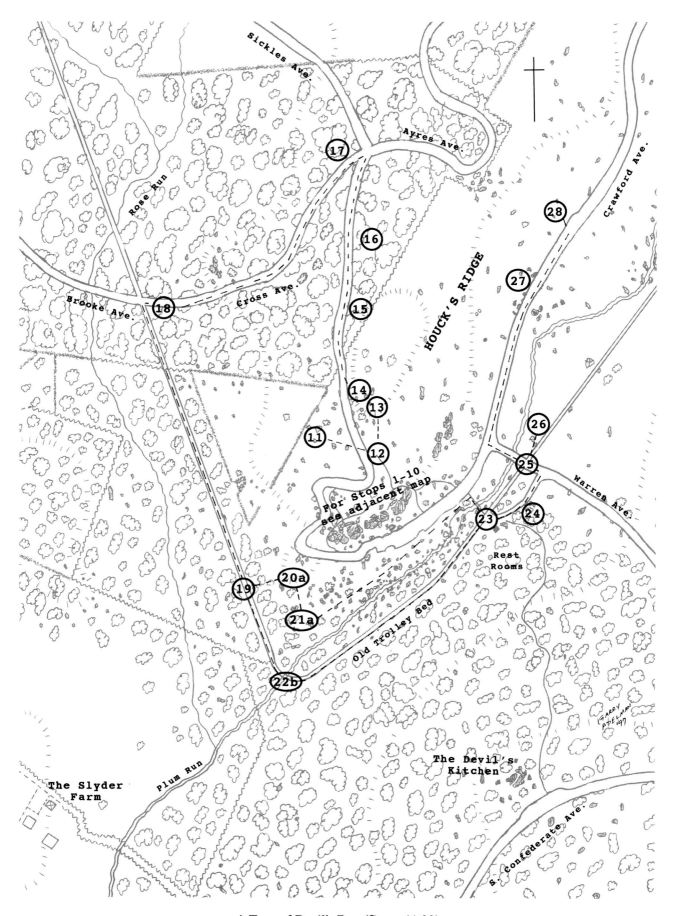

A Tour of Devil's Den (Stops 11-28).

Touring Devil's Den

This section of the book is intended to enhance the reader's understanding of the features around Devil's Den which played such a significant role in the outcome of the battle. It is also designed to follow those who fought here into their later lives, after the war. Additionally, many interesting tidbits will both add to and solidify much of the information previously given in this book. The stops are laid out in order but the reader is encouraged to follow the tour in any sequence which may be convenient or desirable. The entire route, excluding "excursions" is just under two miles.

Walking through the area, it is hard to ignore the natural beauty of the landscape. Whether it be the massive geological formation or the flora and fauna, Devil's Den has it share of interesting scenery. Gettysburg is a National Park, and thus has a wide variety of wildlife, as in any North American woodland.

On cool evenings in the spring, summer or fall, it is not unusual to see people with binoculars studying the birds in the trees around the Den. Vultures make up a large part of the population of birds at the park, but there are about 200 other species that can be observed at different times of the year. Other inhabitants of the Den include a number of snakes, turtles, frogs and lizards. Among the snakes, the Eastern Timber Rattlesnake (rarely seen) and the Northern Copperhead are poisonous and should be avoided. The Five-Lined Skink, a black lizard between five and ten inches long with a brilliant blue tail, is frequently observed. Mammal inhabitants include chipmunks, squirrels, skunks, ground hogs, and a large population of deer. Those visiting this area are encouraged to observe the many forms of wildlife that make Devil's Den their home, but are cautioned not to disturb their habitat.

Due to its rugged terrain, the Den is inherently a dangerous place. Please use caution while following this tour and obey all NPS rules and regulations, which among other things, prohibit rock climbing. Erosion is a major concern in the park. Whenever possible stay on well established trails or paths. Do not leave trash or debris behind. Only through a commitment by all visitors can the Den be kept an enjoyable and scenic location for future generations.

Stop # 1 - The Table Rock. To most tourists who come to Gettysburg, this large and notable boulder represents Devil's Den more than any other terrain feature. Indeed the Table Rock stands sentinel at the very entrance to the rocky bulwark and, due to its picturesque appearance, was the subject of many of the 19th century portraits. Regardless of where the actual Devil's Den is, this group of boulders, quite visible from Little Round Top, remains the most well-remembered feature in the vicinity.

The Table Rock, Tyson, 1867 stereo.
(Timothy H. Smith Collection)

Underneath the Table Rock, Tipton, 1880 stereo. This passage is covered with chisel marks. (Garry Adelman Collection)

The name "Table Rock" actually comes from the caption of an 1867 C. J. Tyson Brothers Stereo view (Negative # 538). Also called the "Balancing Rock" or "Hanging Rocks" in various tourbooks, it has been estimated to weigh between 200 and 600 tons.[1] As late as 1898, it was said that the effect of the battle upon these boulders could still be seen.

> The comet-shaped marks upon the boulders each show where a hostile bullet struck. These to be sure, rebounded, but left a portion of lead adhering to the rock. This, becoming oxidized by time and the rains, ran down upon the face of the rock....[2]

For decades during the late 19th century, this formation served as an open canvas for anyone wanting to carve their initials in the rocks. After the Government purchased the land, these carvings were carefully removed. The result is quite visible today all over the Den but particularly on the formation in front of you. "Scratch-outs," as well, can be seen on the very top of the Table Rock, and in the passages between the rocks. Walk around and underneath the formation before proceeding to the next stop. One particularly deep carving is visible through the chisel marks, on the wall of the eastern boulder, faintly reading "1872."

As You Walk, take the time to examine the coarse-grained, weathered diabase boulders surrounding you which figure prominently in accounts of the fighting.

Stop # 2 - The 4th Maine Monument. Standing in the Valley of Death teaches more about the plight of the 4th Maine than a multitude of Civil War books. The position assigned to them was low in elevation and vulnerable to enemy attack. Little Round Top was a Northern salvation in an abstract sense only. Although it was in Union hands and stood as a symbol of strength for the Yankees, the troops atop had just arrived and had no real means of actually helping the Maine men. As a result, a small regiment of less than 300 soldiers were at the weakest point in Ward's line and were charged with protecting the "trap door" to the Union left.

No regiment of that size, however, could have done its duty better in such a critical situation. Colonel Walker played the part of a military man to the hilt. Protesting the order to move into the valley, he did so despite his personal objections. When it became necessary, without orders, he led a charge back to the top of Devil's Den and formed the core of the final Union defense there. Although wounded, he retained command until the 4th Maine fell back.

Walker returned to the regiment a few months later and led it, and occasionally the brigade, through the summer of 1864, when he was again wounded at North Anna. Cold Harbor was the last battle for the 4th Maine; its term having finally expired after three years of intense and bloody fighting. Walker continued to be active in veterans' affairs until the time of his death in 1905. He wrote of the unit's history, compiled the final list of Gettysburg casualties and even designed the regimental monument at this tour

The 4th Maine Monument, Mumper, c. 1889 Stereo. (Garry Adelman Collection)

stop. On October 10, 1888, Walker addressed a "few" survivors of the regiment and turned the monument over to the Gettysburg Battlefield Memorial Association, "with the fervent hope that when the stone shall have yielded to the disintegrating hand of time, our flag will still be floating over an undivided country and a free people."[3] However, there were problems with the monument. In a short time it was in danger of leaning, snow and water had collected atop its boulder base, the red granite diamonds came loose and the flank markers were placed incorrectly. Through Walker's efforts, cement and stone chips, still visible today, were placed underneath to steady the monument, a groove was cut into the boulder to promote drainage, the diamonds were refastened with cement and the flank markers were relocated.[4] Well aware that his unit had made history, Walker wanted his 4th Maine Volunteers remembered with the same respect that it had commanded on the battlefields of the Civil War.

An additional tribute to the "4th ME" in the form of a rock carving is visible about twelve yards northeast of the monument.

Stop # 3 - The Slaughter Pen. Although the term "Slaughter Pen" is a tag sometimes attached to areas of carnage, history remembers but one such place at Gettysburg. The name was undoubtedly first used by those who had the misfortune of seeing the mangled corpses twisted among the rocks at the base of Big Round Top. Whether those who coined the term were soldiers or early visitors such as Alfred Waud or Alexander Gardner, will never be known for sure. Waud offers some insight, however, when he describes a sketch he drew in the area, "called by the soldiers the Slaughter Pen." Gardner used the

Slaughter Pen designation no fewer than six times in describing his own work in the area. Despite this recognition, the Pen remained largely obscure until William Frassanito located the site precisely and greatly popularized the "Slaughter Pen" term with the publication of his *Gettysburg: A Journey in Time* in 1975.

Like Devil's Den, the area of the Slaughter Pen has no certain boundaries. It seems reasonable, however, to include all of that area between the woodline at the base of Big Round Top, the Elephant Rock to the south, the modern road through Devil's Den to the west and roughly the footbridge over Plum Run to the north. Within these boundaries, Gardner recorded no fewer than fifteen bodies in addition to the one which Waud drew in his sketch.[5] Near the center of the Pen lies the Pond of Plum Run, the centerpiece of many 19th century views.

Stop # 4 - The Waud Rock. Alfred Waud came to Devil's Den as a sketch artist for *Harper's Weekly*. While there, he ran into Alexander Gardner's photographic crew.   Both Gardner's crew and Waud decided to momentarily ignore the general carnage and potentially profitable scenes surrounding them to expose the now-classic photograph of Waud upon this rock. Waud did in fact draw at least one scene near Devil's Den, but if he was working on one while this photo was taken, it has not survived in the Library of Congress collections with the remainder of his drawings.[6]

Unlike cameramen who were burdened with heavy equipment, sketch artists such as Waud traveled light, often accompanying the armies. Artists' renderings, unlike photographs, could show soldiers in action and did not require ideal atmospheric con-

The Slaughter Pen looking south, Tipton, c. 1888. The pond is in the foreground. (ACHS)

(Left) *Alfred Waud at Devil's Den, Gardner, July 1863. (Courtesy of William A. Frassanito,* Gettysburg: A Journey In Time*)*

(Below) *"Vincent's Brigade, Driven In," Waud, July 1863. The sketch for this engraving is on file at the Library of Congress. Waud's original title made no mention of Devil's Den, but later, someone penned the words "Devil's Den" onto the drawing. Although the scene is clearly not Devil's Den, it was used as such in* Battles and Leaders of the Civil War *and the mistake has remained until the present day. (Battles and Leaders)*

ditions. As far as Waud is concerned; he made precise, accurate drawings as his sketchwork repeatedly attests. His brother William was also a competent sketch artist.

The National Park Service plaque next to the rock portrays one of Waud's drawings. It was drawn at Gettysburg, but it was not sketched at the Devil's Den as is suggested by the plaque. It depicts a scene on Big or Little Round Top but, unfortunately, the site has not been precisely located.[7]

Stop # 5 - The Devil's Bath. It is not known when the "Devil's Bath" received its name, but it was presumably styled as such to conjure an image of the giant snake slithering out of its Den to bathe itself in the collected rainwater. Battlefield guides have called it the Devil's Bath or the "Devil's Basin" for decades but this pool might have been a relatively new addition at the time of the battle. Emanuel Bushman explained:

> By the way, it is not generally known that there was a large rock knocked off by lightning, which, perhaps, would have weighed 20 tons. The late Rev. Jos. Sherfy told me that he recollected the night very well when it was split off by a thunderbolt. He saw it the next morning. It was immediately to the right of the open cavern.[8]

It is speculation that this is the rock of which he spoke, but the evidence is compelling. It is clear that this rock was originally attached to the one above it, for they fit together like pieces in a puzzle.

This area saw horrible fighting as the men of the 2nd and 17th Georgia passed through it while Yankees poured fire down onto them from the rocks above. One man remembered two of his comrades being "shot through the top of the head by the almost vertical fire." He even located the site precisely. "The Government Avenue passes directly over the spot where they fell, and just beyond it is an iron sign with the words 'Devil's Den' on it." This sign is visible about 25 feet from the Devil's Bath.[9]

Stop # 6 - The Devil's Den. Whether viewing it in the daylight hours or after dark, one can easily understand how this place is named. This perpetually dark cave sparks the imagination with visions of evil things lurking inside. The person who pinpointed the exact spot for the Devil's Den was the man who largely popularized the name—Gettysburg historian John Bachelder. He described the Den as, "a hole in the ground" which is "very difficult to get into." According to Bachelder, as well as Emanuel Bushman, a spring once flowed though the cave. But the laying of the modern roadway has apparently disrupted the flow of water.[10]

The Devil's Den, Mumper & Co., c. 1888 stereo. (Timothy H. Smith Collection)

Anyone who cares to journey into and through the Devil's Den, is encouraged to bring a flashlight and to use caution. The quarters are cramped, the rocks are plentiful and, the large snake which supposedly lived here has never been found. Perhaps the "Devil" yet inhabits these rocks, amusing itself with its immense notoriety as it feasts upon those who dare to venture inside. For the bold-hearted, depending on body size, there are up to six different ways to enter and exit the Den.

Bachelder stated that very few people go near the Den because it is "masked by a big bowlder, and you cannot see it until you get within ten feet of it." In 1891, Samuel Wiley Crawford intended to place a plaque containing the Gettysburg Address upon this boulder, but the plans were never carried out.[11]

Stop # 7 - The Southeast Den. In the surrounding rocks Union skirmishers were positioned early in the fight, and Confederate "Sharpshooters" were there after the Den was taken. This area richly represents the unique rock formations which make up Devil's Den. Many tourists have enjoyed this vista over the years and took the time to make several rock carvings, as evidenced by the numerous "scratch-outs" in the vicinity.

Al Waud and John Bachelder both chose this angle to sketch the eerie nature of Devil's Den. Gettysburg photographers also recorded stereo views of this locale, one of which is reproduced here.

Stop # 8 - The Top of the Den. From the modern footbridge, gaze northeastward toward Little Round Top and imagine hundreds of hostile enemies shoot-

"The Southern Entrance to Devil's Den,"
Tyson, 1867 stereo. (GNMP)

Soldier gazing from Devil's Den toward Big Round
Top, Tipton, c. 1880 stereo. This is not a wartime
photograph as some have assumed. Apparently Tipton
hired someone to act the part of a soldier. The location
of this view can be found atop the Den. (Garry
Adelman Collection)

"...ravine from which the Rebels were driven by the 3rd Corps, called by the soldiers the
Slaughter Pen." Waud, July 1863. (Courtesy of William A. Frassanito, Gettysburg: A
Journey In Time)

ing down at you from that hill. So it was for the Confederates after they captured the Den.

To the east and south, the terrain is far more wooded than it was at the time of the battle. The woods to the east were thick, but the woodline was much farther up the slopes of Big Round Top. The woods to the south were largely absent at the time as well.[12]

Peering downward, you can see the many chasms which became temporary grave sites for many Confederate soldiers who, due to the rocky terrain, were simply tossed into the crevices in lieu of burial. Also, upon examination, the rock carving of "J. Tipton" is yet visible on top of the large group of rocks to the south of the footbridge. Incidentally, this bridge is but a replacement for several which came before it, but the type or date of the first bridge atop the Den remains a mystery.

Stop # 9 - The Dead "Sharpshooter." One of the most famous views of the entire Civil War was recorded at this spot. Comparison of the photograph to the actual site is verification that the photograph was taken here. Every crack in each rock is visible and, on certain days, the pool of water in the bottom of the view is evident. Unfortunately, the entire basis for this otherwise moving scene is fictional. The story of the "Dead Sharpshooter," killed about 70 yards away and moved by the photographers to this site, was researched and popularized by William Frassanito.[13]

In a 1925 article in the *Confederate Veteran*, it was said that the boy was recognized as an Andrew Hoge of the 4th Virginia, who was killed at Gettysburg. Unfortunately, the 4th Virginia fought far from Devil's Den—on Culp's Hill.[14]

The identity of this soldier will never be known for certain. Nonetheless, his sacrifice will always be remembered. The spot where he was initially photographed (four times) and at which he was almost certainly killed is southwest about 70 yards.

Stop # 10 - The Texas Brigade. Although the 1st Texas and 3rd Arkansas (half of Robertson's Brigade) were largely isolated for a time, they distinguished themselves in the fighting for the Den. Colonel Manning, in his official report just six days later, praised the conduct of his men:

> It would be invidious to make special mention of gallantry with either officers or men when all did so well, fighting greatly superior numbers and at a great disadvantage. I might safely assume that the bearing of the entire command was of the highest credible character.[15]

Colonel Work, who occasionally commanded the brigade, wrote:

> The success of the Texan regiments was not due to the training of Hood or any other commander, but that they were composed of the very pick and flower of an intelligent, educated, adventurous and high spirited people. Infused with the spirit of chivalry, the Texans on every battlefield displayed the sublime, fearless, exalted courage of the heroes of the

"The Dead Sharpshooter," Gardner, July 1863. (Courtesy of William A. Frassanito, Gettysburg: A Journey In Time)

Alamo and San Jacinto, adoring their Lone Star flag and guarding it with its unsullied record as a dutiful son [in] the name of an honored father.[16]

General Jerome Bonaparte Robertson continued to head the brigade, but his days in the field were numbered. Of his performance at Gettysburg, Lieutenant Colonel Work was extremely critical saying that Robertson "was not an eye witness to anything that occurred" during the fight on July 2nd.[17] Accompanying Longstreet westward after Gettysburg, he failed to distinguish himself and was soon transferred to Texas where he had charge of the reserve corps. Robertson busied himself in many occupations after the war, including railroads, until he died at Waco, Texas in 1891.[18]

The 3rd Arkansas took the heaviest casualties of any of the regiments around Devil's Den. Although outflanked and outnumbered, they rendered valuable service and performed valiantly until help arrived in the form of Anderson's Georgia Brigade.

Colonel Manning recovered from his Gettysburg wound only to receive another (in the thigh) at the Wilderness, where he was also captured. Released at the end of the war, he became an Arkansas lawyer and later a U.S. Congressman for three terms. He resumed the practice of law in Washington D.C., and died in November 1892.[19]

The plaque at which you are standing (erected in 1907) uses the term "Rocky Ridge." This is the name that Bachelder preferred for this elevation and, although obscurely, it remains over 100 years later.

Stop # 11 - The Triangular Field. Through this triangular-shaped field crossed the 1st Texas, the 20th Georgia and the 124th New York. Scores of writhing and dead soldiers of both armies littered the ground after the fight. This land-locked tract, owned by George W. Weikert, was of little value before the battle. The substantial stone walls on the north and southwest boundaries suggest that it was used as a pen for hogs or cattle.

It is not known if the eastern stone wall existed in that form at the time of the battle. Early maps of the field show it as a worm fence. If it were made of stone, it is difficult to explain why the 124th New York does not mention this wall in their accounts.

Notice the relatively limited scope of view from here. The knoll in the field to your left prevented troops from seeing and cooperating with those on the other side.

It has recently been written that a strange, ghostly phenomenon prevents modern tourists from taking successful photographs inside the boundaries of this field. However, numerous views have been shot within its borders with no supernatural interference.[20]

Stop # 12 - The 4th New York Independent Battery. This impressive monument was dedicated by Captain James E. Smith and several survivors of the battery 25 years after the battle. In his oration on that day, Smith, much enfeebled by rheumatism, lauded his own deeds as well as those of his battery at Gettysburg. That his men did good service in the Civil War is not in question, but James Edward Smith remains an enigma. He spent his remaining years justifying the actions for which he was never censured.

The placement of this monument is most certainly wrong. (See Appendix III.) Near the left flank marker of the 4th New York Battery is the rock containing the impressive carving "P. Noel.

Stop # 13 - The 99th Pennsylvania. You are now standing at the key to the Devil's Den position—a place where few soldiers had the desire or courage to stand at about 5:00 p.m. on July 2, 1863. It was around and for this spot that the battle for Devil's Den was fought. The 99th Pennsylvania, brought to this location as a reinforcement, was formed facing south and east, overlooking the Gorge. These Pennsylvanians fought hard at Gettysburg, losing almost 40% of their men. This only furthered their reputation as warriors and solidified their nickname, "the bloody 99th."[21]

Major John W. Moore was slightly wounded during the battle but retained command until the 99th retired. On September 10, 1864, Moore was awarded the colonelcy of the 203rd Pennsylvania. The beginning of 1865 marked the conclusion of this bright officer's life. In the assault on Fort Fisher, Moore led his men, flag in hand, to the parapet when he was "pierced by a rebel bullet." And so, "his spirit took its flight to join the boys of the Ninety-ninth 'gone before,' and his life blood mingled with the sands that were swept by the great Atlantic."[22]

Despite its modern appearance, this monument was dedicated on September 11, 1889. Initially, another monument stood in its place, having been erected three years before. When the Commonwealth of Pennsylvania allocated additional funds to each regiment for the purpose of erecting monuments, the current, larger one replaced the original. The 1886 monument presently stands about two miles to the north near the Angle.

This regiment also has the distinction of having in its ranks the only Medal of Honor winner for action around Devil's Den. Color bearer Harvey M. Munsell was recognized by General Ward as well as Major Moore, who commended him in his official report:

> The courageous conduct of Color Sergeant Harvey M. Munsell, and the manner in which he bore the regimental colors during the con-

The 99th Pennsylvania Monument at Devil's Den, Tipton, c. 1888 stereo. This monument was later moved and replaced by the current one. (ACHS)

flict, has induced me to make special mention of his case as one worthy of the most decided approval.[23]

He was given the Medal of Honor in 1866 for "gallant and courageous conduct as Color Bearer." His personal accomplishment is impressive, yet the entire regiment was deserving of the laurels of which Captain Albert Magnin spoke at the 1889 monument dedication. "Proud is the man who can say, 'I was at Gettysburg, and I wore the Kearny patch, and fought with the Ninety-ninth.'"[24]

Before moving on to the next stop, take a moment to consider the impregnable nature of Little Round Top. There were no trees on the eastern slope of Houck's Ridge at the time of the battle, making the view unobstructed.

Stop # 14 - The 124th New York. Dedicated exactly twenty-one years after the battle, this monument was both the first one built to honor a New York regiment at Gettysburg and the first at the Den. Erected before the State of New York had appropriated funds for monumentation, it was paid for by survivors of the regiment and the citizens of Orange County. The monument depicts none other than Colonel Augustus Van Horne Ellis himself. Ellis was brevetted a Brigadier General dating to the date of his death.[25]

The losses at Gettysburg for the 124th were crippling. Although it was the smallest Union regiment that fought atop the Devil's Den, it lost more men killed than any other in that area. It also lost all three of its original field officers—two killed and one wounded. Major Cromwell died with a gold locket on his breast containing a portrait of his young wife. After Gettysburg, Francis Cummins recovered from his wounds and became the second Colonel of the 124th New York, a position he held until severely wounded in the Battle of the Wilderness.[26]

The 124th served for the remainder of the war until mustered out on June 14, 1865. Five Medal of Honor recipients were within its ranks. The veterans of the 124th formed a society and made annual pilgrimages to Gettysburg to ponder the impossibility of events at that place. Over twenty men survived into the 1930s to deliver their legacies to future generations.[27]

Stop # 15 - Ward's Brigade. This plaque, erected by the GNMP Commission around 1912, is situated at roughly the center of Ward's line. Ward praised the numerous deeds of his brigade in his official report:

> This brigade, with the exception of Antietam, has been engaged in every battle fought by the Army of the Potomac, and has been frequently mentioned for its gallantry, but on this occasion it eclipsed all its former actions....The Third and Fourth Maine, Twentieth Indiana, and Ninety-ninth Pennsylvania Volunteers, the veterans of this brigade, to their world-wide reputation have added new laurels, and, if possible, excelled themselves. The First and Second U.S. Sharpshooters and the Eighty-sixth and One Hundred twenty-fourth New York Volunteers, recently assigned to this brigade, have richly earned the title to wear the "Kearny Patch."[28]

In the fight for Devil's Den, only six of Ward's eight regiments were engaged, and of those six, five of the commanding officers were killed or wounded. Almost 37% of the men in these six regiments became casualties during the battle, considerably more than the 24.3% for the entire Union army.

Had this brigade been under the command of a lesser man, casualties and accomplishments might have been fewer. But Ward performed his duty so fully on that afternoon that, in addition to being active all along his brigade's line, he kept his command together—by all means a difficult task. After the wounding of General Sickles, General Birney took charge of the Third Corps. Command of the 'red diamond' division then devolved upon Ward.

Veterans of the 124th New York at their monument on September 5, 1897, Tipton, 1897. It was during this visit to Devil's Den that previously unlocated graves of members of this unit were found. (USAMHI)

After Gettysburg, the division was moved into the Second Corps and Ward maintained his status as a brigadier, occasionally commanding the division. Fighting through the Wilderness and wounded at Spotsylvania he was highly regarded by most of his superiors. Surprisingly, Ward was placed under arrest on May 12, 1864 for alleged, "misbehavior and intoxication in the presence of the enemy." One even said that he was under arrest for "running away in the Wilderness battle." This does not sound like the General Ward of Gettysburg. Many prominent persons requested and demanded his reinstatement, but for reasons unexplained, he was never given a trial and was honorably mustered out of service on July 18, 1864.[29]

Ward returned to civilian life to become Clerk of the Superior and Supreme Courts of New York. Having just celebrated his eightieth birthday, he took a vacation in Orange County where one of his daughters was buried. On July 24, 1903, 40 years and three weeks after the Battle of Gettysburg, Ward was run over by a train and killed. Having kept his life through dozens of hard-fought battles, it is somehow fitting that Ward would be killed in Orange County—the final resting place of his daughter, and also the home of the old 124th New York Infantry—the "Orange Blossoms."

As You Walk toward Stop # 16, look into the woods on your right notice the flank marker which the 86th and 124th New York share. It is one of the few on the entire battlefield which is done in such a way. The same is true for the left of the 124th, which is coupled with the right of the 99th Pennsylvania.

Stop # 16 - The 86th New York. The monument in front of you was dedicated on July 2, 1888, exactly 25 years after the battle and commemorates

the deeds of the 86th on this field. At Gettysburg, the unit was commanded by Lieutenant Colonel Benjamin L. Higgins. Promoted to command of the regiment on the eve of battle, he performed well at Gettysburg until wounded by a shell fragment in Rose Woods. Higgins recovered to fight later that year at Mine Run. There he was shot through the "flesh of both thighs" and was "totally incapacitated." Higgins never returned to active duty and was mustered out seven months later.[30]

The 86th, however, continued to fight with the Army of the Potomac. Reenlisting in 1864, most of the men fought until the bitter end. They were present at Appomattox to witness the surrender of the Army of Northern Virginia. One remembered the excitement:

> Men who an hour before had been unable to stand from fatigue, capered about and cut "pigeon wings" with frantic glee. Bands played, flags waved, hats filled the air, the host of artillery and infantry joined in one grand, wild symphony of cannon and musketry that made those in the rear who had not yet heard the good news, think that the greatest battle of the war had commenced.[31]

The 86th was mustered out of duty in June 1865. Despite the horror of the Civil War and the loss in killed and wounded of 60% of its total number, a certain regret accompanied the muster out of the regiment:

> We bade adieu to the stirring life of camp and field to return once more to the peaceful monotony of rural life ... We bade farewell to comrades as brave as any that wore the blue, and as chivalrous as any knight that ever wore plate of Milan steel.[32]

As You Walk on the modern road through Rose Woods remember that at the time of the battle this area was a woodlot. In such a place, the trees are many but the current undergrowth was not present, allowing for a much better field of vision. Turn left onto Cross Avenue and halt at the 20th Indiana monument.

Stop # 17 - The 20th Indiana. Erected on October 28, 1885, the same day as almost all of the Indiana monuments at Gettysburg, this memorial stands near the right-center of the 20th's line. As the inscription reads, its colonel at Gettysburg, John Wheeler, was "killed near by." Someone painted that fact on a boulder about 40 feet from the monument. General Ward had only the most praiseful words for the fallen colonel.

A more gallant and efficient officer did not exist. The great State of Indiana may well feel proud of John Wheeler, the hero, the patriot, and the honest man. He was worthy to command the glorious 20th, and his command was proud of him.[33]

Wheeler remains the highest ranking officer from the state of Indiana killed at Gettysburg.

The woods between the monument and the Wheatfield to the north and west is the space which two companies of this regiment had to occupy when the 99th Pennsylvania was moved to the fighting atop the crest. Suffering the greatest total casualties of any Union regiment which fought around the Den, the 20th lost its Colonel (killed) and Lieuten-ant-Colonel (wounded) as well as 154 more men. Although the Lieutenant-Colonel, William Calvin Linton Taylor, was wounded at Gettysburg, he led the regiment until it was mustered out in the fall of 1864.

As you walk down Cross Avenue, you are advancing much as the men of the 86th New York (to the left) and 20th Indiana (to the right) did at the outset of the fight. Stop at the intersection of the old trolley path, which crosses the modern avenue and is now a peaceful trail through the woods. If you cross the bridge, you've gone too far.

Stop # 18 - Cross Avenue and the Trolley Bed. At this stop, turn around and look at the ridge behind you. Men of the 86th New York and 20th Indiana were the first troops to arrive on that ledge, but did not remain very long once the 3rd Arkansas entered the fray. Although unable to advance much further, and occasionally forced back, the men of the 3rd Arkansas reached and held this position during the early stages of the fight for Devil's Den. This is a spot that Colonel Van Manning of that regiment should have well-remembered, for it was in the vicinity of these rocks that a shell exploded in his face. Bleeding from his nose and forehead, he was dragged to the rear and Lieutenant-Colonel Robert S. Taylor took over. Hence, as the 3rd Arkansas and the 20th Indiana fought elements of each other, both lost their commanding officers and both had as a second in command a man named Taylor.

The trail ahead is what remains of the roadbed for the Gettysburg Electric Railway. Construction started here in 1893, and by the following year the trolley was in full swing. It operated under various names and owners until 1916, and the tracks themselves were removed in 1917. Today it serves as a walking trail, and is part of the Billy Yank Hiking Trail, used by the Boy Scouts of America.

As You Walk along this trail, the Triangular Field is visible as the clearing a few yards through the woods to your left. As the men of the 1st Texas advanced into this vicinity, the scene became one of disorderly frustration. With Rose Woods to their left and the knoll to their right, they were essentially isolated and exposed to the deadly fire from atop the hill. Unaware of the approaching Alabamians just a few hundred yards to the southeast and painfully aware that the Arkansans were at a stand-still to the north, the brave Texans charged onward against the "Orange Blossoms" and Smith's rifled guns, which looked all the more impressive perched atop the smoky, rock-strewn height.

Look to your right and notice the swampy ground upon which the trolley bed was laid. Tons of boulders were used in building up this roadway.

Boulder where Colonel John Wheeler of the 20th Indiana fell, Tipton, c. 1885 stereo. (ACHS)

Continue to walk some distance until you reach the steep ledge on your left which appears in the accompanying photograph. If you cross Plum Run, you have gone too far.

Stop # 19 - The Devil's Den Quarry. At this stop the reader can make a choice. The peculiarities of the ground here necessitate two separate paths, both of which have much to offer, but are difficult to see in an organized fashion. The first option, (a) more physically strenuous than the next, is to advance up the ledge, onto "Benning's Knoll," up the Gorge and then back to the trolley path. The alternative (b) is to simply remain on the trolley bed, cross Plum Run at the "trolley curve" and view the Slaughter Pen from the east. In any event, both routes will meet at Stop # 23 — Tipton Park.

The name of this stop refers to the numerous boulders which have evidently been quarried. The rock was used for the trolley, battlefield monuments, roads, bridges, steps and flank markers. In fact, the stone denoting the site where General Meade took command of the Army of the Potomac at Frederick, Maryland was quarried in this area. The large marks from chisels and the man-made edges are clearly visible on hundreds of rocks on both sides of the trolley path.

Stop # 20 - Benning's Knoll (option a). Standing atop what is herein referred to as "Benning's Knoll" one can obtain a fresh perspective of the fight for Devil's Den. Much of the slope of the Triangular Field is not visible and the terrain in all directions is difficult. Over this hill advanced

the left of the 44th Alabama and elements of the 2nd and 17th Georgia. It is plain to see how the main formation of Devil's Den forced Benning's Brigade, as well as the 44th Alabama, to split into two wings.

A U.S. government plaque stands at the northern side of the knoll. Erected in 1907, it tells a brief story of Benning's Georgians. "Old Rock" retained command of his brigade through the end of the war, and was severely wounded at the Battle of the Wilderness. In later life he resumed his law practice until he fell ill on the way to court and died shortly thereafter on July 10, 1875. Fort Benning, near Columbus, Georgia, is named in his honor.[34]

Of Benning's regimental commanders at Gettysburg, two were killed in action (Harris and Jones). One, like Benning, was wounded at the Wilderness (Hodges) and the last (Dudley DuBose) became a brigadier-general in November 1864. All of these men remain in Georgia with their former commander; in fact, all but DuBose are buried in Linwood Cemetery in Columbus.[35]

Stop # 21 - The Elephant Rock (option a). By far the tallest boulder in the Slaughter Pen, this split rock does not resemble much of anything unless viewed from the south. From that vantage point, however, it has been called the "Elephant Rock" and the "Turtle Rock."[36]

Its precipitous sides are difficult to climb, but people have been doing so for quite some time. In fact, the oldest existing rock carving on the battlefield is atop this chunk of diabase. It reads: "D. Forney 1849."

This rock formation is along the trolley bed at the base of Benning's Knoll.

The Elephant or Turtle Rock, Tyson, 1867 stereo. (Timothy H. Smith Collection)

Note: *At this point, you can advance up the Gorge by either taking the road or advancing through the rocks themselves, as the soldiers did. Either way, cross Plum Run near the modern comfort station in the Slaughter Pen.*

As You Walk up the Gorge: It may seem a reasonable assumption that the men of the 44th (in the Gorge) and 48th Alabama (in the woods to the east),

after having endured a plethora of physical hardships, were lucky that they were not ordered to attack the intimidating height of Little Round Top on July 2nd. But when one considers where they ended up instead, the supposition is questionable. There has never been a body of troops in history who could charge through this area, under fire, without losing formation. Such was the case for the Alabamians who attempted to do that very thing that summer afternoon. Suffering a greater percentage of casualties than the Alabama regiments which assaulted Little Round Top, these two regiments did their duty wholly.[37]

The right wing of William F. Perry's 44th Alabama advanced through this treeless ground in the Gorge. After Gettysburg, Colonel Perry continued as commander of the 44th, a position he held for over 20 months. In June 1864, he was promoted to the command of the brigade. Although he was in charge of the brigade until Appomattox, he would not earn the title of brigadier general until six weeks before the surrender. After the war, Perry returned to his former occupation as a professor at Ogden College in Kentucky. He survived until December of 1901.[38]

Spend as much time as you would like in this fascinating locale. The tour will pick up again at Tipton Park.

Stop # 22 - The "Trolley Curve" (option b). Despite the controversy that surrounded it, the electric trolley was a popular and effective means of seeing the battlefield. Like all modes of transportation, however, it had its share of problems. Cars passed

The Gorge. Walter Lane, c. 1965. Alabamians and Georgians moved through this area in their advance.

through this area only to arrive at Devil's Den and Little Round Top, unload, reload and turn back. Hence, a mechanism was placed on both sides of this curve to warn cars of others approaching. August 15, 1910 was an extremely busy day as Gettysburg and the Electric Railway employed extra cars to handle the more than 12,000 visitors in town. On that day the system failed and two cars collided head-on at this spot. No one was killed but six people were seriously injured. [39]

The most notable change to the area since the battle is the substantial growth of the woods. At the time of the fight, this place was only dotted with scattered trees. The modern footbridge is an addition as well, built in 1995 and subsequently swept away by rains and replaced, twice, in 1996. This is but one of a series of crossings to span Plum Run through the decades. Interestingly, this tour stop is just 40 yards north of the confluence of Plum and Rose Runs which figure so prominently on maps of the area. Also, within a stone's throw of this stop is a small marker with the letter "T" carved upon it, presumably denoting a boundary of Tipton's property.

As You Walk Along the trolley path: Hugging the base of Big Round Top was James L. Sheffield's 48th Alabama before it formed into line to duel with the 4th Maine. Sheffield commanded Law's Brigade at Gettysburg after Law ascended to divisional command. Sheffield's adjutant at Gettysburg said of him just five days after the battle, "I never saw a braver

man."[40] *He retained his position as Colonel until he resigned in May of 1864. He died, ironically, on July 2, 1893—exactly thirty years after the battle. One Confederate had the following to say of him, upon passing by his grave:*

> *Loyalty to the cause was one of the shining traits of his character. He fought its battles, and he honored its memory. He loved to meet and talk with Confederate soldiers. His character and his high record for bravery were all that he could leave his children.*[41]

Stop # 23 - Tipton Park. If you were standing in this vicinity a century ago, you would not see the comparatively peaceful area which we enjoy today. This tour stop is at the heart of Tipton Park, a booming tourist center consisting of several structures as well as a playground for children. During its heyday the trolley unloaded visitors here to enjoy their day around Devil's Den while visiting Tipton's photographic gallery, his restaurant and dance pavilion. Originally owned by Levi Mumper, the park lands were condemned by the GNMP Commission in 1901 and the buildings dismantled shortly thereafter.

The modern comfort station is a more recent addition, built in 1935.

Stop # 24 - The Trough Rock. Although not a particularly important feature, mystery surrounds this rock, for it is unknown as to when, or specifically why, the large trough was cut into it. By ex-

The Flowing or Trough Rock, Tipton, c. 1890. Notice the shadow at the lower right caused by the photographic studio. (GNMP)

amining photographs which include this rock, it seems that the trough was not present just after the battle, although some have asserted to the contrary.[42] This being the case, it seems reasonable that the cut was designed as a watering hole for horses. In fact, one photograph in an 1898 tourbook is captioned the "Flowing Rock," and shows a horse using the trough for just that purpose.[43] It is curious, however, that such a trough would be needed in close proximity to Plum Run. Incidently, the photographic studio built by Levi Mumper and later used to great advantage by William Tipton stood just a few feet south of this rock.

As You Walk, note that you are no longer on the trolley roadbed. This is part of the old vehicular road which wound its way toward Devil's Den from Little Round Top.

Stop # 25 - The Trolley Path and Warren Avenue. It was here that the trolley crossed the modern road. Looking southward toward the comfort station, the path of the old bed (somewhat easier to follow in the winter months) can still be seen. As the automobile became a more affordable means of transportation, the popularity of the battlefield trolley declined. It was at this spot on the fourth of July, 1909, that the two forms of transportation met in a "disastrous collision." A party of visitors from Chester, Pennsylvania, was touring the battlefield with a guide named William McCleary. Traveling west down Warren Avenue, the vehicle suddenly slammed into a trolley crossing the road in front of it. No one in the automobile or the trolley was seriously injured, but the guide, who was standing on the running board, was thrown with such force against the side of the trolley that three of his ribs were broken.[44]

Just south of this stop is one boulder which, for unknown reasons, was preserved in the face of destruction during the construction of the trolley. More than sixty holes were drilled in preparation for its demise. A broken-off drill bit is yet visible in one of its holes and the top portion of the boulder is missing.

As You Walk up the valley, look to your left and imagine the charge of the 4th Maine Regiment as they pulled out from the valley and surged up Houck's Ridge.

Stop # 26 - The 40th New York. Standing where they fought, in the Valley of Death, both the danger and the importance of the 40th's position can be appreciated. Losing 23 men killed and 120 wounded, there were but seven men reported as missing.

The 40th was to have its share of costly glory during the two years after Gettysburg. Colonel Egan was promoted to Brigadier and, dating to October 1864, was brevetted to the rank of Major General,

but not before he was twice wounded. Most of Egan's men re-enlisted and the regiment was not mustered out until June 27, 1865 —exactly four years to the day after its muster-in. Gettysburg represents but 12% of the 40th's casualties for the war. Its 1244 killed, wounded, and missing ranks 11th among all Northern regiments.[45]

The monument you see was dedicated exactly twenty-five years after the heroic deeds of the 40th occurred. At a cost of $2225 the regimental association chose to depict a soldier hiding behind a boulder in the valley. As is evident, the scores of boulders were not enough to shelter the large number of exposed men receiving fire on two fronts. Of interest is a carving upon a rock just to the south of the monument, which was probably done by a veteran.

As you walk, please return to the vehicular bridge, cross it and then proceed to the next stop. Crossing the marshy, winding, Plum Run is one of those things that sounds much more enjoyable than it actually is.

Stop # 27 - The 6th New Jersey. Based on their relatively low casualty figures, the 6th New Jersey might seem as if they had little share in the fighting which occurred here. Indeed they suffered fewer casualties, in total and percentage, than any other infantry regiment that fought in the area, Union or Confederate. A quick study of their position, however, explains, at least partially, the smaller casualty numbers in this unit. The men had the luxury of a virtually natural breastwork of large boulders. Houck's Ridge rose high above the men on the right of the line and the 40th New York was near their left.

The 6th fought on until August 1864 when it was mustered out as a mere skeleton of its former self. Only 200 men remained of the 898 who left the Garden State in 1861. Lieutenant Colonel Gilkyson, who was wounded before and after Gettysburg, once in each arm, recorded that during the war "their battle-scarred colors, ...were never dishonored".[46]

Stop # 28 - Smith's Rear Section. Placed in 1900, seven years after the death of James E. Smith, these two guns are almost certainly placed incorrectly (see Appendix III). Whether the position was here or about 120 yards to the south and west as some suggest, the devastation caused by these cannons was substantial. Only used during the period following the 4th Maine's departure from the valley until the 6th New Jersey's arrival, the effective fire of these Parrotts was felt by many Confederates near the Slaughter Pen and admired by Yankees on Little Round Top.[47]

Unknown to most visitors is the presence of the right flank marker to Smith's Battery. It is difficult to locate, but if you like a challenge, it can be found about 75 yards to the northwest of the 6th New Jersey Monument.

The 40th New York Monument, Tipton, c. 1888. The rock that partially blocks Mumper's photographic gallery is the same one mentioned at the previous stop. Note the presence of another early monument (the pole with the plaque attached) and the carving to the 40th New York on the rock at the base of the pole. (Boardman Collection)

The 6th New Jersey Monument in the Valley of Death, Mumper & Co., c. 1888 stereo. (Timothy H. Smith Collection)

Smith's Rear Guns, Tipton, c. 1900. The trolley and the monument to the 6th New Jersey can be seen in the background. (USAMHI)

Dotting the valley to the west and north are some markers to the United States Regular Infantry units which fought in this area. Arriving after Ward's men pulled out, the Regulars were roughly handled on July 2. All of the land around you at one time belonged to Samuel Wiley Crawford, whose monument is located some distance up the valley.

Excursions

Not part of the tour route, the following sites are included should the reader choose to visit them. Like most of the places on the Gettysburg Battlefield, they are worthwhile points of interest.

The Devil's Kitchen. This site is most easily visited by crossing the modern footbridge at the parking area, and walking up the slopes of Big Round Top on the path just to the left of the comfort station at Devil's Den. This trail leads through the heart of Tipton Park. About 175 yards up the path, a smaller trail branches to the right. Follow this trail until you come to the large formation of rocks. Walk around to the top of the formation for a more commanding view.

Somewhere between here and Little Round Top, skirmishers of Vincent's Union Brigade first engaged elements of the 4th and 5th Texas as they clamored over these rocks in their advance on that hill. Captain Lucius S. Larabee of Company B, 44th New York was killed on this skirmish line.[48] A visit to the Kitchen is a must during the winter season for the view through the leafless trees is excellent. It is not certain what type of view could be obtained from this vantage point in 1863, but the two 1880s views provided here show that it

was certainly more open at that time. Just to the south of the Kitchen can be found the remnants of a stone wall built by Confederate Soldiers on the evening of July 2 and the morning of July 3, 1863. On the Warren Map, this wall continued down the hill to the edge of the Slaughter Pen, but the section of the wall that ran through Tipton Park is now missing. Like the Devil's Den, Devil's Bath and Devil's Slipper, it is not entirely certain when or how this formation was named. It is referred to, however, in an 1898 tourbook:

> The Devil's Kitchen is about midway between Big Round Top and Devil's Den, and is the last point occupied by the Confederate Sharpshooters - being much more elevated than Devil's Den the sharpshooters had a clear range on Devil's Den and Little Round Top.[49]

The Slyder Farm. A direct, but somewhat difficult route to the farm is to simply follow Plum Run from the Gorge at Devil's Den south through the woods to the Slyder Lane. Although the ground is swampy and covered with thorn bushes, the advantage of this route is an opportunity to visit the "confluence" of Plum Run and Rose Run. This spot is clearly delineated on every map of the Gettysburg Battlefield, but rarely visited. It was also through this valley that the 44th Alabama moved in its assault on Devil's Den.

Another way to the Slyder Farm is to drive around to South Confederate Avenue. Just before reaching Plum Run, there will be a pullout on the left which affords a excellent view of the Slyder Farm. You may wish to stop here for a few minutes, as you are in close proximity to the Devil's Slipper. When

The "Devil's Kitchen," Tipton, c. 1888. (GNMP)

View looking toward the Valley of Death from the Devil's Kitchen, Tipton, c. 1888 stereo. The monument to the 6th New Jersey can be barely detected in the valley beyond the boulders in the foreground. (Boardman Collection)

you are ready, cross the bridge over Plum Run and head up the hill toward the Big Round Top parking lot. Before you reach this parking area however, a trail will be seen heading into the woods off to the left. This path, once called Kilpatrick Avenue, will take you past the monument to the 1st Vermont Cavalry, and down across Plum Run to the Slyder Lane, and Slyder farm.

A third alternative is to start at the Alabama or Texas Monument on Seminary Ridge and simply walk the route of the attack. This is not an easy task, but there is no better way to learn about the difficulties of the advance than to actually experience them. This is an extremely informative exercise on a hot summer day, even without marching twenty miles beforehand.

The John Slyder Farm sat directly in the path of Hood's Division when it advanced against the Union left on July 2. It must have been an impressive sight for the men of the 2nd United States Sharpshooters who were positioned in this area. A monument to Companies E and H from Vermont, and one to Company D from Maine, can be seen along the Slyder Lane. It was also in this vicinity that Evander M. Law detached the 44th and 48th Alabama regiments and sent them toward the Devil's Den. On the third day of the battle this area would be in the center of "Farnsworth's Charge" and after the battle the farm was used as a temporary field hospital for wounded of both armies.

There is some mystery as to when the Slyder house was erected, but it was most likely between 1849, when John Slyder purchased the land, and 1852. At the time of the battle the Slyder family included, John, his wife Catherine, and their children; William, Matilda, John, Hannah, and Jacob. In fact, one of the large stones around the house bears a carving, "W. J. Slyder 1852." This would be John's oldest son William James Slyder born April 19, 1836.[50] Nicknamed the "Granite Farm" by the NPS, a few scenes of the movie "Gettysburg" (Turner Pictures Inc., 1993) were filmed on this site.

The Challenge

Much of the new material upon which this book is based came about through the study of rare photographs. In terms of the Civil War, there can be no doubt that William Frassanito is the pioneer of this method of research. Under his tutelege, the authors have developed an intense passion for locating the exact camera positions from which these views were taken. It is only with practice that one begins to realize how challenging and exciting this exercise can really be. We have therefore included a group of seven previously unpublished photographs and challenge the reader to discover their locations. Good luck! (Hint: They are all located in the Devil's Den area.)

1. Tipton, 1867 stereo. (Timothy H. Smith Collection)

4. *Mumper & Co., c. 1878 stereo. Mumper entitled this view "Reflection scene." (Fields of Glory)*

2. *Mumper & Co., c. 1878 stereo. (Boardman Collection)*

3. *Mumper & Co., c. 1888 stereo. Something dramatic will be discovered when this location is found. (Timothy H. Smith Collection)*

5. *Tipton, c. 1890. Occasionally, the view is obscured in some manner. One must learn how to use the size and shape of rocks (as well as the cracks in them) to help find the location. (ACHS)*

6. *Tipton and Myers, 1869 stereo. The most difficult of the views presented here, its original caption is "Glen on Plum Run—Near the base of Round Top." (Boardman Collection)*

7. *Unknown photographer, c. 1900. What rock is the party sitting on?*
(Timothy H. Smith collection)

Appendix I

Order of Battle

The Army of the Potomac

Major General George Gordon Meade

First Corps—Maj. Gen. John F. Reynolds
First Division—Brig. Gen. James S. Wadsworth
Brigades: Meredith and Cutler
Second Division—Brig. Gen. John C. Robinson
Brigades: Paul and Baxter
Third Division—Maj. Gen. Abner Doubleday
Brigades: Rowley, Stone and Stannard
First Corps Artillery—Col. Charles S. Wainwright

Second Corps—Maj. Gen. Winfield S. Hancock
First Division—Brig. Gen. John C. Caldwell
Brigades: Cross, Kelly, Zook and Brooke
Second Division—Brig. Gen. John Gibbon
Brigades: Harrow, Webb and Hall
Third Division—Brig. Gen. Alexander Hays
Brigades: Carroll, Smyth and Willard
Second Corps Artillery—Capt. John G. Hazard

Third Corps—Maj. Gen. Daniel E. Sickles
First Division—Maj. Gen. David B. Birney
Brigades: Graham, Ward and DeTrobriand
Second Division—Brig. Gen. Andrew A. Humphreys
Brigades: Carr, Brewster and Burling
Third Corps Artillery—Capt. George E. Randolph

Fifth Corps—Maj. Gen. George Sykes
First Division—Brig. Gen. James Barnes
Brigades: Tilton, Sweitzer and Vincent
Second Division—Brig. Gen. Romeyn B. Ayres
Brigades: Day, Burbank and Weed
Third Division—Brig. Gen. Samuel W. Crawford
Brigades: McCandless and Fisher
Fifth Corps Artillery—Capt. Augustus P. Martin

Sixth Corps—Maj. Gen. John Sedgwick
First Division—Brig. Gen. Horatio G. Wright
Brigades: Torbert, Bartlett and Russell
Second Division—Brig. Gen. Albion P. Howe
Brigades: Grant and Neill
Third Division—Maj. Gen. John Newton
Brigades: Shaler, Eustis and Wheaton
Sixth Corps Artillery—Col. Charles H. Tompkins

Eleventh Corps—Maj. Gen. Oliver O. Howard
First Division—Brig. Gen. Francis C. Barlow
Brigades: Von Gilsa and Ames
Second Division—Brig. Gen. Adolph von Steinwehr
Brigades: Coster and Smith
Third Division—Maj. Gen. Carl Schurz
Brigades: Schimmelfennig and Krzyzanowski
Eleventh Corps Artillery—Maj. Thomas W. Osborne

Twelfth Corps—Maj. Gen. Henry W. Slocum
First Division—Brig. Gen. Alpheus S. Williams
Brigades: McDougall, Lockwood and Ruger
Second Division—Brig. Gen. John W. Geary
Brigades: Candy, Kane and Greene
Twelfth Corps Artillery—Lt. Edward D. Muhlenberg

Cavalry Corps—Maj. Gen. Alfred Pleasonton
First Division—Brig. Gen. John Buford
Brigades: Gamble, Devin and Merritt
Second Division—Brig. Gen. David M. Gregg
Brigades: McIntosh and I. Gregg
Third Division—Brig. Gen. Judson Kilpatrick
Brigades: Farnsworth and Custer
Horse Artillery—
Brigades: Robertson and Tidball

Artillery Reserve—Brig. Gen. Robert O. Tyler
Brigades: Ransom, McGilvery, Taft,
Huntington and Fitzhugh

The Army of Northern Virginia

General Robert Edward Lee

First Army Corps—Lt. Gen. James Longstreet
McLaws' Division—Maj. Gen. Lafayette McLaws
Brigades: Kershaw, Barksdale, Semmes and
Wofford
Artillery—Col. H.C. Cabell
Pickett's Division—Maj. Gen. George E. Pickett
Brigades: Garnett, Kemper and Armistead
Artillery— Maj. James Dearing
Hood's Division—Maj. Gen. John B. Hood
Brigades: Law, Robertson, Anderson and
Benning
Artillery—Maj. Mathis W. Henry

Second Army Corps—Lt. Gen. Richard S. Ewell
    Early's Division—Maj. Gen. Jubal A. Early
        Brigades: Hays, Smith, Avery and Gordon
        Artillery— Col. Hilary P. Jones
    Johnson's Division—Maj. Gen. Edward Johnson
        Brigades: Steuart, Williams, Walker and Jones
        Artillery— Maj. James W. Latimer
    Rodes' Division—Maj. Gen. Robert E. Rodes
        Brigades: Daniel, Iverson, Doles, Ramseur and
          O'Neal
        Artillery—Col. Thomas H. Carter

Third Army Corps—Lt. Gen. Ambrose P. Hill
    Anderson's Division—Maj. Gen. Richard H. Anderson
        Brigades: Wilcox, Mahone, Wright, Lang and
          Posey
        Artillery— Maj. John Lane
    Heth's Division—Maj. Gen. Henry Heth
        Brigades: Pettigrew, Brockenborough, Archer
          and Davis
        Artillery— Col. John Garnett
    Pender's Division—Maj. Gen. William D. Pender
        Brigades: Perrin, Lane, Thomas and Scales
        Artillery—Maj. William T. Poague

Stuart's Cavalry Division—Maj. Gen. J.E.B. Stuart
    Brigades: Hampton, Lee, Robertson, Jones
        Chambliss and Jenkins
    Horse Artillery—Maj. Robert F. Beckham
    Imboden's Command—Brig. Gen. John D. Imboden

Artillery Reserve—Brig. Gen. William N. Pendleton
    First Corps Artillery—Col. J.B. Walton
        Battalions: Alexander and Eshleman
    Second Corps Artillery—Col. J. Thompson Brown
        Battalions: Dance and Nelson
    Third Corps Artillery—Col. R. Lindsay Walker
        Battalions: Pegram and McIntosh

Appendix II

CASUALTIES FOR UNITS ENGAGED AROUND DEVIL'S DEN

These figures include casualties incurred by those units which fought at and around Devil's Den. In all of the units but one, the bulk of the casualties were inflicted on July 2nd, 1863. The exception is the 15th Georgia who suffered some 101 casualties on July 3rd, 1863. Strengths and losses come from Busey and Martin's, *Regimental Strengths & Losses at Gettysburg.*

UNITED STATES TROOPS

Regt.	Commander (Brigade)	Engaged	Killed	Wounded	Missing	Total	%
99 PA	Maj. John. W. Moore (Ward)	277	18	81	11	110	39.7
86 NY	Lt. Col. Benjamin L. Higgins (Ward)	287	11	51	4	66	22.9
124 NY	Col. A. Van Horne Ellis (Ward)	238	35	58	5	98	41.2
4 ME	Col. Elijah Walker (Ward)	287	11	59	74	144	50.2
20 IN	Col. John Wheeler (Ward)	401	32	114	10	156	38.9
2 USSS	Maj. Homer Stoughton (Ward)	169	5	23	15	43	25.4
40 NY	Col. Thomas W. Egan (DeTrobriand)	431	23	120	7	150	34.8
6 NJ	Lt. Col. Stephen Gilkyson (Burling)	207	1	32	8	41	19.8
4 NYLA	Capt. James E. Smith (Randolph)	126	2	10	1	13	10.3
TOTAL		2423	138	548	135	821	33.9

CONFEDERATE STATES TROOPS

Regt.	Commander (Brigade)	Engaged	Killed	Wounded	Missing	Total	%
44 ALA	Col. William F. Perry (Law)	363	24	66	4	94	25.9
48 ALA	Col. James L. Sheffield (Law)	374	9	66	27	102	27.3
1 TX	Col. Phillip A. Work (Robertson)	426	29	46	22	97	22.8
3 ARK	Col. Van H. Manning (Robertson)	479	41	101	40	182	37.9
4 TX Co. I	Lt. J.R. Loughridge (Robertson)	44	2	2	1	5	11.4
2 GA	Lt. Col. William T. Harris (Benning)	348	25	66	11	102	29.3
15 GA	Col. Dudley DuBose (Benning)	368	14	58	99	171	46.5
17 GA	Col. Wesley C. Hodges (Benning)	350	22	70	11	103	29.4
20 GA	Col. John A. Jones (Benning)	350	25	84	28	137	39.1
TOTAL		3102	191	559	243	993	32.1
COMBINED TOTALS		5525	329	1107	378	1814	32.9

Appendix III

Where Were Smith's Guns?

No serious attempt has been previously made to discuss precisely where Captain James Smith's guns stood on the afternoon of July 2, 1863. Researching the actions of the 4th New York Independent Battery on that day is frustrating, because Smith alluded many times to the battery's location, but only difinitively stated where it was not located, as opposed to where it actually stood.

The basic and undisputed fact is that Smith had six rifled guns in action around the Devil's Den. Four guns were located atop the hill and the remaining two were in the rear, covering the Plum Run Gorge.[1] Both positions are currently marked but are almost certainly done so incorrectly. As the rear section is only described in relation to the guns atop the hill, it is necessary to place the front sections first.

Several clues are helpful in an attempt to crack the frustrating code which has been left behind.

— Brigadier General Henry Hunt, Captain Smith and the Association of the 4th New York Independent Battery all condemn the location of the current monument and its guns. Smith described the monument's location as "in a hole." The site of the monument, nonetheless, was chosen in 1888 by James R. Hill and Frederick W. Watkins, both veterans of Smith's Battery who were present at the battle.[2]

— The two sections were in front and to the left of the 124th New York as well as in front of the 4th Maine for a time. Smith stated that during the bombardment the 124th "were in line directly in rear, below the crest of the ridge, and not being engaged, had a good opportunity to witness the conduct of the artillerists who were stationed on the rock bound crest of Devil's Den." Smith said that, at the outset, the 4th Maine was formed in rear as a support "under cover of a hill."[3]

— Smith also stated that there was only room for four guns atop the crest. He was very specific. "From the termination of the ridge at the "Den" to the woods dividing the "wheatfield" from the valley of Plum Run, the distance was not more than fifty yards. Here I could not place more than four guns on the crest. In rear of this ridge the ground descended sharply to the east, leaving no room

for the limbers on the crest, therefore, they were posted as near to the guns as the nature of the declivity permitted" The fifty yards that he discussed coincides closely with army standards of having artillery pieces 14 yards apart.[4]

— Smith wrote that during the charge of the 124th "they advanced to the crest like one solid line, boldly charging the enemy, who were about to capture the guns.[5]

— During the dedication of the 99th Pennsylvania monument Albert Magnin related to his comrades: "In a desperate effort to save Smith's New York Battery, and with your colors resting against one of the guns you made it the rallying point and saved the day.[6]

— Colonel Walker of the 4th Maine was "convinced that the key to the whole position [at Devil's Den] rested at the battery, although the possession of the guns themselves amounted to nothing." Walker stated that he was able to see the Rebels capturing Smith's battery while he was moving along his line in the Valley of Death. He further stated that when his men charged back to the top of the hill, they "halted on a line with the N.Y. Smith's guns."[7]

If the guns were not located where they stand today, there are only two possible locations for them— either in the field between Sickles Avenue and the Triangular Field, or on the crest of Houck's Ridge near the 99th Pennsylvania monument. Although most writers over the years, have aurgued in favor of the former position, the evidence available clearly points toward the latter. First, the eastern and more elevated site is arguably a better artillery position with at least as good a field of fire. There are more rocks at this position and one member of the 124th New York recalled that Smith went, "into position amid the rocks on [the] crest..."[8] Next, Smith discussed the "termination of the ridge at the Den". There does exist a termination at the eastern point where the western one lacks one if it is roughly fifty yards from the woods, and capable artillerymen know distances. Also, the eastern position coincides more with the left flank marker of the 124th New York as well as with the positions the 99th Pennsylvania and 4th Maine claim to have occupied during the fight.

Smith stated that he did not leave the limbers atop the hill because there was no room.[9] If the guns were in the forward position, there would have been plenty of room for the limbers atop the crest. Certainly Smith would have preferred to avoid the necessity of carrying the ammunition up the eastern slope of Houck's ridge if his guns were near the Triangular Field. Finally, and most importantly, Smith later recalled that he was with General Hunt at the position in 1888. Together they occupied the same large rock that they had occupied together 25 years earlier. Hunt said to Smith:

> Captain, get a painter and have painted upon this rock the fact that your left piece rested within a few feet , and to the north, of this point, and you will have a historical monument located upon the ground occupied by your guns on this ridge. If you had placed your pieces down where the monument stands, I would have arrested you for incompetency. It is not flattering to my intelligence as an artillerist to infer that I did countenance such a position while a better one was to be had.[10]

Today, we are left without a painted rock and no precise description. The word "down", however, is a key to the puzzle. In no other place around the monument can one properly refer to it as "down" other than east of the road on the higher ground.

The forward (or western) position has other problems as well. First, if the monument is "in a hole"

then so is the western position. It is not as good an artillery position as the rear one since it is lower in elevation and it is closer to the Triangular Field, where the enemy could come right up to the guns under cover of the slope. Also, there is probably room for more than four guns at this position and Smith repeatedly said that there was only room for four.

At the termination of the ridge at the eastern position there exist several large rocks, upon which two people may stand comfortably. At this position the ridge is approximately 60 yards from the woods and it is very plain to see how Smith had only room for four guns along it.

To further bolster the weight of evidence, Colonel Walker of the 4th Maine recalled that the key to the Devil's Den area was the position occupied by Smith's guns. The position closer to the Triangular Field can in no way be considered the key to Devil's Den, whereas the eastern position is far more commanding. Nor can one in any way observe what is happening at the western position from the vantage point of the 4th Maine's line in the Valley of Death, as Walker did. It is also important to note that the research has failed to unearth one contemporary source which places the guns in the field west of Sickles' Avenue. The weight of the evidence certainly lies toward the position nearer the crest of the Devil's Den Hill.

The rear section is somewhat of a puzzle as well. The position which is currently marked in the valley

A sketch drawn by James E. Smith showing the position of his guns. (A Famous Battery)

was placed in 1900, after Smith, Hunt and Bachelder had all passed away. It is approximately 320 yards in rear of the crest of Devil's Den. Yet Smith said that the rear section was only 75—150 yards in rear. He wrote 150 yards in his official report and later reduced the distance to "about seventy five yards" in the battery's history. It is plausible that he might have erred by some distance but not by 200%. In 1886 Smith wrote the that the section "occupied a hillock more in rear, and from that position raked the Plum Run gorge." Also, Smith made a drawing, supposedly near the time of the battle, which places the rear guns directly below the crest as opposed to far to the north; up the valley. Third Corps chief of artillery Captain George Randolph recalled, "The remaining two were placed in position a few yards in rear..." . With Randolph being an artilleryman as well, it is highly unlikely that he would refer to a sixth of a mile as "a few yards."[11]

One little-known facet of the Devil's Den area is the presence of Smith's right flank marker, which perhaps indicates the location of his rear guns, caissons and horses. Interestingly, this marker is about 200 yards in rear of the crest and is about 120 yards south and west of the current placement of the rear guns. The position of the guns near the flank marker fits in with all available evidence as to its location during the battle. Smith recalled firing "obliquely through the gully" with these guns, something he could well do from this position. The 6th New Jersey was said to have advanced directly in front of the guns, which is just how it appears in relation to their monument.

The above exercise is frustrating, since there are a few eye-witnesses and elusive but occasionally concise statements from Captain Smith. His words must be appraised and pieced together with the other known writings of the position of his guns.

A competent officer by all accounts and a newly-wed in 1863, his defining moment was at Gettysburg when he heroically guarded the Union left flank and lost three of his guns as a result. From 1863 until the day he died, he vehemently defended his actions during the battle and constantly justified the loss of his guns. No written document, official or unofficial, has surfaced that censures him or his battery in the least for the loss of the guns at Gettysburg. In fact, Third Corps Artillery Chief Captain George Randolph praised Smith's actions.

I regret the loss [of the guns], but from my knowledge of the position and of the gallantry displayed by Captain Smith, I am convinced that it was one of those very unpleasant, but yet unavoidable, results that sometimes attend the efforts of the most meritorious officers.[12]

Although correspondence reveals nothing but heroic mentions of Smith's actions at Gettysburg, many pages in his book, *A Famous Battery and its Campaigns*, are dedicated to defending the loss of his guns. Smith's writing is generally accurate but his personal defense renders many of his statements questionable. Unfortunately, he seems to have been the only member of the battery to have published anything on the performance of the 4th New York in the summer of 1863.

The plot thickens when one considers Smith's officers. 1st Lieutenant Thomas Goodman and 2nd Lieutenant Jeremiah S. Clark, both of whom were attached to the battery from other commands, are conspicuously absent from all of Smith's writings. In fact, he praised all men in the battery except the officers by saying in his official report, "The non-commissioned officers and privates conducted themselves throughout the day with commendable bravery." Despite any of Smith's personal short-comings, he and his battery rendered valuable service on July 2. Perhaps Smith would have been better served by ending the matter the way he closed his official report: "I trust no blame will be attached to me for the loss of my guns. I did that which in my judgment I thought best."[13]

Notes

Pre-Battle History

1. Over the years a great many people have made this mistake. See The Wolf Family, *A Simplified Tour of the Gettysburg Battlefield* (Gettysburg: Audio-Tronic Tape Tours, 1975), 21; B. Keith Toney, *Gettysburg: Tours & Tales with a Battlefield Guide* (Publishers Press, Inc., 1994) 92.

2. Michael Jacobs, "Later Rambles Over The Field Of Gettysburg," *United States Service Magazine* (New York: 1864), Vol. 1, 67-68. Another early reference to the geology of the area was written by Aaron Sheely and appeared in the *1886 History of Adams County, Pennsylvania* (Chicago: Warner, Beers & Co., 1886), 44-54. Page 48 deals specifically with the formations on the southern end of the battlefield.

3. Andrew Brown, *Geology and the Gettysburg Campaign* (U.S. Geological Survey, 1962), 1; George W. Stose, *Geology and Mineral Resources of Adams County Pennsylvania* (Harrisburg: 1932), 72; William R. Shirk, *A Guide to the Geology of Southcentral Pennsylvania* (Chambersburg: 1980), 66.

4. Brown, 9.

5. Stose, 66. Diabase is "composed dominantly of white or gray plagioclase and black pyroxene, with accessory quartz and magnetite, and in places hypersthene, biotite, and olivine." The abundance of dark minerals gives the diabase its dark-gray appearance. In early accounts of the Den, this diabase is often incorrectly refered to as "granite" or "syenite."

6. Stose, 66-70; *Big Round Top Loop Trail*, A pamphlet published by Eastern National Park & Monument Association (April, 1987).

7. Shirk, 74-75.

8. Ibid.

9. "Found Tomahawk," Gettysburg *Star & Sentinel*, October 10, 1906. John Thorn was the son of Peter and Elizabeth Thorn, caretakers of the Evergreen Cemetery at the time of the battle.

10. "The Country Around Gettysburg," Gettysburg *Compiler*, August 20, 1869.

11. *Relics of the First Battle of Gettysburg; Pre-Columbian Era of American History* (Gettysburg: Star & Sentinel Book And Job Office, 1869), 7. A copy of this rare pamphlet can be found in the Natural History File 190, Adams County Historical Society (ACHS).

12. Antique, "The Indian Field," *Compiler*, January 29, 1880. From the content of the article it is clear that "Antique" is actually Emanuel Bushman.

13. Ibid.; Emanuel Bushman, "Interesting Local History," *Compiler*, April 19, 1887, and "Indian Field," *Adams County Independent*, February 6, 1897.

14. Bushman, "The Indian Field;" *1886 History of Adams County*, 237. In his 1880 article, Bushman wrote that for "traditions and facts I mostly owe to my immediate ancestors and the two Armstrongs and the Works and Woodses." In an 1884 article he credited his family, the Armstrongs, and the Sherfys.

15. Emanuel Bushman, "Devil's Den," *Compiler*, August 19, 1884.

16. Bushman, "Interesting Local History." One of Bushman's ghost stories (not concerning Round Top) appears in the *Compiler* for January 12, 1886.

17. Antique, "The Indian Field."

18. Bushman, "Devil's Den."

19. Robert L. Bloom, *History of Adams County, Pennsylvania: 1700-1990* (Gettysburg: ACHS, 1992), 5-6; *1886 History of Adams County*, 12-23.

20. Charles H. Glatfelter and Arthur Weaner, *The Manor of Maske: Its History And Individual Properties* (Gettysburg: 1992), 7-21. For even more detail see Glatfelter and Weaner, *Monographs on the Individual Properties within the Manor of Maske*, ACHS.

21. Glatfelter and Weaner, *Manor of Maske*, 14, 59. According to Glatfelter, considering the nature of the ground "it is understandable that the first settlers in the manor would look elsewhere for desirable tracts on which to locate themselves and their families."

22. Glatfelter and Weaner, *Manor of Maske*, 32, 38, 39, 41; Emanuel Bushman, *Compiler*, November 2, 1886; Bushman, "The Indian Field;" Bushman, "The Devil's Den." In his various recollections, Bushman remembered the early settlers as his grandfather Jacob Bushman, the elder Sherfy, his great uncles, Michael Miller and Andrew Bushman, the Armstrongs, Works, and Woodes. This list of settlers is by no means intended to be complete, and includes only those who were well-known residents of the area.

23. In 1873 Bachelder wrote that the "hill was nameless prior to the battle, but has since been known as Little Round Top." John B. Bachelder, *Gettysburg:What to See and How to See It* (New York: Lee, Shepard, & Dillingham, 1873), 11. For more information concerning the naming of the Round Tops see William A. Frassanito, *Early Photography At Gettysburg* (Gettysburg: Thomas Publications, 1995), 242-246.

24. The height of Big Round Top is taken from the USGS map of the Gettysburg area published by the Department of the Interior. The *1886 History of Adams County*, 237, records Big Round Top as being 799 feet high. The Warren Map (c. 1869) gives the hill the ominous height of 666 feet, but that survey is based on a benchmark at Cemetery Hill of 500 feet. Cemetery Hill is actually 620 feet, making a difference of about 120 from the actual elevations and those on the Warren Map.

25. Glatfelter and Weaner, *Manor of Maske*, 16, 33.

26. *Adams County Deed Book F*, 486-488; *Will Book I-J*, York County Court House, 146; Glatfelter and Weaner, *Manor of Maske*, 39; Recital Deed, Andrew Guinn to William and John Guinn, April 26, 1832 (original at GNMP).

27. Emanuel Bushman, "Round-Top on Fire," *Compiler*, November 2, 1886; McPeak Family File, ACHS; Glatfelter and Weaner, *Manor of Maske*, 40. A letter

in the McPeak Family File, ACHS, also relates that Big Round Top was once known as "McPeak's Hill." Sarah McPike (also recorded as McPeak) was the daughter of Daniel McPike who came to this area from Chester County about 1767 and died in Cumberland Township in 1787. He probably owned Big Round Top after Adam Linn and then bequeathed it to his daughter. It should be pointed out that on the Reading Howell Map of Pennsylvania published in 1792, two places are indicated as "Round Top" in what is now Adams County, and neither is the Big Round Top on the battlefield.

28. Emanuel Bushman, "Letter to the Editor," *Compiler,* March 15, 1887.
29. Bushman, "Round-Top on Fire." The Armstrongs, who appear in many of Bushman's stories, were early property owners south of Devil's Den.
30. Tax Records of Cumberland Township, 1858-1863; Kathleen R. Georg, 1863 Land Ownership Map for the properties on the Gettysburg Battlefield, GNMP; Estate Papers of Hugh Guinn Scott, ACHS.
31. Glenn Tucker, *High Tide At Gettysburg* (Indianapolis: The Bobbs-Merrill Company, 1958), 248. According to USGS Maps, Little Round Top is 550 feet above sea level. A 1906 guide book states that "the west face of [Little Round Top] had been cleared of timber the year before the battle, as though to prepare it as the bloody altar it became on the 2nd of July '63, when 500 brave men there shed their blood that the Union might survive. See William A. Scott, *The Battle of Gettysburg* (Gettysburg: Wm. A. Scott, 1906), 17.
32. See Frassanito, *Early Photography,* 242-245.
33. William H. Swallow, "The Second Day at Gettysburg," Southern Bivouac (January 1886), No. 4, 494.
34. Glatfelter and Weaner, *Manor of Maske,* 38.
35. Today this stone structure (built c.1820) is known as the Rose Farm. For more information on the Jacob Sherfy family (owners of Devil's Den from 1805-1845) see Kathleen R. Georg, *History of Rose Farmhouse and Farm* (GNMP, 1982), 2-25; and Wm. Emory Sherfey, *The Sherfy Family in the United States 1751-1948* (Greensburg, Indiana), 195.
36. *Adams County Deed Book S,* 301-307; Georg, *History of Rose Farm,* 25-26.
37. Tax Records of the Borough of Gettysburg and Cumberland Township, Adams County, Pennsylvania, 1848; *Adams County Deed Book MM,* 201; Georg, *Rose Farm,* 26-27. The early tax records of Adams County can be examined at the ACHS.
38. Obituary of John Houck, *Star and Sentinel,* August 10, 1881. At the time of his death he was the oldest citizen of Gettysburg at 94 years of age. John Houck was married to Samuel McCreary's sister.
39. Tax Records, 1848-1863; *Adams County Deed Book MM,* 201.
40. *Star and Sentinel,* August 10, 1881; *Compiler,* March 25, 1867; Tax Records, 1863.
41. 1860 United States Census, Gettysburg, Adams County, Pennsylvania, 196; Agnes Barr, Civilian Accounts, ACHS. This is a handwritten, untitled account of the battle of Gettysburg. Agnes Barr was Houck's next door neighbor.
42. *Star and Sentinel,* August 6, 1881; *1886 History of Adams County,* 93, 96, 191, 192.
43. Georg, 1863 Land Ownership Map.
44. It was referred to as "Houck's Ridge" as early as 1873. For examples see Bachelder, *Gettysburg,* 12; *1886 History of Adams County,* 48; In "The Pennsylvania Reserves at the Battle of Gettysburg," an article by Samuel W. Crawford which appeared in the Philadelphia *Weekly Press* on September 9, 1886, the high ground north of Devil's Den is referred to as "Houck's Hill." This hill or ridge varies in height, it highest point being 440 feet above sea level, 110 feet lower than Little Round Top.
45. Glatfelter and Weaner, *Monographs on the Individual Properties,* ACHS, Tract 57A, 57002.
46. *Map of Adams & York Counties* (D. Small & W. Wagner, 1821); J. D. Rupp, *The History And Topography Of Dauphin, Cumberland, Franklin, Bedford, Adams, and Perry Counties* (Lancaster City: 1846), 525.
47. *Map of Pennsylvania: Constructed from the county surveys authorized by the state and other original documents* (John Melish, 1832); and *Map of Pennsylvania* (Philadelphia: R. L. Barnes, 1848 and 1850). It should be noted that Plum Run is a common name for a stream. On early maps of the area there are three other Plum (or Plumb) Runs in Adams County alone, one each in Freedom, Reading and Mount Joy Townships.
48. Copies of these maps can be found at the ACHS.
49. Bachelder, *Gettysburg,* 11-12. For a discussion of early cartography on the Gettysburg Battlefield see Frassanito, *Early Photography,* 7-19. It should be mentioned that the official report of Joshua Chamberlain, dated July 6, 1863, which appears in the printed version of the *Official Reports Of The Union And Confederate Armies* (Washington, 1889), Series 1, vol. 27, Part 1, 623 (Hereafter cited as OR), does mention "Plum Run," "Little Round Top," and "Granite Spur," by name. If this report actually dates from July 1863, it would be the first recorded reference for all three place names. Documents recently uncovered at the National Archives, however, now call into question the origin and date of this document. More than likely, what appears in the OR is a postwar revision of Chamberlain's original report, in which he made no reference to Little Round Top or Plum Run, and mistakenly referred to Big Round Top as "Wolf's Hill." A copy of the original report is on file at the Maine State Archives.
50. John M. Butler, *The Battle of Gettysburg: A Historical Account* (Philadelphia: 1885), 36; Jacob Hoke, *A Guide to the Battle-field of Gettysburg* (Dayton: 1887), 21-22. Butler's 1885 guide book states, "In between the Devil's Den and the Round Tops, the valley is called the Valley of the Shadow of Death. Such indeed it proved!" As prevalent as the "Valley of Death" nickname appears to be in early tour books, the term "Bloody Run" is conspicuously absent. No reference for the term could be found in any early tourbook. The story seems to have been fabricated much more recently than previously thought.
51. For early use of the term "Gorge" see *OR* 27, Part 1, 509, 588, and Part 2, 420, 425. See also Harry W. Pfanz, *Gettysburg: The Second Day* (Chapel Hill and London: University of North Carolina Press: 1987), 501.

52. For early references to the name "Slaughter Pen" see Alexander Gardner, *Gardner's Photographic Sketch Book Of The Civil War* (Washington, D.C.: Philp & Solomons Publishers, 1866), Vol. 1, plate 44; Anchor, "A Visit To Gettysburg," *Army and Navy Journal*, June 8, 1867. Anchor is actually the pseudonym of John Watts De Peyster. Besides early postwar accounts, the term Slaughter Pen was not used to describe this area until its resurrection from oblivion by William Frassanito in 1975 with the publication of *Gettysburg: A Journey in Time* (New York: Charles Scribner's Sons, 1975), 173-175. The terms "Slaughter Pen" and "Gorge" describe basically the same area and are used interchangeably in this book.

53. Tax Records, 1863; 1860 Agriculture Census, Cumberland Township, Adams County, Pennsylvania; Kathleen R. Georg Harrison, "Our Principal Loss was in this Place," *Gettysburg: Historical Articles of Lasting Interest* (Dayton: Morningside Bookshop, July, 1989), No. 1, 48. From the lack of underbrush or tall grass in an 1863 Brady photograph of Houck's property, it appears that the cattle were in the valley for some time preceding the battle, and not just hidden there to avoid capture by the southern army.

54. *1886 History of Adams County*, 48.

55. Ibid. There are many small quarries still visible in the Devil's Den area. It is difficult, however, to tell if any are pre-battle. After the war, diabase in this area was used "for monuments and tablets to mark positions on the battle-field." This stone, called "Gettysburg Granite," by locals, was used mostly for flank markers and the bases of several monuments around the field. The 91st Pennsylvania monument erected on Little Round Top in 1883, the marker that today designates the spot where Weed and Hazlett fell, was carved from a block of "Gettysburg Granite from Devil's Den." See "Gettysburg Granite," *Compiler*, April 24, 1888; *Compiler*, August 29, 1883; untitled newspaper clipping from J. Howard Wert Scrapbook, Vol. 32, 212, ACHS.

56. Journal of Anna Cecilia Keller Haupt: December 18, 1842-December 18, 1843, *Herman Haupt Papers*, Yale University, 27 (transcribed copy in Haupt Family File, ACHS).

57. "The Methodist Church in Adams County," *Compiler*, February 26, 1880.

58. Holman D. Waldron, *With Pen And Camera On The Field Of Gettysburg In War And Peace* (Portland: 1898).

59. *OR* 27, Part 1, 558.

60. F. M. Stoke to J. M. Stoke, October 26, 1863, Special Collections, Gettysburg College. F. M. Stoke was more than likely Francis M. Stoke, a member of Co. F, 1st Battalion, Pennsylvania Militia. This unit was "organized just previous to the invasion of the State...and...performed guard and provost duty at various points in the State." Upon the expiration of its term, it was reorganized as part of the 187th Pennsylvania. Stoke, a resident of Cumberland County, served with this unit to the end of the war. See Samuel P. Bates, *History of the Pennsylvania Volunteers, 1861-1865* (Harrisburg, Pa: 1870) Vol. 5, 222, 230, 238.

61. John B. Bachelder, *Descriptive Key To The Painting Of The Repulse Of Longstreet's Assault At The Battle Of Gettysburg* (New York: 1870), 50-51; John Bachelder Sketchbook, in the Gilder Lehrman Collection on deposit at the Pierpont Morgan Library. Another sketch, of Hanover Junction, PA, is dated July 11, 1863. It is therefore probable that he arrived on the field by at least July 12.

62. Bachelder, *Descriptive Key*, 50-51; John B. Bachelder, *Isometrical Map of the Battlefield* (Philadelphia: 1864).

63. Bachelder, *Gettysburg*, 12.

64. *The United States Vs. A Certain Tract of Land in Cumberland Township, Adams County, State of Pennsylvania*, In The Circuit Court of The United States for the Eastern District of Pennsylvania, October Sessions 1894, Third Circuit, 288-289. The testimony was given between Setember 11 and 19, 1894. A bound transcript of the testimony can be found in the historian's office at the GNMP.

65. Benson Lossing, *Pictorial History of the Civil War in the United States of America* (Hartford: Thomas Belknap, 1868), 67. The engraving is very well drawn, and one has little trouble finding this formation on the side of Little Round Top today.

66. Comte De Paris, *History of the Civil War In America* (Philadelphia: Porter & Coates, 1883), 542. This is a translation of the French edition that was originally published in 1874.

67. Wm. Y. W. Ripley, *Vermont Riflemen in the War for the Union, 1861-1865. A History of Company F, First United States Sharp Shooters* (Rutland: Tuttle & Co., 1883), 115.

68. Butler, *The Battle of Gettysburg*, 36.

69. *Maine At Gettysburg, Report of Maine Commissioners Prepared By The Executive Committee* (Portland: Lakeside Press, 1898; Reprint, Gettysburg: Stan Clark Military Books, 1994), 160.

70. William F. Perry, "The Devil's Den," *Confederate Veteran*, (April, 1901), Vol. 9, 161.

71. Francis Trevelyan Miller, *Gettysburg: A Journey to America's Greatest Battleground in Photographs* (New York: The Review of Reviews Company, 1913).

72. William F. Fox, ed., *New York at Gettysburg*, (Albany: J. B. Lyon Company, 1902), 37. For more information concerning the use of the term Devil's Den, see Frassanito, *Early Photography*, 266-268.

73. "Col. Egan's Charge," *Compiler*, July 1, 1884; "Round-Top, "*Compiler*, August 5, 1884.

74. Bushman Family File, ACHS; 1860 United States Census, Adams County, Gettysburg, 181; Obituary of Emanuel Bushman, *Star and Sentinel*, December 19, 1899. At the time of the battle, a tenant farmer resided at the farm. The Bushman Farm still stands today.

75. Emanuel Bushman, "Devil's Den."

76. Ibid.

77. "Stories Of The War," newspaper clipping dated February 13, 1886, from a J. Howard Wert scrapbook, 119, ACHS. It is intriguing to note that both Captain Smith's OR and the Comte De Paris' account state that the Devil's Den is a "Cave" or a "Cavern." Another early Gettysburg visitor wrote in 1865 that

Devil's Den was "a dark cavity in the rocks." See J. T. Trowbridge, "The Field Of Gettysburg," *Atlantic Monthly* (November, 1865), No. 16, 622.

78. Devil's Den," *Compiler*, March 2, 1886. This article was originally published in the Lancaster *Intelligencer*.

79. *United States Vs. A Certain Tract of Land*, 288-289. In this statement, Bachelder seems to contradict his earlier 1873 account as to what the Devil's Den consists of. Bachelder's term "Rocky Ridge" never caught on, and like "Weed's Hill," his preferred name for Little Round Top, and "Buford's Ridge," his preferred name for eastern McPherson's Ridge, is not used by historians.

80. Emanuel Bushman, "Big Snake," *Compiler*, August 12, 1875. Other articles that talk of giant snakes can be found in newspapers at the time. See "The Boss Snake Story," *Compiler*, July 18, 1883 (this article claimed that a skin from a blacksnake found in Codorus Township, York County, measured over 14 feet), and "As Big As A Stove Pipe," newspaper clipping in Henry Stewart scrapbook, ACHS no. 31, 35. This article, from the turn of the century, tells of a hunter on Wolf's Hill encountering a 14 foot snake.

81. *Inventorying and Monitoring Protocols of Vertebrates in National Park Areas of the Eastern United States* (Gettysburg National Military Park and Eisenhower National Historic Site: June, 1995), i, 90-91. The seven other snakes are; the Ringsnake, Black Rat, Eastern Hognose, Northern Water, Garter, Northern Copperhead, and Timber Rattlesnake. Because of the popularity of Devil's Den since the battle, very few snakes are seen among its rocks. However, more snakes than ghosts have been observed in the area.

82. Roger Conant and Joseph T. Collins, *A Field Guide to Reptiles and Amphibians* (Boston: Houghton Mifflin Company, 1991), 183-184; Raymond L. Ditmars, *The Reptiles Of North America* (New York: Doubleday & Company, 1936), 191-194. The Black Rat Snake is similar in size and appearance to the Northern Black Racer and shows many of the same characteristics.

83. Salome Myers Stewart File, ACHS. For more information see Sarah Sites Rodgers, *The Ties of the Past: The Gettysburg Diaries of Salome Myers Stewart, 1854-1922* (Gettysburg: Thomas Publications, 1996).

84. Salome Myers Stewart "Reminiscences of Gettysburg," Chattanooga *News*, October 30, 1913. Copy of original letter to the Chattanooga *News* in the Salome Myers Stewart File, ACHS. In Jack McLaughlin's, *Gettysburg: The Long Encampment* (New York: Appleton-Century, 1963), 92, Devil's Den during the battle is described as an "eerie place of rocks and gullies, and if anyone happened to be looking, poisonous snakes."

The Battle for Devil's Den

1. Ezra J. Warner, *Generals in Blue* (Baton Rouge and London: Louisiana State University Press, 1964), 537, 538, 669; Mark Mayo Boatner III, *The Civil War Dictionary* (New York: David McKay Company, Inc., 1959), 889; John W. Busey and David G. Martin, *Regimental Strengths and Losses at Gettysburg* (Highstown, N.J.: Longstreet House, 1986), 50. Un-less otherwise stated, the strength of units as well as casualty figures for the remainder of this book come from the latter source.

2. Edmund J. Raus, Jr., *A Generation on the March: The Union Army at Gettysburg* (Lynchburg, Va.: H. E. Howard Inc., 1987, 80, Reprint. Gettysburg, Pa: Thomas Publications, 1996); Charles H. Weygant, *History of the One Hundred and Twenty-Fourth Regiment*, N.Y.S.V. (Newburg, N.Y.:Journal Printing House, 1877), 170; Robert A. Braun, "The Fight for Devil's Den," *Military Images*, July-August, 1983, 5-12.

3. Raus, 22; Boatner, 61-62; *Maine at Gettysburg*, 185.

4. Raus, 73; *New York at Gettysburg*, 700-701.

5. Raus, 128; John P. Nicholson, ed., *Pennsylvania At Gettysburg, Ceremonies At the Dedication of the Monuments Erected by the Commonwealth*, Vol. 1, 532-541.

6. Raus, 20.

7. Ibid., 156; Boatner, 736.

8. Raus, 90; *New York at Gettysburg*, 1294; June 30, 1863, Muster Roll of the 4th New York Independent Battery, National Archives and Records Administration, Washington, D.C. (hereafter cited as NARA).

9. Raus, 59; Warner, *Generals in Blue*, 31, 139, 140, 237.

10. Raus, 52.

11. Harold B. Simpson, *Hood's Texas Brigade: A Compendium* (Hillsboro, Texas: Hill Jr. College Press, 1977), 10; Boatner, 703.

12. Simpson, 251; Robert K. Krick, *Lee's Colonels* (Dayton, Ohio: Press of Morningside Bookshop, 1991), 262.

13. Ezra J. Warner, *Generals in Gray* (Baton Rouge and London: Louisiana State University Press, 1959), 236-237; Boatner, 642.

14. Krick, 340.

15. Ibid., 184; Lillian Henderson, *Roster of the Confederate Soldiers of Georgia 1861-1865* (Hapeville, Georgia: Longino & Porter Inc., 1955-1958), Vol. 1, 373-437.

16. Ibid., Vol. 2, 409-558; *Generals in Gray*, 76.

17. Ibid., 25-26; Henderson, Vol. 2, 558-614; Krick, 194.

18. Ibid., 215; Henderson, Vol. 2, 769-838.

19. Weygant, 171.

20. Ibid., 170.

21. Henry Leach, Pension Records, NARA.

22. OR, Part 3, 463.

23. Ibid., Part 1, 530. Birney's men took the Emmitsburg Road while Humphreys' soldiers used a parallel route about two miles to the west.

24. Weygant, 171; Peter B. Ayars, "The 99th Pennsylvania," *National Tribune*, February 4, 1886.

25. Ibid. Many men of the 3rd Corps remembered it to be a ninety-degree day, but the actual tempature was lower. As recorded by Michael Jacobs, professor of Pennsylvania College, the thermometer read as follows during the battle.

   July 1, 1863. 7 A.M.-72, 2 P.M.-76, 9 P.M.-74.
   July 2, 1863. 7 A.M.-74, 2 P.M.-81, 9 P.M.-76.
   July 3, 1863. 7 A.M.-73, 2 P.M.-87, 9 P.M.-76.
   See: "Meteorology of the Battle," *Star and Sentinel*, August 11, 1885.

26. Weygant, 172.

27. Ayars, "The 99th Pennsylvania."

28. This overnight picket duty is described in detail by Colonel Elijah Walker in *Maine at Gettysburg*, 180.

29. J. Harvey Hanford, "The Experiences of a Private of the 124th N.Y. in the Battle," National *Tribune*, September 24, 1885.

30. Theodore T. Fogle to his sister, July 16, 1863, Theodore Fogle Papers, Special Collections, Robert W. Woodruff Library, Emory University.

31. W. C. Ward, "Incidents and Personal Experiences on the Battlefield at Gettysburg" *Confederate Veteran*, (1900) Vol. 8, 346.

32. *OR*, Part 2, 358.

33. William T. Fluker, "A Graphic Account of the Battle of Little Round Top Hill at Gettysburg," a brochure produced by his great grandaughter, Terri Lee Fluker, 15th Georgia File, GNMP Vertical Files.

34. Ibid.

35. *OR*, Part 2, 358.

36. Fluker, "A Graphic Account of the Battle."

37. *OR*, Part 2, 358.

38. Ward, 346. Law's Brigade marker and a tablet to the 4th Alabama, both placed on Warfield Ridge along South Confederate Avenue in the early 1900s, place the time of departure from New Guilford at 3:00 a.m.

39. Using Route 30 West and the Old Cashtown Road we charted an actual distance of seventeen miles from New Guilford to Marsh Creek. This figure is often exaggerated.

40. *New York at Gettysburg*, 1289.

41. *OR*, Part 1, 511.

42. Ibid., 513, 506. Colonel Elijah Walker, whose 4th Maine was still on the advanced skirmish line stated that the reconaissance that morning was originally intended to move directly westward from the Emmitsburg road to the Confederate position, but upon his suggestion to Colonel Hiram Berdan that "it would be foolhardy to make the attempt" its direction was changed. See *Maine At Gettysburg*, 180.

43. These Southerners belonged to the brigade of General Cadmus Wilcox.

44. Hanford, "The Experiences of a Private."

45. Some troops marched around four miles and some marched slightly more but the operation, nonetheless, took up valuable time.

46. Daniel E. Sickles, "Further Recollections of Gettysburg," *North American Review* (March, 1891), No. 412, 263-264.

47. Ibid. For a very detailed study of this subject see Richard Sauers' *A Caspian Sea Of Ink: The Meade-Sickles Controversy* (Baltimore: Butternut and Blue, 1989). See also Pfanz, *Gettysburg-The Second Day*.

48. Weygant, 173.

49. A. W. Tucker, "Orange Blossoms," *National Tribune*, January 21, 1886.

50. *Maine At Gettysburg*, 181.

51. Charles H. Fasnact, *Speech Delivered at Dedication of 99th Pennsylvania Monument, Gettysburg, Pa. July 2, 1886* (Lancaster, Pa.: Examiner Steam Book & Job Print), 9. Lieutenant Henry P. Ramsdell of Company C, 124th New York remembered that "About noon, our Colonel gave orders to drive in some cows which we found near there, which were slaughtered and dealt out to the regiment which we needed very much as we had short rations for some days. While we were engaged in cooking this unexpected ration, the enemy commenced with tremendous cannonding

along the whole line." See "Account of Civil War Service," dated April 16, 1918, in Henry Ramsdell's Pension File, NARA. A copy is in the 124th New York File, GNMP Vertical Files.

52. *OR*, Part 1, 588.

53. Robert U. Johnson and Clarence C. Buel, eds. *Battles and Leaders of the Civil War* (Secaucus, New York: Castle, 1884-1889; Reprint. New York: Thomas Yoseloff, 1956), Vol. 3, 304-305.

54. James E. Smith, *A Famous Battery and its Campaigns, 1861-'64* (Washington: W. H. Lowdermilk & Co., 1892), 102. In his official report, Smith said that his rear section was 150 yards away but cut that distance in half when he wrote his battery's history.

55. Ibid., 104; *OR*, Part 1, 588.

56. *Battles and Leaders*, 305.

57. *Maine At Gettysburg*, 160; Weygant, 173; Francis M. Cummins to John B. Bachelder, February 21, 1884, published in *The Bachelder Papers*, edited by David L. and Audrey J. Ladd (Dayton, Ohio: Morningside House Inc., 1994), Vol. 2, 1023-1024. Hereafter cited as *Bachelder Papers*. According to the regimental history, from left to right, the companies of the 124th were situated atop Houck's Ridge as follows: B, G, K, E, C, H, I, D, F, A.

58. Ibid., 173. In his address at the dedication of the 124th monument, Weygant reduced the gap in the lines to "an unoccupied space of fifty yards or more."

59. *OR*, Part 1, 511.

60. Dean S. Thomas, *Ready...Aim...Fire!* (Biglerville, Pa.: 1981), 61.

61. *OR*, Part 2, 407, 412.

62. *OR*, Part 2, 393. Perry said in his official report that his regiment formed the "second battalion in the line formed by the brigade." John Bachelder's situation map published in 1876 places the 48th rather than the 44th in the rear. Other than that no additional evidence has surfaced to place Law's Brigade in two battalions.

63. Notes of Henry L. Benning in data gathered by E. P. Alexander for a history of Longstreet's Corps, Southern Historical Collection, Chapel Hill, North Carolina.

64. Busey and Martin, 234. These were the three most common types of cannon used by both sides at Gettysburg.

65. John Bell Hood, *Advance and Retreat* (New Orleans: 1880), 55.

66. Ibid., 57. In his postwar writings Law also favored this flanking movement.

67. Longstreet wanted to position the entire Confederate army between Meade's army and Washington and remain on the defensive.

68. The movements of Lee, Longstreet, and Hood on the eve of the attack are discussed in Glenn Tucker, *Lee and Longstreet at Gettysburg* (Dayton, Ohio: Morningside Bookshop, 1982), 59-62.

69. John O. Scott, "Heroic Acts in Texas History," in *Unveiling and Dedication of Monument to Hood's Texas Brigade* (Houston, Texas: F. B. Chilton, 1911), 311.

70. James Longstreet, "The Mistakes of Gettysburg", Philadelphia *Weekly Times*, February 23, 1878.

71. Russell C. White, ed. *The Civil War Diary of Wyman S. White* (Baltimore: Butternut and Blue, 1991), 164.
72. *OR*, Part 1, 518.
73. Ibid.
74. *OR*, Part 2, 395. The 47th Alabama detatched three unspecified companies while the 48th detailed Companies A and H for this purpose. See *OR*, Part 2, 408. The 1st and 4th Texas each sent its company I on skirmsh duty.
75. Busey and Martin.
76. Hanford, "The Experiences of a Private."
77. Hood, 56.
78. *OR*, Part 1, 588. Ward's aides included Lt. S. J. Leigh and Lt. A. M. Raphall. Since Smith identified Leigh elsewhere in his report, it is likely that Raphall delivered this order. Accounts also suggest that Smith's Battery had earlier fired a much-fabled shot by order of General Gouverneur K. Warren. See Oliver W. Norton, *The Attack and Defense of Little Round Top* (New York: Neale Publishing Company, 1913), 309; Benjamin F. Rittenhouse, *The Battle Of Gettysburg As Seen From Little Round Top* (Washington D.C.: Judd and Detweiler Printers, 1887).
79. Thomas Bradley, "At Gettysburg," *National Tribune*, February 4, 1886; Smith, *A Famous Battery*, 102. It is questionable whether all of Smith's ammunition was at the base of the ridge. Smith stated that the limbers were placed "as near to the guns as the nature of the declivity permitted." Perhaps a few chests were left on a less steep portion of the ridge.
80. Smith, *A Famous Battery*, 148.
81. *OR*, Part 1, 588.
82. Smith, *A Famous Battery*, 102-103; Tucker, "Orange Blossoms."
83. Maj. John P. Bane of the 4th Texas, Lt. Col. K. Bryan of the 5th Texas, Lt. Col. P.A. Work of the 1st Texas, and Brig. Gen. Henry L. Benning all mention in their official reports having seen this force atop Houck's Ridge.
84. *Battles and Leaders*, 305.
85. *OR*, Part 2, 414.
86. A.C. Sims, "Recollections of Private A.C. Sims," Robert L. Brake Collection, United States Army Military History Institute (USAMHI), Carlisle, Pennsylvania. From Confederate Research Center, Hill College, Texas.
87. J. B. Polley, *Hood's Texas Brigade: Its Marches, Its Battles, Its Achievements* (New York: Neale Publishing Co., 1910), 167.
88. Ibid., 176.
89. Ibid., 168.
90. Simpson, *Hood's Texas Brigade*, 167-168. James O. Bradfield, who told this story, stated that the shell came "from the mountain in front." In his official report Colonel Work singled out Dick Childers as one of only two men of the 1st Texas who did not prove themselves heroes during the battle. Soon after his capture, he took the oath of allegiance to the Union and joined the 3rd Maryland Cavalry, USA.
91. Smith, *A Famous Battery*, 147.
92. Tucker, "Orange Blossoms."
93. John C. West, "Incidents at Gettysburg," in *Unveiling and Dedication of Monument to Hood's Texas Brigade*, 275.
94. Tucker, "Orange Blossoms."
95. Ibid.
96. Smith, 103.
97. *Maine At Gettysburg*, 161.
98. *OR*, Part 2, 404; J. B. Robertson to John B. Bachelder, *Bachelder Papers*, Vol. 2, 860-861.
99. *OR*, Part 2, 404.
100. Scott, 339.
101. Evander McIver Law was a South Carolinian by birth and an 1856 graduate of the South Carolina Military Academy. He had received command of the Alabama Brigade shortly after the battle of Antietam.
102. In a 1908 letter written by Lieutenant Colonel Work to a comrade, he states he received an order from Brigadier General Law at 5:00 p.m. on July 2, placing him in command of the 3rd Arkansas as well as his own 1st Texas. This is entirely incongruent with all else that is known of that afternoon. In this lengthy and bitter letter Work asserts that Brigadier General Robertson played no significant part in the battle on July 2 and complains of injustices throughout the text. Much of the information in the letter, regrettably, is faulty and hence must be discounted. See P.A. Work to "Tom" Langley, Esq, 1st Texas File, GNMP Vertical Files.
103. It is sometimes asserted that elements of the 99th Pennsylvania and 20th Indiana assisted the sharpshooters on the skirmish line. But while Major Moore of the 99th speaks of "supporting Berdan's Sharpshooters" late in the afternoon, in his official report it is clear that he was describing the movement of Ward's right regiments upon the advance of the enemy.
104. *OR*, Part 2, 391.
105. Ibid., Part 1, 518.
106. C. A. Stevens, *Berdan's United States Sharpshooters in the Army of the Potomac, 1861-1865* (St. Paul: Price-McGill Company, 1892; Reprint, Dayton, Ohio: Morningside Bookshop, 1972), 325.
107. Ward, 347.
108. *OR*, Part 2, 395.
109. *Battles and Leaders*, 320.
110. Ibid., 324; *OR*, Part 2, 382. Years later, Law made no mention as to why the shift of the Alabamians was ordered, or that it was ordered at all, but did claim that he "threw Benning's Georgia brigade" into the gap between the Texans.
111. *OR*, Part 2, 406, 410.
112. *OR*, Part 1, 588.
113. Elijah Walker to John Bachelder, January 5, 1885, *Bachelder Papers*, Vol. 2, 1094-1095.
114. Ibid.; *Maine At Gettysburg*, 181.
115. *OR*, Part 1, 509; *Maine At Gettysburg*, 161, 162, 181. Adjutant Sawyer, who reported the second day's fight on behalf of the 4th Maine, stated that "one company (F)" was left "on the brow of the hill." Company F contained 3 officers and 33 men. To complicate matters however, Colonel Walker states in *Maine at Gettysburg*, that after moving to the low ground, he moved "also a strong line of skirmishers" to his "front" (p. 181). The skirmish line is given a strength of "about 70 men, with 3 officers" deployed "south of Devil's Den," (p. 162). This number may include the men of the 2nd United States Sharpshooters who had

fallen back into the rocks of the Den, or Company H of the 4th, who were apparently ordered to the skirmish line after the regiment was positioned in the Gorge. Before Company H was in position however, "a fresh regt" of the enemy appeared before the movement was completed. Lieutenant Nathaniel Robbins of Company H described the above movement but his account is unclear as to where or how his company was to deploy. See: Nathaniel Robbins to Adjutant General, December 23, 1895, Records of the Adjutant General of Maine, Box 110, Maine State Archives. From the information available the authors have constructed the following logical senerio. Company F was left on top of the Den. After the regiment moved to the valley, Company B was sent into the woods on the slopes of Big Round Top to the left, and shortly afterward Company H was sent forward to cover the Gorge in front.

116. *OR*, Part 1, 509-510.
117. Fluker, "A Graphic Account of the Battle of Little Round Top."
118. Tout-Le-Monde, "Letter from the Army," The Savannah *Republican*, July 7, 1863.
119. Tucker, "Orange Blossoms."
120. *OR*, Part 1, 493.
121. Tout-Le-Monde, "Letter from the Army;" Margaret Harper, "Their Last Chance," *Confederate Veteran* (March, 1919), Vol. 27, 93.
122. *OR*, Part 2, 421.
123. *OR*, Part 1, 588; Smith, 103.
124. John Malachi Bowden, "Journal of Private John Malachi Bowden," Emory University, copy in Robert L. Brake collection, USAMHI.
125. *OR*, Part 1, 493.
126. Ibid.
127. H. W. Berryman to his family, July 9, 1863, letter in Robert L. Brake collection, USAMHI.
128. *OR*, Part 2, 407.
129. Val. C. Giles in Polley, *Hood's Texas Brigade*, 175.
130. Benjamin L. Higgins, pension records, NARA; *OR*, Part 1, 511.
131. Smith, 111-112.
132. Scott, "Heroic Acts in Texas History," 340.
133. Ibid.
134. Polley, 169.
135. Hanford, "The Experiences of a Private."
136. *OR*, Part 1, 520, 522, *Maine At Gettysburg*, 193. In the latter source Captain George W. Verrill states, "The regiment took position just in time to receive the first and furious attack made by the enemy on that part of the line. This was made by Robertson's Brigade of Hood's Division, and the first struggle of the Seventeenth was with the 3rd Ark. regiment."
137. *OR*, Part 2, 407. This ledge of rocks is accessible today. See Tour Section.
138. *OR*, Part 2, 404-405.
139. Ibid., 408.
140. Ibid., 407.
141. Fasnact, 10.
142. *OR*, Part 1, 506.
143. Erasmus C. Gilbreath, "Account of Erasmus C. Gilbreath," Gilbreath Papers, Indiana State Library, copy at GNMP; Francis A Osbourn, Gilbreath Papers. Indiana State Library, copy at USAMHI.
144. Ibid.
145. Francis A Osbourn, Gilbreath Papers.
146. Weygant, 175.
147. Ibid., 176; Tucker, "Orange Blossoms."
148. Ibid. It is interesting that the Texans chose not to mention the charge of the 124th in their accounts of the battle.
149. Weygant, 176.
150. Bradley, "At Gettysburg."
151. Weygant, 176.
152. Ibid., 177; Cummins to Bachelder, *Bachelder Papers,*, 1023-1024. Exactly when in the battle Captain Smith and his gunners abandoned the guns on the crest and proceeded to the rear section is unclear. In Smith's postwar writings he tries to give the impression that his men stayed on top of the hill even after the charge of the 124th was repulsed and that they alone held the enemy at bay for another 30 minutes before reinforcements arrived. This scenario, however, does not jive with other known accounts. Most likely, Smith and his men left the crest about the time that they pulled the disabled gun off the hill. After the war, Smith would go to great lengths to justify his actions. In 1886 he wrote: "When driven from the crest three guns were left in position to make a show of defense after removing implements and ammunition. The result of this was their loss, but it did not expose our weakness. Had the guns been run to the rear when it was possible to save them the enemy would have been encouraged, and very likely would have made a more vigorous charge, which we were not in condition to repel." See James E. Smith, "The 'Devil's Den,'" *National Tribune*, March 4, 1886.
153. Ibid., 176. The Newburgh *Weekly Telegraph* reported on July 9, 1863, that "Major Cromwell was shot just at the moment the rebels began to break and retreat. He was one of the first to perceive their retrograde movement and exclaimed 'The day is ours.' Just as those words passed his lips, a rifle-ball pierced his heart and he fell lifeless to the ground."
154. Ibid.
155. Weygant, 179.
156. James Scott, Pension Records, NARA.
157. Weygant, 176. One of these men was killed and one was wounded.
158. Ibid.
159. Ibid., 188; Noah B. Kimbark, Pension Records, NARA.
160. Charles J. LaRocca, ed. ,*This Regiment of Heroes*, (1991), 165. This information is from a letter printed in the Middletown *Whig Press* on July 22, 1863.
161. Ibid, 164.
162. Hanford, "The Experiences of a Private."
163. Bradley, "At Gettysburg."
164. Hanford, "The Experiences of a Private."
165. Tucker, "Orange Blossoms."
166. A.W. Tucker, "From Comrade Tucker," *National Tribune*, February 4, 1886.
167. Bradley, "At Gettysburg."
168. *OR*, Part 2, 393-394.
169. Ibid., 394.
170. William F. Perry, "The Devil's Den," 161.
171. *OR*, Part 2, 394.
172. Perry, "The Devil's Den," 161.
173. *OR*, Part 2, 394.

174. Perry, "The Devil's Den," 161.

175. Ibid.

176. *OR*, Part 2, 394.

177. Perry, "The Devil's Den," 161.

178. *OR*, Part 2, 394.

179. Perry, "The Devil's Den," 161. The enemy they saw "escaping" were probably members of the 2nd USSS, and skirmishers of the Company H, 4th Maine. As a matter of fact, Lieutenant Nathaniel Robbins, the commander of Company H, was captured in this action.

180. *Bachelder Papers*, 1095.

181. "Col. George W. Cary," *Confederate Veteran* (April 1909), Vol. 17, 242; Perry, "The Devil's Den," 161.

182. H. H. Sturgis, "Little Billy Fort," *Confederate Veteran* (September 1922), Vol. 30, 345.

183. 2nd Lieutenant George M. Bragg of Company F was actually in temporary command of Company K at Gettysburg and was mortally wounded.

184. Companies F and A suffered the highest number of captured in the 4th Maine.

185. Perry, "The Devil's Den," 162. Two of these swords were more than likely those of Captain George G. Davis and 1st Lieutenant Solomon S. Stearns, both of Company F, 4th Maine.

186. Ibid.

187. Ibid.

188. *OR*, Part 1, 509-510. In *Maine at Gettysburg*, Walker mistakes the 48th for the 44th Alabama (181).

189. *Maine At Gettysburg*, 164.

190. *OR*, Part 1, 510.

191. *OR*, Part 2, 396.

192. *Maine At Gettysburg*, 182; John W. Busey, *These Honored Dead* (Hightstown, New Jersey: Longstreet House, 1988), 35.

193. *OR*, Part 2, 396. To get an accurate idea of where the woodline along the slopes of Big Round Top was at the time of the battle, and hence an idea of where the 48th spent much of its time on July 2, see Frassanito, *Early Photography*, 241, 262-265, 279-294, 306-311. Many histories of the battle indicate that the 48th Alabama charged up the slopes of Little Round Top (a few also have suggested the 44th charged as well). The 48th Alabama did, in fact, assist in the attack on Little Round Top, but did not actually charge up its slopes. While the left of the 48th was engaged with the 4th Maine, the right wing of the regiment exchanged fire with the troops atop the hill from their position near the "Finger Like Ridge." The official report of Major John P. Bane of the 4th Texas is the primary source for those who claim these units ascended that hill. He states that after failing to capture Little Round Top during several attempts and "being re-enforced by the Forty-eighth Alabama, commanded by the gallant Colonel [James L.] Sheffield, and the Forty-fourth Alabama, whose commander I did not learn, we again charged their works, but were repulsed...." See *OR*, Part 2, 411. Bane does not actually discuss the role that these units played in the charge, but many writers have had no problem adding these two regiments to the Confederate assault, making the stand on Little Round Top seem all the more dramatic.

194. *OR*, Part 2, 405.

195. Scott, "Heroic Acts In Texas History," 340.

196. *Maine At Gettysburg*, 166.

197. *Bachelder Papers*, 1095.

198. Ibid.

199. *Maine At Gettysburg*, 182; Elijah Walker, Pension Records, NARA.

200. Ayars, "The 99th Pennsylvania."

201. *OR*, Part 1, 513.

202. *Pennsylvania At Gettysburg*, 538.

203. Fasnact, 10. Fasnact describes: "The left of our regiment extended down over the slope in front of the Devil's Den to near Plum Run, in the direction of Little Round Top." In *Maine at Gettysburg*, Colonel Walker is even more specific: "...the 99th Pennsylvania monument stands on ground from which that regiment did not fire a shot July 2, 1863. Their right was their left flank marker is now placed, and extended along the brow of the hill" (185). In either case, the 99th held a most commanding position.

204. *OR*, Part 1, 589.

205. Smith, 104.

206. Ibid., 105. Smith says that Hazlett's guns began firing while he was at his rear guns. He later called the report of the first gun, "the sweetest music I ever heard." See Benjamin F. Rittenhouse, *The Battle of Gettysburg*.

207. *Bachelder Papers*, 1095.

208. Weygant, 179.

209. Ibid., 178.

210. Tucker, "Orange Blossoms."

211. *OR*, Part 1, 511; Bangor *Daily Whig & Courier*, July 21, 1863; *Maine At Gettysburg*, 182; Henry O. Ripley, Pension Records, NARA. The official report of the 4th Maine recorded that there were 31 bullet holes in the flag. During the dedication of the monument Colonel Walker said it was pierced by 32 bullet holes and two pieces of shell. Take your pick. Ripley, who was already wearing the Kearny Cross at Gettysburg for past gallantry, was given special mention for "meritorious conduct" in the reports of both General Ward, and Captain Edwin Libby of the 4th Maine. In December 1863 he was commissioned as a Lieutenant and on June 7, 1864, he died of wounds received in action at the Battle of Po River a month earlier. An obituary for Henry O. Ripley appears in a book entitled *The Old Soldier* , a collection of bound newspaper clippings concerning the 4th Maine, located at the Maine State Library.

212. *Maine At Gettysburg*, 182.

213. Theodore F. Rodenbough, *The Bravest Five Hundred of '61* (New York: G. W. Dillingham, 1891), 186-187.

214. Ibid., 187.

215. *Bachelder Papers*, 1095.

216. Perry, "The Devil's Den," 162.

217. *OR*, Part 2, 415.

218. Ibid.

219. *OR*, Part 2, 408-409.

220. Ibid., 421.

221. Fluker, "A Graphic Account of the Battle of Little Round Top."

222. *OR*, Part 2, 426.

223. Ibid., 415.

224. J. W. Lokey, *My Experiences in the War Between the States,* 15, copy in 20th Georgia File, GNMP Vertical Files. A very similar narrative by Lokey appeared in *Confederate Veteran* (September, 1914), Vol. 22, 400.

225. *OR*, Part 2, 420.
226. Houghton, William R., *Two Boys in the Civil War and After* (Montgomery: Paragon Press, 1912), 220. This quote was taken from a GNMP transcription of that page.
227. Bowden, "Journal of Private John Malachi Bowden," 6.
228. John H. Martin, "Accurate Historic Records," *Confederate Veteran* (March, 1904), Vol. 12, 113-114. It is possible that the 17th Georgia was split by the rocks of the Den, much as the 44th Alabama had been.
229. Tout-Le-Monde, "Letter from the Army."
230. Smith, 106.
231. *OR*, Part 1, 577.
232. Ibid.
233. Ibid., 526.
234. Ibid. This may explain why Colonel Egan made no mention of the 6th New Jersey in his report.
235. *OR*, Part 1, 589.
236. Ibid., 526.
237. Ibid., 527; Busey, *These Honored Dead*, 105; Madison M. Cannon, Pension Records, NARA. Cannon was wounded in the left side, received a twenty day leave of absence as a result and returned as the new lieutenant colonel of the 40th.
238. *OR*, Part 1, 526.
239. Ibid., Part 2, 420. Shepard was a major when he entered the fight but was promoted to lieutenant colonel upon the death of Lieutenant Colonel Harris.
240. Ibid., 425.
241. *OR*, Part 2, 415
242. Ibid., 409.
243. *Maine At Gettysburg*, 167; OR, 512-513. While Major Moore of the 99th mentioned nothing of an order to fall back from General Ward (probably because he was wounded just prior to the retreat), Charles H. Fasnact did recall such an order: "In fact, it was only when General Ward himself came, with a bullet hole through his hat, and ordered the regiment to the rear..." that the unit retreated. See Fasnact, 11.
244. *OR*, Part 1, 494.
245. Ramsdell, "Account of Civil War Service." While this account was written in 1918, over fifty years after the battle, another letter written on July 5, 1863 by Henry M. Howell also claims "We had not fallen back more than twenty or thirty rods, when the 2d corps and part of the 5th came up to our assistance and speedily retook the ground we had lost..." See LaRocca, 164.
246. Only one Union regiment lost more men captured than the 4th Maine on July 2nd. This was the 4th Michigan, Sweitzer's Brigade, Barnes' Division, Fifth Corps, who lost 76 men captured in the Wheatfield.
247. *Maine At Gettysburg*, 182.
248. Rodenbough, 189-192; George Broadbent and George W. Setley, Service Records, NARA. George W. Setley, 20 years old at the time of the battle, died in Libby Prison on February 27, 1864.
249. Ibid. The Sixth Corps unit was probably within the brigade of David Nevin.
250. *Pennsylvania At Gettysburg*, 539-540; James Casey, Pension Records, NARA. At the dedication of the monument it was related that Corporal Casey "was a

brave lad, and the ghouls who robbed his body and thus prevented his identification knew it, for upon his breast he wore the Kearny Badge...."
251. *OR*, Part 1, 514.
252. John R. Nice, Pension Records, NARA. For a complete list of the 99th's casualties at the battle see "Local Intelligence," Lancaster *Daily Evening Express*, July 9, 1863.
253. Scott, 340.
254. Ibid., 339.
255. Polley, 172. The story of Sergeant Barbee is also told in early guide books. See J. Warren Gilbert, *The Battle of Gettysburg Made Plain* (Gettysburg: 1899), 45.
256. Sims, "Recollections of Private A.C. Sims." Veterans of Smith's Battery recalled that the guns were taken by Alabamians. As far as most of Smith's men were concerned, this was the case as the 44th Alabama did, indeed, first capture the guns. See "More Battlefield Notes," Gettysburg *Compiler*, April 24, 1888.
257. Martin, 114.
258. *Report of the Gettysburg Battle-field Commission of New Jersey* (Trenton, N. J.: John L. Murphy Publishing Co., 1887), 104.
259. OR, Part 1, 526.
260. Smith, 105.
261. Many Confederate accounts of the battle describe beating off several counterattacks against their position at Devil's Den. There is no evidence, however, of any direct assault on the hill after its capture, although it is not hard to imagine in the confusion that the Southerners might not have realized this fact. One early tourbook states that on the evening of July 2, "General Fisher's brigade was moved down the ravine between the two Round Tops, and fought their way foot by foot westward across the Valley of Death, until they reached and captured Devil's Den, the stronghold which the enemy had taken from the Third corps of the Union army. At midnight they were ordered back to Round Top...." This incredible story is not corroborated by any other accounts and actually contradicts known facts. See Gilbert, 28.
262. Sims, "Recollections of Private A. C. Sims."
263. *OR*, Part 2, 417.
264. Bowden, "Journal of Private John Malachi Bowden."
265. Ibid.
266. Letter from Theodore T. Fogle to his parents, July 7, 1863.
267. Tout-Le-Monde, "Letter from the Army."
268. *OR*, Part 2, 405.
269. Ibid., Part 1, 494.
270. Polley, 173-176. A slightly different version of Giles' account appears in Mary Lasswell, *Rags and Hope: The Recollections of Val C. Giles, Four Years With Hood's Brigade, Fourth Texas Infantry* (New York: Coward-McCann, Inc., 1961), 173-191.
271. Col. A. H. Belo, "Gettysburg," *Confederate Veteran* (April, 1900), Vol. 8, 165.
272. Scott, 340.
273. Ibid., 341. The 1st Texas passed directly through the Den on the way to their new position.
274. Sims, "Recollections of Private A.C. Sims," 2. Two other men on picket duty that night (one in the 91st Pennsylvania, and one in the 5th Texas), wrote of

employing tobacco in their eyes for the same purpose. See "Josie And I At Gettysburg: On Picket On Little Round Top," undated newpaper clipping in 91st Pennsylvania file, Vertical Files, GNMP, and William A. Fletcher, *Rebel Private: Front and Rear* (Beaumont, Texas: Press of the Greer Print, 1908).

275. Scott, 340. Smith's three guns were among just a handful captured by either side during the battle.

276. A "small cannon, weighing 150 pounds, with one and one-half inch bore," was one of the prized possessions of the Gettysburg GAR, Corporal Skelly Post No. 9. It was said to have been "made from one of the guns of Henry's North Carolina rebel batteries, which exploded during the battle." The gun can be seen today in the basement of the GAR building located on Middle Street in Gettysburg. *1886 History of Adams County*, 202.

277. Tout-Le-Monde, "Letter from the Army."

278. Fluker, 7.

279. *OR*, Part 2, 416.

280. Jacob Hoke, *Reminiscences of The War; Or Incidents Which Transpired In and About Chambersburg, During the War of the Rebellion* (Chambersburg, Pa.: M.A. Foltz, 1884), 100.

281. Ibid.

282. Weygant, 187-188.

283. Ibid., 188-189.

284. Harold B. Simpson, ed., *Touched With Valor, Civil War Papers and Casualty Reports of Hood's Texas Brigade* (Hillsboro, Texas: Hill Junior College Press, 1964), 46. Although there were Southern sharpshooter units at Gettysburg, such as Blackford's Alabama Sharpshooters of O'Neal's Brigade, there was no such organization at the Devil's Den.

285. For a thorough study of the origins and subsequent popularization of the Devil's Den sharpshooter lore, see Frassanito, *Early Photography*, 273-276.

286. Robert Goldthwaite Carter, *Four Brothers in Blue* (Washington: Gibson Bros. Inc., 1913), 313-314.

287. Stevens, 339.

288. Ibid., 340.

289. For additional reading on this subject see Paul M. Shevchuk, "The 1st Texas and the Repulse of Farnsworth's Charge," *Gettysburg: Historical Articles of Lasting Interest* (January, 1990), No. 2, 80-90.

290. *New York at Gettysburg*, 969. Among the generals known to have participated in this meeting were Warren, Sedgwick, Sykes, Pleasanton and Crawford.

291. Samuel W. Crawford, "The Pennsylvania Reserves at Gettysburg," Gettysburg *Star & Sentinel*, August 23, 1887.

292. McCandless' Brigade of Crawford's Division with part of Nevin's Brigade in support did this duty.

293. *OR*, Part 2, 417, 424.

294. John L. Smith, *History of the Corn Exchange Regiment, 118th Pennsylvania Volunteers* (Philadelphia: J. L. Smith, 1888), 254, 261. On July 2 this unit was involved in the heavy fighting at the Wheatfield. On July 3 they were placed on Big Round Top, where they proceeded to create a fortress. The monument of the Corn Exchange Regiment on Big Round Top is off the beaten path and rarely visited today. Hence the site, and the fortress nature of their breastworks are still in pristine condition.

295. Ibid.

296. Ibid., 262. William A. Dunklin was the Captain of Company G, 44th Alabama, and was killed in action on July 2, 1863.

297. *New York at Gettysburg*, 972.

298. Ajax, "The Last of the Dead Buried-Condition of the Wounded-The Battlefield and Relic Gatherers." New York *Times*, July 15, 1863.

299. J. Howard Wert, *Historical Souvenir of the Fiftieth Anniversary of the Battle of Gettysburg, July 1-4, 1913* (Harrisburg: Harrisburg Telegraph, 1913), 31. A slightly different version of his visit to Devil's Den after the battle appears in J. Howard Wert, *A Complete Hand-Book Of The Monuments And Indications and Guide To The Positions On The Gettysburg Battlefield* (Harrisburg, Pennsylvania: R. M. Sturgeon & Co. Publishers, 1886), 92-93.

300. Russle C. White, ed., *The Civil War Diary Of Wyman S. White: First Sergeant of Company F, 2nd United States Sharpshooter Regiment 1861-1865* (Baltimore: Butternut and Blue, 1991), 175.

301. Daniel Alexander Skelly, *A Boy's Experiences During the Battles of Gettysburg* (Gettysburg: D. A. Skelly, 1932), 22.

302. Hoke, 172-173.

303. "The Gettysburg Battlefield," *Daily Patriot and Union*, July 11, 1863. Another article describing an early visit to the area is "The Great Battle," Lancaster *Evening Express*, July 20, 1863.

304. Gardner, *Sketch book*, plates 36 and 37.

305. Ibid. The story of Gardner's photographic activity on the Gettysburg Battlefield is discussed in great detail in Frassanito's *Early Photography*.

306. Gardner, *Sketch book*, plates 41 and 40.

307. Frassanito, *Early Photography*, 273.

308. Michael Jacobs, "Later Rambles Over The Field Of Gettysburg," 71.

309. Andrew Cross, *The War, Battle of Gettysburg and the Christian Commission* (Baltimore: 1865), 25-26.

310. F. M. Stoke Letter.

311. Frassanito, *Early Photography*, 294-306.

312. Ibid., 306. Examples of the misuse of these photographs to show actual dead can be found in the following sources: *Pictorial History of The Battle of Gettysburg* (Gettysburg, PA.: L. E. Smith, 1978), 37; McLaughlin, 104; Pete and Cyndi Dalton, *Into the Valley of Death: The Story of the 4th Maine Infantry at the Battle of Gettysburg, July 2, 1863* (Union, Maine: Union Publishing Co., 1994), 59. An original Weaver view from this series that has recently surfaced refers to the formation as "Stony Point," further indicating that the term Devil's Den was not in common usage at that time.

Post-Battle History

1. "Visit to Gettysburg by Isaac Moorhead," *The American Magazine* (Ann Arbor: University of Michigan, Autumn-Winter, 1985-86), Vol. 1, No. 2, 25-26. Originally printed in *The Occasional Writings of Isaac Moorhead, With a Sketch of His Life*, ed., A. H. Caughey (Erie: 1882).

2. Castine, June 14, 1865, A newspaper clipping in the Edward McPherson Papers, Library of Congress, Box 98, Book 2, 60.

3. Cymon, "The Gettysburgh Battle-field," *New York Times*, July 10, 1865. Cymon was actually one of Lorenzo L. Crounse's pen names. The drowning of wounded soldiers was a popular theme in early tours, and although it did rain heavily just after the battle, these accounts are exaggerated.

4. George J. Gross, *The Battle-field Of Gettysburg* (Philadelphia: Collins, printer, 1866), 14-15. This account originally appeared as an article in the *Philadelphia Press* on November 2, 1865.

5. Henry V. N. Boynton, *Adams Sentinel*, July 17, 1866. This letter was written on June 30, 1866 and originally appeared in the Cincinnati *Gazette*.

6. Anchor, "A Visit to Gettysburg," *Army and Navy Journal*, June 8, 1867. "Anchor" was actually the pen name of John Watts De Peyester.

7. Waldron, *With Pen and Camera; Gettysburg* (Portland, Maine: L. H. Nelson Company, 1905). A postcard of Devil's Den published by the Hugh C. Leighton Co. of Portland, Maine, mailed from Gettysburg on June 9, 1910 also states that sixty-eight dead bodies were found there.

8. James E. Hall, *The 50th Anniversary of the World Famous Battle of Gettysburg* (Gettysburg: Gettysburg Board of Trade, 1913). A study of the casualties at Devil's Den indicates that there may well have been as many as one hundred dead Confederates in the area after the battle (See Appendix B).

9. *Star and Sentinel*, July 17, 1888.

10. "Little Round Top," *Compiler*, October 24, 1899.

11. Gardner, plate 41; Frassanito, *Early Photography*, 276.

12. Postcard entitled "The Devil's Den Ledge" owned by Timothy H. Smith and mailed on August 18, 1910. The exact same story is related in *The Story of Gettysburg in Pictures* (Gettysburg, Pennsylvania: David Blocher, circa 1925).

13. "Devil's Den Is Unchanged," *Gettysburg Times*, 75th Anniversary Edition, July, 1938.

14. Captain R. K. Beecham, *Gettysburg: The Pivotal Battle Of The Civil War* (Chicago: A. C. McClurg & Co., 1911), 190-191.

15. *Pictorial History Of The Battle Of Gettysburg*, 37.

16. Wolf Family, *A Simplified Tour of the Gettysburg Battlefield*.

17. File on the visit of President Carter in GNMP Vertical Files. For more information see "Three Summit Conferees visit Gettysburg Battlefield Sunday," and "Tight Security Provided By Police From 3 Nations During Visit To Field," *Gettysburg Times*, September 11, 1978.

18. For a history of battlefield guiding, see Frederick W. Hawthorne, *A Peculiar Institution: The History of the Gettysburg Licensed Battlefield Guides* (Gettysburg: Association of Licensed Battlefield Guides, 1991).

19. "Never Mind The Guide," *New York Times*, July 9, 1888.

20. *Gettysburg and Vicinity* (Published by the GBMA, 1888). This map appeared in several early guidebooks. A original copy can be found in the Gettysburg Battlefield 190-0 File, ACHS.

21. *The Battle-field Of Gettysburg* (Gettysburg: The Gettysburg & Harrisburg Railroad Company, 1885; reprinted in *Gettysburg by Train*, Thomas Publications, 1989), 25.

22. Ibid., 14.

23. John Reed Scott, "The Gettysburg Desecration," *Harper's Weekly*, July 1, 1893. A *Philadelphia Press* article on July 15, 1894, also mentioned that "Plum Run ran red with soldiers blood." *Gettysburg Newspaper Cuttings*, Vol. 1, 66, GNMP.

24. Herbert L. Grimm and Paul L. Roy, *Human Interest Stories of the Three Days' Battles at Gettysburg* (Gettysburg: Times And News Publishing Co., 1927), 48. This book has gone through many editions and is still very popular in Gettysburg gift shops.

25. McLaughlin, 108. Similar versions also appear in *A Pictorial History Of The Battle Of Gettysburg*, 37, and the Wolf Family, 21.

26. "On The Battlefield Of Gettysburg," newspaper clipping in Henry Stewart Scrapbook No. 31, 16, ACHS.

27. John S. Coleman and James D. Fraser, *Final Report: Home Range, Habitat Use, Behavior, And Morphology of The Gettysburg Vultures*, (Blacksburg, Virginia: Virginia Polytechnic Institute, 1985), 1-2. A copy can be found in the GNMP library.

28. Victoria Brenner Greenlee, "Vulture Research Begins at Gettysburg," *Park Science: A Resource Management Bulletin* (N.P.S., U. S. Department of the Interior, Fall, 1983), Vol. 4, No. 1, 12-13; "What are those Big Birds Anyway? The Vultures of Gettysburg" (GNMP, n.d.). This was a flyer handed out to visitors by GNMP during Vulture studies in the 1980s.

29. Coleman and Fraser, 1; Nancy Di Blasi, "NPS to study battlefield's vulture population," *Gettysburg Times*, September 18, 1982; "Study Contradicts Local Legend: Gettysburg vultures predate battle," undated newspaper clipping from Adams County Natural History File-102, ACHS; *National Tower* (Harrisburg, Pa.: 1978), 16.

30. *The Battle-field of Gettysburg*, 10.

31. *1886 History of Adams County*, 54.

32. Clifton Johnston, *Battleground Adventures* (Boston and New York: 1915), 196. In the past this account has been incorrectly credited to T. D. Carson, but there is little doubt that Samuel Bushman is the man being interviewed.

33. "Albino Crow At Gettysburg," *Compiler*, August 26, 1902. Robert Frank Lott started guiding around 1900. In 1915 he became licensed and guided until his death in December of 1930. See obituary of Robert Frank Lott, *Compiler*, December 20, 1930.

34. "Believe It or Not: Foes Claimed Shots Clashed in Mid-Air," 75th Anniversary Edition of the *Gettysburg Times*, July, 1938.

35. Busey, 262.

36. John T. Campbell, "Sights At Gettysburg," *National Tribune*, September 17, 1908.

37. "Hidden at Gettysburg," *Star and Sentinel*, November 25, 1890.

38. Busey, 363; John Ambrose, Pension Records, NARA.

39. *Gettysburg Newspaper Cuttings*, GNMP, Vol. 2, 58.

40. "Baltimorean Says 'Little' Round Top Named for Her Great-Grandfather," *Gettysburg Times*, July 8, 1938.

41. Obituary of Ephraim H. Little, *Compiler*, July 29, 1916; Obituary of Martha Little, *Compiler*, October 23, 1868.

42. Interview with Mrs. George D. Rosensteel, by Marcella Sherfy and Mike Strock, November 29, 1972, GNMP.

43. McLaughlin, v.

44. "13 Haunted Places of the Civil War: 'It Was A Dark and Stormy Night...,'" *Blue & Gray Magazine* (Columbus, Ohio: October-November, 1986), Vol. 4, No. 2, 8-9. See also "Legends and Folklore Abound," *Gettysburg Times Commemorative Edition*, June 24, 1988, and "The Ghosts of Gettysburg," Lancaster *Sunday News* , October 29, 1995; Mark Nesbitt, *Ghosts of Gettysburg: Spirits, Apparitions and Haunted Places of the Battlefield* (Gettysburg, Pa.: Thomas Publications, 1991) 17-22.

45. "Children Born During Civil War Found Alive! They haven't aged a day since the 1860s," *Weekly World News*, November 10, 1992.

46. "An Act To Incorporate the Gettysburg Battle-field Memorial Association," *Compiler*, May 16, 1864. For a discussion of McConaughy's involvement in the GBMA see Frassanito, *Early Photography*, 142-144.

47. John M. Vanderslice, *Gettysburg Then And Now* (John M. Vanderslice: 1899) 360-363. This book was intended to be the official history of the GBMA. In both 1867 and 1868 the state legislature appropriated the sum of $3,000 to this group for the purchase of important portions of the field.

48. Ibid., 363-364.

49. "Vandals Plead For their Charter," Philadelphia *Press*, August 3, 1893; *Adams County Deed Book MM*, 201.

50. *Compiler*, December 19, 1872.

51. Vanderslice, 364; "The Old Bucktail Regiment," *Star and Sentinel*, October 11, 1905.

52. Vanderslice, 395.

53. *Bachelder Papers*, 979.

54. "Battle-field Monuments," *Compiler*, July 8, 1884; "Veteran Re-Unions and Dedication of Monuments," *Star and Sentinel*, July 8, 1884.

55. "Vandalism," *Star and Sentinel*, July 29, 1884.

56. *Bachelder Papers*, 1077.

57. "The Indiana Monuments," *Star and Sentinel*, November 3, 1885.

58. *Star and Sentinel*, May 25, 1886.

59. *Star and Sentinel*, July 6, 1886.

60. *Pennsylvania At Gettysburg*, v.

61. "Pennsylvania Day," *Star and Sentinel*, September 17, 1889.

62. *Pennsylvania At Gettysburg*, 540.

63. Ibid, 533.

64. "The Great Reunion," *Star and Sentinel*, July 3, 1888.

65. *New York At Gettysburg*, 288-291.

66. *New York At Gettysburg*, 698-699.

67. "More Battlefield Notes," *Compiler*, April 24, 1888.

68. Smith, 148-149. Originally, only two guns were placed near the monument, one on each side. It would not be until 1900 that the park would add another two guns atop Houck's Ridge and mark the position of the rear section. See *Annual Reports of The Gettysburg National Military Park Commission 1893-1904* (Washington; Government Printing Office, 1905), 60.

69. Walker, "Gettysburg Monument."

70. *Maine At Gettysburg*, 164; Journal of William Robbins 1894-1904, Southern Historical Collection, University of North Carolina, entry for December 29, 1897. Robbins was a battlefield commissioner at the time.

71. "Vandal's Plead For their Charter." A circular to the Grand Army Posts of Pennsylvania referred to the property as "'Crawford's Glen,' the title to which is held by General S. W. Crawford, but which is under our care..." Certainly the association felt the land was part of their holdings. See "Property of the Memorial Association," *Compiler*, October 7, 1884. J. Howard Wert also mentioned that the GBMA had "care of 40 acres at Devil's Den and the vicinity, the property of General S. Wylie Crawford...," in *The Two Great Armies at Gettysburg* (Harrisburg, PA: 1892), 30.

72. "The Pennsylvania Reserves," *Star and Sentinel*, October 2, 1888.

73. "The Reserves," *Compiler*, February 14, 1888; undated clipping in Pennsylvania Reserves Monument File, GNMP.

74. "The Memorial Vote," *Compiler*, May 28, 1889.

75. The story of the Memorial Hall is told in *Pennsylvania at Gettysburg,* by William Hayes Grier, 88-91.

76. "Preparations For Reserve Day," *Star and Sentinel*, July 15, 1890. See also "The Reserve Monuments," *Compiler*, July 15, 1890. Today, there are no reserve monuments erected on Crawford's land. They were erected slightly outside the boundary lines.

77. Grier, 87.

78. *Star and Sentinel*, March 12, 1889. This article gave notice that the Memorial Hall was to be erected on Crawford's tract and that Andrew Carnegie had agreed to contribute the steel.

79. Obituary of Samuel W. Crawford, *Star and Sentinel*, November 8, 1892.

80. "General Sickles's Indignation," *Star and Sentinel*, May 30, 1893.

81. "Round Top Road," *Star and Sentinel*, May 6, 1884.

82. "All Aboard," *Compiler*, April 22, 1884; *Compiler*, June 17, 1884.

83. "Railroad Notes," *Compiler*, May 20, 1884.

84. "The New Railroad," *Compiler*, May 6, 1884; "Local Flashes," *Compiler*, June 24, 1884; *Compiler*, June 17, 1884; "Round Top Park, *Star and Sentinel*, May 6, 1884; Cumberland Township Tax Records, 1885. Shortly after its opening, Lewis Bushman constructed a warehouse and store on land adjoining the railroad station and went into a successful business shipping grain, lumber, coal, lime, and groceries. On June 23, 1886, a post office was opened and Bushman was named the postmaster. It continued operation until April 30, 1900, and was named "Sedgewick." See "Round Top Station," *Compiler*, June 23, 1885; *1886 History of Adams County*, 398.

85. "Ox Roast On The Fourth," *Compiler*, June 24, 1884; "The Fourth," *Compiler*, July 8, 1884; The Fourth-Ox Roast," *Star and Sentinel*, July 8, 1884.

86. "The Fourth."

87. "Railroad Notes," *Star and Sentinel*, May 27, 1884; *Star and Sentinel*, July 15, 1884.

88. "Round-Top-Park," *Compiler*, July 15, 1884. Ironically, the first case of serious vandalism to a monument in the park occurred during the same week this warning was printed. See "Vandalism," *Star and Sentinel*, July 29, 1884.

89. John M. Butler, advertisement in end piece.

90. Ibid., 126-127.
91. *Adams County Deed Book PP*, 315-319; *Star & Sentinel*, April 3, 1888. See also "Round Top Park Now Open," *Compiler*, June 22, 1886.
92. Obituary of John H. Rosensteel, *Compiler*, September 13, 1924; Obituary of George D. Rosensteel, *Compiler*, February 28, 1914; Obituary of Margaret Mary Rosensteel, May 31, 1938, Rosensteel Family File, ACHS. For more on the origins of the Rosensteel collection see Stephen W. Sylvia & Michael J. O'Donnell, *The Illustrated History of American Civil War Relics* (Orange, Virginia: Moss Publications, 1988), 146-150; "Glimpses...," Gettysburg *Times*, December 5, 1981; Rosensteel Interview, GNMP.
93. *1886 History of Adams County*, 374; Henry Stewart, "Reminiscences of 70 years in Gettysburg," This was a series of articles printed in the Gettysburg *Times*, from April 17, to June 1, 1946.
94. "A Thousand at Catholic Picnic," *Compiler*, August 19, 1903.
95. "Merry-Go-Round For Sale," *Compiler*, August 14, 1894. John Hugen, who was the proprietor of the merry-go-round stated that he enjoyed a very prosperous business during the season.
96. *Adams County Deed Book QQ*, 520-521.
97. Robbins' Journal, entries for March 30 and August 29, 1896; *Adams County Deed Book YY*, 341; "In Condemnation Proceeding Jury Awards Mr. Tipton $6,150," *Adams County Independent*, May 25, 1901. When Round Top Park closed it was under the ownership of the Pennsylvania and Reading Railroad.
98. Hall, *50th Anniversary.*
99. Report of Major Charles Reed on the conditions at Camp Colt, July 13, 1918, in *Letters to the Surgeon General Office 1917 to 1927*, Record Group 112, Box 12, NARA. This letter was brought to the authors' attention by David Weaver, LBG.
100. *USA Vs. A Certain Tract*, 127, 187.
101. *Adams County Deed Book OO*, 496; Tax records of Cumberland Township.
102. *1886 History of Adams County*, 366-367; Obituary of Levi Mumper, *Compiler*, December 2, 1916; Mumper Family File, ACHS.
103. *United States of America Vs. Two certain tracts of land in Cumberland Township, Adams County, Pennsylvania.* In the Circuit Court of the United States for the Middle District of Pennsylvania, November Sessions, 1901, and Eastern District, No. 45, October session, 1900, 117-124. This is the testimony of Levi Mumper given on May 8, 1901 at the Tipton Park Condemnation hearings. A complete transcript of the proceedings can be found in the historian's office, GNMP.
104. Ibid.
105. "Remains of Soldiers Found," *Star and Sentinel*, July 17, 1888.
106. "Soldier Body Found," *Compiler*, July 17, 1888. This was not the first nor last time skeletons were discovered at the Den. In March 1885 two bodies were found in the "neighborhood of Devil Den" by James Young and Isaiah Trostle. And in 1897 veterans of the 124th New York were visiting the Den when a "discussion arose as to the exact location of" sixteen men of the unit who were killed during the battle and "buried by friends." The "captain who assisted in burying them...asked for a pick and shovel. He started in and soon came upon a number of skulls, bones, canteens, ect., proving that he had not forgotten the exact spot of burial." See "Bodies Found," *Compiler*, April 21, 1885; *Adams County Independent*, September 11, 1897.
107. *Adams County Deed Book QQ*, 339-340; "Sales," *Star and Sentinel*, March 12, 1889; *USA Vs. Two Certain Tracts*, 124.
108. Ibid.
109. "Wm H. Tipton to A. M. Collins Mfg. Co.," April 29, 1922, Copy of letter in Tipton Family file, ACHS.
110. Tipton's early life and his achievements as a battlefield photographer are detailed in Frassanito, *Early Photography*, 37-40 and 231-235.
111. "W. H. Tipton, Who Died Week Ago, Set Up Fund for Poor Of Gettysburg In His Will," *Compiler*, September 28, 1929; "William H. Tipton Dies Friday Night After Long Illness," *Star and Sentinel*, September 28, 1929. For more biographical information on Tipton see *1886 History of Adams County*, 374-375; Charles H. Tipton, William H. Tipton: "The Battlefield Photographer," unpublished manuscript, Sheads Papers, ACHS; "Out of the Past," Gettysburg: Alumni Issue (January, 1979), Vol. 69, No. 4, 30-31.
112. "The Power of Street Railway Companies," *Star and Sentinel*, August 11, 1891; "The Gettysburg Electric Railway Charter," *Star and Sentinel*, August 4, 1891.
113. "The Electric Railway," *Star and Sentinel*, August 18, 1891; Minutes of the Gettysburg Borough Council: 1887-1912, 92-97 (on microfilm at the ACHS). In a special meeting held on July 25, William Tipton moved that the council grant permission to the railway company for the use of the streets of Gettysburg if their charter was accepted. The motion was passed unanimously. At another meeting on July 31, the ordinance was passed. It originally called for the town to receive $10,000 in return, but this clause was not included in the bond. The issue would cause much controversy in town politics for years to come. See "Harrisburg Warning Gettysburg," *Star and Sentinel*, September 22, 1891; "The Electric Railway Company, *Star and Sentinel*, November 17, 1891; "The Electric Road Not To Pay A License," *Compiler*, May 8, 1894.
114. "The Electric Railway and the Battlefield Association," *Star and Sentinel*, September 1, 1893; *Hummelstown Sun*, April 14, 1893 and March 23, 1894; "Trolley Case," *Star and Sentinel*, September 18, 1894. Edward M. Hoffer (a former dealer in farming implements) was a shrewd businessman, and during the research for this section of the book became the perfect villain for the authors.
115. "The Electric Railway Company," *Star and Sentinel*, September 15, 1891.
116. "The Electric Railway and the Battlefield Association," *Star and Sentinel*, September 1, 1893.
117. "The Electric Railway Company," *Star and Sentinel*, September 15, 1891.
118. Ibid., "The Electric Railway Company," *Star and Sentinel*, November 17, 1891.
119. "Gen. Crawford's Gift," *Star and Sentinel*, December 22, 1891.

120. "The Attorney General on Gettysburg," *Star and Sentinel*, August 15, 1893.

121. *Adams County Deed Book SS*, 294-297. As for W. Harvey Gelbach, his name would fall into obscurity as quickly as it arose into the history of Gettysburg photography. Shortly after he moved to Catonsville, Maryland, where he is known to have resided as late as 1945.

122. "The Electric Railway," *Star and Sentinel*, March 22, 1892.

123. "Gettysburg Battlefield Park," *Star and Sentinel*, March 22, 1892.

124. "Gettysburg National Military Park," *Star and Sentinel*, April 26, 1892. See also: "Events Confirm our Views," *Star and Sentinel*, May 22, 1893.

125. In the meantime, the trolley company was working behind the scenes to stack the Gettysburg Borough Council in its favor, and also to get a bill through the State Legislature giving trolley companies the power of eminent domain. The bill failed. See: "The Electric Railway," *Star and Sentinel*, February 9, 1893; *Star and Sentinel*, May 16, 1893; "The Trolley At Gettysburg," *Philadelphia Inquirer*, May 29, 1893; "Electric Railroad Legislation," *Star and Sentinel*, May 30, 1893.

126. "Electric Road Notes," *Star and Sentinel*, April 18,1893; "Electric Railway," *Compiler*, April 18, 1893.

127. "Electric Road Notes, *Star and Sentinel*, April 25, 1893; "Electric Railway," *Compiler*, April 25, 1893.

128. "The Grading of the Electric Railway," *Star and Sentinel*, May 9, 1893.

129. "Gettysburg Field Despoiled," New York *Times*, June 17, 1893.

130. "The Spoilization Of Our Field," *Star and Sentinel*, May 23, 1893.

131. "Gettysburg National Park," *Compiler*, May 9, 1893.

132. *Star and Sentinel*, May 23, 1893.

133. "The Trolley Likely to be Stopped by the War Department," *Star and Sentinel*, May 23, 1893. Other articles voicing outrage against the trolley include: "Protests Against the Vandalism That is Ruining the Battleground," from the *Williamsport Times*, "The Despoilers Should Be Ousted," from the *Chester News*, "A Stain Upon Gettysburg," from the *Scranton Truth*, and "Clear the Vandals Away," from the *Harrisburg Telegraph*, all printed in the *Star and Sentinel* on May 30, 1893. See also: "Condemning the Vandals," and "Ex-Gov. Curtin Shocked," *Star and Sentinel*, June 6, 1893.

134. "Gettysburg Field Despoiled," New York *Times*, June 17, 1893.

135. John Reed Scott, "The Gettysburg Desecration," *Harper's Weekly*, July, 1893.

136. "Hensel's Reasons for His Inaction," *Star and Sentinel*, August 15, 1893.

137. *Hummelstown Sun*, June 9, 1893 and August 11, 1893.

138. "The Gettysburg Desecration," *The Evening Star*, May 27, 1893; "Electric Road Notes," *Star and Sentinel*, April 18, 1893.

139. "The Trolley Road," *Star and Sentinel*, June 13, 1893. There is some indication that William Tipton was also a stockholder of the Electric Railroad. See Robbins' Journal, July 30, 1895.

140. "Trolley Notes," *Star and Sentinel*, June 6, 1893. Another who wrote defending the trolley was George B. Fairchild, "Much Ado About Nothing," *Compiler*, July 18, 1893.

141. "Would Wreck The Trolley," New York *Times*, June 26, 1893; *New York At Gettysburg*, 193-266.

142. *Compiler*, July 11, 1893; "Dedication of the 44th Monument-General Sickles Sued," *Star and Sentinel*, July 11, 1893.

143. "The Association Protest," *Star and Sentinel*, May 23, 1893.

144. "Vandalism At Gettysburg," New York *Times*, May 26, 1893.

145. "The Secretary of War Advised to Enjoin the Trolley-General Maxwell's Opinion," *Star and Sentinel*, July 18, 1893; "Secretary Lamont Acts Promptly," *Philadelphia Press*, May 26, 1893.

146. "Petition to the Attorney-General," *Star and Sentinel*, July 11, 1893; "The Electric Railway and the Authorities," *Star and Sentinel*, July 18, 1893.

147. "Gettysburg Field Despoiled," New York *Times*, June 17, 1893.

148. "The United States Government in Motion," *Star and Sentinel*, July 25, 1893; "The U.S. Commissioners Assert their Power, Work on Trolley Suspended," *Star and Sentinel*, July 25, 1893.

149. "Attorney General Hensel Refuses to Interfere," *Compiler*, August 15, 1893; "The Attorney General on Gettysburg," *Star and Sentinel*, August 15, 1893; "Hensel's Reasons for His Inaction," *Star and Sentinel*, August 15, 1893.

150. "More Avenues," *Compiler*, July 18, 1893; "To Preserve the Gettysburg Field," *Star and Sentinel*, July 11, 1893.

151. "Proceedings of the United States Jury of Condemnation," *Star and Sentinel*, August 7, 1894.

152. "The U.S. Case Against Our Trolley Railway Heard," *Star and Sentinel*, May 22, 1894; "Gettysburg Trolley Line Victorious," New York *Times*, May 30, 1894; "The Secretary of War Checked in his Effort to Mark the Confederate line of Battle," *Star and Sentinel*, June 5, 1894; Annual Reports of The GNMP, 15. At one point David Wills (of National Cemetery fame) was acting as an attorney for the railway company.

153. "Battlefield Notes," *Star and Sentinel*, June 12, 1894.

154. "The Trolley Case," *Star and Sentinel*, September 18, 1894; "The Trolley Case," *Star and Sentinel*, November 6, 1894. A bound transcript of these proceedings can be found in the historian's office at the GNMP.

155. "The Trolley Case," and "The Divided Court," *Star and Sentinel*, April 30, 1895; "Notice On The Dallas Opion," *Star and Sentinel*, May 7, 1895.

156. "Justice Peckham Begins Work," *New York Times*, January 28, 1896; "The Right to Condemn," *Compiler*, January 28, 1896; "The Freeing Of Gettysburg Field;" "The Prediction Verified;" and "Judge Dallas Reversed," all in the *Star and Sentinel*, February 4, 1893; "Gettysburg Decision," *Star and Sentinel*, February 11, 1896.

157. "Hoffer Sells Out," *Star and Sentinel*, January 22, 1895.

158. "A Trolley Concession," *Star and Sentinel*, February 26, 1895.

159. "The Trolley Starts," *Compiler,* July 18, 1893. Initially, the fare was ten cents, five out and five back, 25 cents with a guide.

160. William Wible and his wife Rosanna purchased the Rose Farm in 1880. Wible was a "guide and driver over the field." He would entertain clients at his home as a sort of bed and breakfast. He even built a pond and kept it stocked with "some fine specimens of German carp." See *1886 History of Adams County,* 54, 404; J. Howard Wert, "Little Stories of Gettysburg," *Harrisburg Star and Independent,* September 5, 1907.

161. "Hoffer Sells Out," *Star and Sentinel,* January 22, 1895.

162. "St. Francis Xavier Church Pic-Nic,"*Compiler,* August 8, 1893; "A Big Success," *Compiler,* August 8, 1893.

163. *USA Vs. Two Certain Tracts,* 5.

164. Gettysburg Electric Railway Company File-150, ACHS. This file has much helpful information on the trolley controversy.

165. *Gettysburg Newspaper Cuttings,* GNMP, Vol. 2, 10.

166. Emanuel Bushman, "History: The Drought of Forty Years Ago," *Compiler,* July 17, 1894.

167. *Adams County Independent,* September 11, 1897; *USA Vs. Two Certain Tracts,* 4-9.

168. Ibid., 15, 59.

169. While the evidence is overwhelming that Tipton did in fact operate a tintype gallery at the Den, examples of his work are rarely seen today. The fact that tintypes seldom have backmarks and are usually recorded in front of a generic backdrop make if difficult for them to be distinguished from each other.

170. *Annual Reports of the GNMP,* 72.

171. Charles F. Tipton, William H. Tipton, "The Battlefield Photographer."

172. *USA Vs. Two Certain Tracts*; "Land Condemnation," *Star and Sentinel,* May 15, 1901; "Land Condemnation," *Compiler,* May 14, 1901; "Condemnation Proceedings," *Compiler,* May 21, 1901; "In Condemnation Proceedings Jury Awards Mr. Tipton $6,150," *Adams County Independent,* May 25, 1901. It is interesting that during the hearing one of the improvements that Tipton claimed to make was the filling in of holes (one as big as a house) to level off the property. He did this by hauling stones from Round Top and throwing them into the depressions. It just so happens that about this same time the stone breastworks built by the Confederate soldiers on the evening of July 2 and morning of July 3, that crossed Tipton's land seem to have disappeared.

173. *Annual Reports of the GNMP,* 72; Robbins' Journal, December 6, 1901; "Land Condemnation Case," *Compiler,* December 17, 1901.

174. "Last of Tipton's Park," *Compiler,* August 12, 1902; Robbins' Journal, March 10, 1902.

175. Ibid; "Terrible Accident,"*Compiler,* June 3, 1884; "'Blind Davy' Goes West: A Familiar Figure at Round Top for a Generation,"*Compiler,* May 13, 1920. David was the grandson of Jacob Weikert, the man who owned the eastern slopes of Little Round Top at the time of the battle. For more information see: Edward L. Weikert Jr., *The History of the Weikert Family from 1735 to 1930* (Harrisburg: Telegraph Press, 1930), 240.

176. "Want 30,000 To Purchase Land of Trolley Line," *Gettysburg Times,* February 1, 1917; "Expect Purchase of Trolley Line," *Gettysburg Times,* May 10, 1917; "Start to Lift Trolley Tracks," *Gettysburg Times,* July 11, 1917; "Tracks are Gone," *Gettysburg Times,* July 18, 1917.

177. "Trolley - Thing of the Past," *Compiler,* June 30, 1917; Tear Up Tracks, *Gettysburg Times,* June 26, 1917.

178. Frassanito, *Journey In Time,* 24-34, 48, 183-192; Frassanito, *Early Photography,* 20-25, 41-49.

179. Frassanito, *Early Photography,* 35, 45-49.

180. Ibid., 37-40, 405.

181. W. H. Tipton, *Catalogue of Tipton's Photographic Views of the Battlefield Of Gettysburg* (J. E. Wible, Steam Printer, Gettysburg: 1894).

182. Stewart, "Reminiscences of 70 Years."

183. "Gen. Crawford's Gift," *Star and Sentinel,* December 22, 1891.

184. *U.S.A. Vs. Two Certain Tracts,* 135.

185. This was a common statement in all of Williams' advertisements. See M. Jacobs, *Notes on the Rebel Invasion of Maryland and Pennsylvania and the Battle of Gettysburg, July 1st, 2nd, and 3rd, 1863* (Seventh Edition, Revised and Enlarged, The Times Printing House, Gettysburg, PA.: 1909). The early tour and guidebooks are filled with advertisement and provide much otherwise unobtainable information on the activities of these photographers.

186. A original copy of this notice can be found in *Gettysburg Newspaper Cuttings,* Vol. 3, 33.

187. Robbins' Journal, entries for June 4, August 17, October 31, 1896, and December 8, 1897.

188. Over the years, these group views have been sold, framed and unframed, for anywhere from $5 to $240, without regard to their significance or setting. There has been no true market value assigned to these photographs.

189. Adams County Photographers 150-File, ACHS. There are a few examples where regiments brought their own photographer with them to record the dedication of their monument. For instance Rile & Kerns of Philadelphia recorded a view at the dedication of the 75th Pennsylvania monument in the National Cemetery on July 2, 1886. A copy of this view is on display at the ACHS .

190. This is probably a conservative estimate, based on an examination of negative numbers of these firms from various collections.

191. For a biography of Tipton's early life, see Frassanito, *Early Photography,* 37-40.

192. Advertisement in *Gettysburg by Train.*

193. Tipton, 1894 *Catalogue.* Two other Tipton catalogs have survived in the files of the ACHS. Both are undated, but both predate 1894.

194. Frassanito, *Early Photography,* 403-405; *1886 History of Adams County,* 366-367; Obituary of Levi Mumper, *Compiler,* December 2, 1916.

195. Mumper Family File, ACHS; Mumper Photography File, ACHS; Robbins' Journal, May 17, 1897. Competing advertisements for both "J. I. Mumper" and his "L. Mumper" appear in *Danner's Pocket Guide Book, with History of the Battle of Gettysburg* (Sev-

enteenth Edition, Gettysburg: no date). A copy of this booklet is in the files at the ACHS.

196. *Adams County Deed Book QQ*, 339-340.

197. *Danner's Pocket Guide Book*; Advertisement in booklet, *27th Annual Convention of the State Fireman Association* (1906), ACHS. Besides guidebooks, another source for advertisements is the Gettysburg College yearbook entitled the *Spectrum*. Printed yearly it was an outlet for these firms to compete in the portrait trade.

198. "Curious Visitors Persuaded Robert C. 'Bob' Miller to Open Jenny Wade Museum," *Gettysburg Times*, October 29, 1952; Mumper Family File, ACHS; Obituary of John A. Mumper, *Gettysburg Times*, September 9, 1957.

199. Williams Family File, ACHS; Williams Photograph 150-File, ACHS. Max's father served in Company C, 16th New York infantry.

200. Robbins' Journal, entries for June 4, August 17, October 31, 1896, and December 8, 1897; Obituary of Marion F. Williams Jr., *Compiler*, March, 30, 1929; *Gettysburg Newspaper Cuttings*, GNMP, Vol. 2, 22. At this point the firm was referred to as Williams and Co.

201. Obituary of Ira L. William Jr., Williams Family File, ACHS.

202. M. Jacobs, *Notes on the Rebel Invasion*.

203. A photograph in *Laney's Gettysburg Battlefield and its Monuments* (Laney Souvenir Company, Cumberland, MD: 1895), clearly shows the blotches and indicates that the inscriptions had been entirely removed by that time. A copy of this guide book can be found at the ACHS.

204. Holman D. Waldron, *With Pen And Camera*. The removal of the carvings is also mentioned in Robert G. Miller, *Historic Views Of Gettysburg* (Gettysburg, PA: Jennie Wade House Museum, c. 1925).

205. Ibid., Because of the appearance of white blotches in early photographs, some have speculated that a chemical of some sort was used to cover the carvings. Actually, the blotches look white because the chisels have exposed a fresh surface of unweathered diabase.

206. A few sources indicate that the GBMA had some arrangement to look after the Crawford Tract, but from the abundance of Rock Carving on its boulders, it does not look as if they enforced the same rules as on their own lands. This also might further suggest that some of the carvings were already there.

207. *Funk and Wagnall's New Encyclopedia* (R. R. Donnelley & Sons Company: 1981), Vol. 7, 291.

208. "Coxeyites Here," *Compiler*, July 17, 1894; "Coxey Representatives," *Star and Sentinel*, July 17, 1894.

209. *Gettysburg Newspaper Cuttings*, GNMP, Vol. 1, 66. This article is from the *Philadelphia Press*, July 15, 1894.

210. Obituary of Park Noel, *Compiler*, February 28, 1942.

211. Jack Bochar & Bob Wasel, *Haunted Gettysburg* (Gettysburg, Pa.: Donny Bayne, 1996), 17.

212. Forney Family File, ACHS; 1850 Gettysburg Census; Obituary of David S. Forney, *Compiler*, October 11, 1911.

213. Trostle Family File, ACHS; 1850 Cumberland Township Census.

214. "Gettysburg Battlefield," *Potter Journal*, September 11, 1879.

215. Obituary of Maurice C. Fox, *Compiler*, December 5, 1914. An Advertisement for his photography firm appears in *Danner's Pocket Guidebook*. "Maurice C. Fox, Photographer, 34 North Stratton Street, Gettysburg, PA."

216. Charles Morris Young File, ACHS.

217. The Gettysburg Battlefield," *Star and Sentinel*, June 6, 1893.

218. "Gettysburg Battlefield Park," *Star and Sentinel*, March 21, 1892.

219. An excellent seven part series on the formation of Gettysburg National Military Park and Park Commission was written by Kathy Georg Harrison, "Preview of Park Centennial, 'On the Road To Park Establishment,'" *Gettysburg Quarterly*, Vol. 1, No. 2 (April, 1993) through Vol. 3, No. 4 (November, 1994). The *Gettysburg Quarterly* is the Newsletter of the GNMP.

220. Ibid., *Annual Reports of the GNMP*, 7.

221. *Annual Reports of the GNMP*, 15; *Adams County Deed Book UU*, 449.

222. This notice was printed in the *Compiler*, August 14, 1894.

223. "Gettysburg National Park," *Compiler,* May 9, 1893.

224. "The National Park," *Star and Sentinel*, December 11, 1894.

225. Vanderslice, 19.

226. *Annual Reports of the GNMP*, 60. The authors have long believed the position of Smith's rear section to be inaccurate (See Appendix C).

227. David G. Martin, *Confederate Monuments At Gettysburg* (Hightstown, New Jersey: Longstreet House, 1986), 129, 132.

228. Kathy Georg Harrison, *The Location of the Monuments, Markers, and Tablets on Gettysburg Battlefield* (GNMP), 23.

229. *Annual Reports of the GNMP*, 21.

230. Scott, 19. It should be noted however, that accessibility, especially among aging veterans, was a main concern in the early days of the park.

231. "Naming The Avenues," *Compiler*, November 8, 1887.

232. *Annual Reports of the GNMP*, 29.

233. Ibid., 37, 40. The hitching posts were removed by the NPS and replaced by the modern stone wall, but both ends of the hitching rail can still be seen embedded in the rocks. It is also interesting that, as of the time of this writing, the hitching rails have not left the Den area. They were apparently just tossed into the "Pond" a few feet from where they were removed and can still be seen.

234. Ibid., 47.

235. Ibid., 77; "National Park Notes," *Compiler*, July 29, 1902.

236. This stands in stark contrast to Little Round Top, Culp's Hill, and the angle, where roads have been removed during the NPS years. See "Will Eliminate Curves on Little Round Top Soon," *Compiler*, June 15, 1935; "Expects $50,000 for Roads, Trails on Battlefield," *Compiler*, June 19, 1935. For those who like specifics Sickles Avenue is said to be 6,515 feet long from Devil's Den to the Emmitsburg Road. Crawford Avenue is 3,530 feet long from Devil's Den to the

Wheatfield Road. And Warren Avenue is 1,550 feet from Sykes Avenue to Crawford Avenue. *Annual Reports of the GNMP*, 90.

237. *Star and Sentinel*, October 11, 1892.
238. *Annual Reports of the GNMP*, 97.
239. *Star and Sentinel*, July 9, 1895.
240. Correspondence of the Gettysburg National Military Park Commission, Records of the National Parks, RG 79, NARA.
241. Ibid.
242. Frassanito, *Early Photography*, 258-262. The significance of this photo was first discovered by William Frassanito in 1975, and in 1979 was revealed to the general public. See Jerry L. Gleason, "Devil's Den Ridge Was Pasture Land In 1863," Harrisburg *Patriot News*, February 4, 1979.
243. A recent controversy over the way in which the park should be restored was the concept of memorial landscape. For more information see: Timothy H. Smith, "The Concept of Memorial Landscape," *Battle Lines: The Official Newsletter Of The GBPA*, Vol. 2, No. 1; Bobbie Platt, "Gettysburg National Military Park a 'Memorial Landscape' Controversy," *Gettysburg Times*, December 15, 1993.
244. GNMP Vertical Files-17M-0090. In this file there are photographs of the comfort station taken during its construction. At the time of this writing it is still in use, but long range park plans as early as 1985 have called for its removal. A photograph by Ira Williams showing the removed cannon balls, chains and paths in front of Devil's Den appears in *Gettysburg: Blue And Gray Reunion in 1938* (Gettysburg: Pennsylvania State Commission), 39, giving evidence that the work had been completed by that time.
245. *Draft Development concept Plan/Environmental Assessment Supplement, Little Round Top/Devil's Den*, (United States Department of the Interior/National Park Service: May, 1986), 3. One report to the park in 1978 actually suggested roping off the area around the Balancing Boulder or Table Rock, because of the fear that it might fall on someone. See John L. Rundle Jr., "The Balancing Boulder in Devil's Den: A Brief Report on Its Conditional Stability," Vertical Files, GNMP.
246. For more information on this subject see Draft Development Concept.
247. "Group opposes Devil's Den/Little Round Top plan," Gettysburg *Times*, April 15, 1988; "Group mounts battle over Devil's Den plan," Hanover *Evening Sun*, May 6, 1988; "Keep Devil's Den Avenues," *Gettysburg Times*, June 2, 1988.
248. Recently, the NPS has placed large rocks around two of the pullouts in the Devil's Den parking lot. The same type of rocks have been placed in front of the Texas monument, across the side of Barlow's Knoll, and around the parking area on top of Culp's Hill. The reason for their placement is obviously to prevent automobiles from pulling off, or driving on those areas. But with the significance of rocks, and their ability to help us identify the locations of early photographs, the authors are somewhat disturbed by the generic movement of what some consider historic features on the field.
249. Correspondence of the GNMP Commission, NARA.

Touring Devil's Den

1. John L. Rundle, "The Balancing Boulder in Devil's Den." Endnotes will only be provided in the tour section for information not mentioned elsewhere in this book.
2. Waldron, *With Pen and Camera*.
3. *Maine At Gettysburg*, 178-186.
4. Ibid., 164; Walker, "Gettysburg Monument," from *The Old Soldier*.
5. These include some nine in and around the Pond as well as six bodies inside the woodline along the slopes of Big Round Top. See Frassanito, Gettysburg: *A Journey in Time*, 172-183, and *Early Photography*, 275-293, 306-309.
6. Ibid., 182-183.
7. This conclusion is based on the fact that the background of the drawing shows the South Mountain range, which is impossible to see from Devil's Den— one needs to be at a much higher elevation. Additionally, the rock formation in the drawing cannot be found in the area.
8. Emanuel Bushman, "Devil's Den."
9. Houghton, 220.
10. *The United States Vs. A Certain Tract*, 288-289; Emanuel Bushman in a letter to the editor, *Compiler*, March 15, 1887.
11. "Gen. Crawford's Gift," *Star and Sentinel*, December 22, 1891.
12. The woodline, as it was at the time of the battle, has been thoroughly researched by Frassanito in *Early Photography*, 241-315.
13. Frederick Ray initially discovered the bodies were identical, but did not realize the extent of the move. See: "The Case of the Rearranged Corpse," *Civil War Times*, October, 1961, 19. For greater detail see Frassanito's *A Journey in Time*, 186-195, and *Early Photography*, 273-278.
14. Jane Nellie Hoge, "The Tragedy of Devil's Den," *Confederate Veteran* (1925) Vol. 33, 20.
15. *OR*, Part 2, 407.
16. Scott, 338-339.
17. Work to Langley, 1st Texas File, GNMP.
18. Warner, *Generals in Gray*, 261-262.
19. Krick, 260. A wartime photograph of Manning appears on page 261 of Krick's book.
20. For plenty about the "ghosts" of the Triangular Field, see Mark Nesbitt, *Ghosts of Gettysburg: Spirits, Apparitions and Haunted Places of the Battlefield* (Gettysburg: Thomas Publications, 1991), 17-22.
21. Fasnact, 15.
22. *Pennsylvania at Gettysburg*, 537.
23. *OR*, Part 1, 514.
24. *Pennsylvania at Gettysburg*, 534.
25. Roger D. Hunt & Jack R. Brown, *Brevet Brigadier Generals in Blue*, (Gaithersburg, Maryland: Old Soldier Books Inc., 1990), 191. That would make Ellis the only general officer killed in the action at Devil's Den.
26. For more on all of the field officers of the 124th, see Weygant, *History of the One Hundred Twenty Fourth Regiment*.
27. Ethel B. Gage, "Orange County in the Civil War," *Views*, (April, 1963), 3-7.

28. *OR*, Part 1, 494.
29. Warner, *Generals in Blue*, 537-538, 669.
30. Benjamin L. Higgins, Pension Records, NARA.
31. *New York at Gettysburg*, 704.
32. Ibid.
33. *OR*, Part 1, 494.
34. Warner, *Generals in Gray*, 25-26; William C. Davis, ed., The Confederate General (The National Historical Society, 1991), 100-101.
35. Krick, 184, 194, 215.
36. The caption of an 1867 Tyson Brothers photograph refers to this formation as the "Turtle Rock," while a 1897 tourbook refers to it as "The Twin Elephant Rocks." See Luther W. Minnigh, *The Gettysburg Knapsack* (Gettysburg: 1897), 29.
37. According to Busey & Martin, *Regimental Strengths and Losses*, the 4th, 15th and 47th Alabama suffered casualties of 25.3% at Gettysburg, while the 44th and 48th Alabama suffered 26.6%.
38. Warner, *Generals in Gray*, 237.
39. "12,000 Visitors in Town Sunday," *Compiler*, August 15, 1910, "Wreck on Trolley Line," *Star & Sentinel*, August 17, 1910.
40. Henry L. Figures to his parents, July 8, 1863. Copy in 48th Alabama File, GNMP.
41. "Col. J. L. Sheffield," *Confederate Veteran* (1900), Vol. 8, 544.
42. For an example see: Kathleen Georg Harrison, "Our Principal Loss was in This Place," 66.
43. Waldron, *With Pen and Camera*. This book also suggests that "One of the curiosities of the field is the Flowing Rock...a natural watering-trough in a crevice of a great boulder." There is little doubt however, that the trough is man-made. The authors have also heard of a recent dish specific to this boulder, containing Tomatoes, Lima beans, corn and one vial of water form the trough, known as "Trough Rock Stew." The reader is by no means encouraged to embark upon this dangerous culinary expedition.
44. "Trolley And Auto Collide," *Star and Sentinel*, July 7, 1909; "Auto And Trolley Collide, *Compiler*, July 7, 1909. It is interesting to note that the *Complier* article blames the accident on the driver of the automobile, William MacFarlane, stating that he "lost his head in the face of the impending collision," causing his accelerator to stick. The *Star and Sentinel* article blames the trolley company, claiming that "trees and underbrush on either side of the avenue," had grown too high, "it was impossible to stop," and "there is no danger sign," at the crossing.
45. *New York at Gettysburg*, 296.
46. *Report of the Gettysburg Battle-field Commission of New Jersey* (Trenton, N. J.: The John L. Murphy Publishing Co., Printers, 1887), 46.
47. The 4th Texas, 48th Alabama and the 2nd and 17th Georgia received the brunt of this fire. An excellent account, as seen from Little Round Top, can be found in Smith, *A Famous Battery*, 141-146.
48. Eugene Arius Nash, *A History of the Forty-fourth Regiment, New York Volunteer Infantry in the Civil War* (Chicago: R. R. Donelly & Sons Company, 1911), 154.
49. Waldron, *With Pen and Camera*.
50. Slyder Farm File, Verticle Files, GNMP; Slyder Family File, ACHS.

Appendix III

1. *OR*, 27, Part 1, 588; *OR*, 27, Part 1, 588.
2. Smith, 147; *Compiler*, April 24, 1888.
3. *OR*, 27, Part 1, 588; Tucker, "Orange Blossoms;" Smith, "The 'Devil's Den.'"
4. Smith, 102.
5. Smith, "The 'Devil's Den.'"
6. *Pennsylvania at Gettysburg*, 538.
7. *Maine at Gettysburg*, 166; *Bachelder Papers*, 1095.
8. Bradley, "At Gettysburg."
9. Smith, 102.
10. Ibid., 149.
11. *OR*, 27, Part 1, 582; Smith, "The 'Devil's Den.'"
12. *OR*, Part 1, 583.
13. Ibid., 589. Lieutenant Goodman was attached from the 6th New Jersey and Lieutenant Clark came from Turnbull's 3rd U.S. Artillery, Batteries F and K consolidated. See June 30, 1863 Muster Roll for the 4th New York Independent Battery, NARA.

Selected Bibliography

During the research for this book, it became apparent that five places stood out as major repositories for information on the battle of Devil's Den: The Adams County Historical Society, Gettysburg, Pa.; the Gettysburg National Military Park; the United States Army Military History Institute, Carlisle, Pa.; the National Archives; and Library of Congress in Washington, D.C. Without the help of any one of these institutions, this study would not have been possible.

The Gettysburg Electric Railway is one of most interesting and least written about subjects in all of Gettysburg literature, and warrants its own book. For that reason, as much information and as many sources as possible were added to the notes in that chapter.

Athough there are many books and articles written on the Battle of Gettysburg, few have focused specifically on Devil's Den. It has been decided therefore, to present a selected bibliography of those sources that focus, or have unique information on, the area in question.

Annual Reports of The Gettysburg National Military Park Commission 1893-1904. Washington: Government Printing Office, 1905.

Ayars, Peter B. "The 99th Pennsylvania." *National Tribune*, February 4, 1886.

Bachelder, John B. *Gettysburg: What To See And How To See It.* New York: Lee, Shepard, & Dillingham, 1873.

Bradley, Thomas W. "At Gettysburg." *National Tribune*, February 4, 1886.

Bushman, Emanuel. "The Devil's Den," August 19, 1884.

Dalton, Pete and Cyndi. *Into the Valley of Death: The Story of the 4th Maine Infantry at the Battle of Gettysburg, July 2, 1863.* Union, Maine: Union Publishing Co., 1994.

Fasnact, Charles H. *Speech Delivered at Dedication of 99th Pennsylvania Monument, Gettysburg, Pa. July 2, 1886.* Lancaster, Pa.: Examiner Steam Book & Job Print, 1886.

Draft Development Concept Plan/Environmental Assessment Supplement, Little Round Top/Devil's Den. United States Department of the Interior, National Park Service, May, 1986.

Frassanito, William A. *Early Photography At Gettysburg.* Gettysburg: Thomas Publications, 1995.

_____. *Gettysburg: A Journey in Time.* New York: Charles Scribner's Sons, 1975.

Grimm, Herbert L. and Paul L. Roy. *Human Interest Stories of the Three Days' Battles at Gettysburg.* Gettysburg: Times And News Publishing Co., 1927.

"The Gettysburg Battlefield." *Daily Patriot and Union*, July 11, 1863.

Harrison, Kathleen R. Georg. "Our Principal Loss was in this Place," *Gettysburg: Historical Articles of Lasting Interest.* Dayton: Morningside Bookshop, July, 1989.

_____. "Preview of Park Centennial, 'On the Road To Park Establishment.'" *Gettysburg Quarterly*, Vol. 1, No. 2, April, 1993 through Vol. 3, No. 4, November, 1994.

Hanford, J. Harvey. "The Experiences of a Private of the 124th N.Y. in the Battle." *National Tribune*, September 24, 1885.

Jacobs, Michael. "Later Rambles Over The Field Of Gettysburg." *United States Service Magazine*, Vol. 1, 1864.

Johnson, Robert U. and Clarence C. Buel, eds. *Battles and Leaders of the Civil War.* Secaucus, New York: Castle, 1884-1889; Reprint. New York: Thomas Yoseloff, 1956.

Ladd, David L. and Audrey J., eds. *The Bachelder Papers.* Dayton, Ohio: Morningside, 1994.

Pfanz, Harry W. *Gettysburg: The Second Day.* Chapel Hill and London: University of North Carolina Press, 1987.

Perry, William F. "The Devil's Den." *Confederate Veteran*, Vol. 9, April, 1901.

Polley, J. B. *Hood's Texas Brigade: Its Marches, Its Battles, Its Achievements.* New York: Neale Publishing Co., 1910.

Relics of the First Battle of Gettysburg: Pre-Columbian Era of American History. Gettysburg: Star & Sentinel Book And Job Office, 1869.

Sauers, Richard. *A Caspian Sea Of Ink: The Meade-Sickles Controversy.* Baltimore: Butternut and Blue, 1989.

Scott, John Reed. "The Gettysburg Desecration." *Harper's Weekly*, July 1, 1893.

Smith, James E. *A Famous Battery and its Campaigns, 1861-'64*. Washington: W. H. Lowdermilk & Co., 1892.

_____. "The 'Devil's Den.'" *National Tribune*, March 4, 1886.

Stose, George W. *Geology And Mineral Resources Of Adams County Pennsylvania.*. Harrisburg: 1932.

Tout-Le-Monde, "Letter from the Army." *The Savannah Republican*, July 7, 1863.

Tipton, W. H. *Catalogue of Tipton's Photographic Views of the Battlefield Of Gettysburg*. J. E. Wible, Steam Printer, 1894.

Tucker, A. W. "Orange Blossoms." *National Tribune*, January 21, 1886.

Tucker, Glenn. *High Tide At Gettysburg*. Indianapolis: The Bobbs-Merrill Company, 1958.

Wert, J. Howard. *Historical Souvenir of the Fiftieth Anniversary of the Battle of Gettysburg, July 1-4, 1913*. Harrisburg: Harrisburg Telegraph, 1913.

Weygant, Charles H. *History of the One Hundred and Twenty-Fourth Regiment, N. Y. S. V.* Newburg, N. Y.: Journal Printing House, 1877.

Index

About the Authors

Timothy H. Smith is a native of Baltimore, Maryland. A lifelong student of the American Civil War, he is currently employed as a Licensed Battlefield Guide at the Gettysburg National Military Park. He volunteers as a reference historian at the Adams County Historical Society, teaches noncredit classes on the battle at the local community college, and is a board member of the Gettysburg Battlefield Preservation Association. He has frequently lectured at Civil War round tables and seminars concerning the battle. He has written numerous articles pertaining to Gettysburg, and has also written a book entitled: *The Story of Lee's Headquarters, Gettysburg, Pennsylvania.* He currently resides with his wife Diane in Gettysburg, less than a mile from Devil's Den.

Garry E. Adelman was born and raised just outside of Chicago, Illinois. He received his bachelor's degree from Michigan State University in hotel, restaurant and institutional management. Relocating to Gettysburg in 1992, where he opened the Food For Thought Cafe & Coffeehouse, he currently works as a Licensed Battlefield Guide at the Gettysburg National Military Park and is a board member of the Gettysburg Battlefield Preservation Association. He has been published in the *Gettysburg Magazine* and his maps appear in other publications as well.

The authors conducting a tour at the Devil's Kitchen. (Larry Fryer)